Dubossary Memorial Book (Dubasari, Moldova)

Translation of

Dubossary: Sefer Zikaron

Originally Published in Tel-Aviv, 1965
in Yiddish and Hebrew
Edited by: Y. Rubin

Translation Project Coordinator:
Sarah Faerman

Published by JewishGen

**An Affiliate of the Museum of Jewish Heritage - A Living Memorial to the Holocaust
New York**

Dubossary Memorial Yizkor Book (Dubasari, Moldova)
Translation of *Dubossary; Sefer Zikaron*

Copyright © 2014 by JewishGen, Inc.
All rights reserved.
First Printing: December 2014, Kislev 5775
Second Printing, March 2019, Adar II 5779

Editor of the Original Yiddish and Hebrew Yizkor Book: Y. Rubin
Translation Project Coordinator: Sarah Faerman
Layout: Sheldon Lipsky
Editors: Lynn Mercer
Cover Design: Rachel Kolokoff Hopper
Yiddish and Hebrew Consultant: Josef Rosin
Contributor: Yefim Kogan, Bessarabia SIG Leader and Coordinator

Published by JewishGen, Inc.
An Affiliate of the Museum of Jewish Heritage
A Living Memorial to the Holocaust
36 Battery Place, New York, NY 10280

"JewishGen, Inc. is not responsible for inaccuracies or omissions in the original
work and makes no representations regarding the accuracy of this translation.
Digital images of the original book's contents can be seen online at the New York
Public Library Web site."

The mission of the JewishGen organization is to produce a translation of the
original work and we cannot verify the accuracy of statements or alter facts cited.

Printed in the United States of America by Lightning Source, Inc.

Library of Congress Control Number (LCCN): 2014958621
ISBN: 978-1-939561-29-9 (hard cover: 342 pages, alk. paper)

Cover photograph: From the cover of the original Yiddish Yizkor book
Back Cover Credit: Ozias Ukshteyn, Director of Dubossary Jewish Community
Cover background photo by Rachel Kolokoff Hopper. Detail from "The Last
March", a sculpture in Warsaw, Poland by artist Nathan Rapoport.

JewishGen and the Yizkor-Books-in-Print Project

This book has been published by the **Yizkor-Books-in-Print Project,** as part of the **Yizkor Book Project** of **JewishGen, Inc.**

JewishGen, Inc. is a non-profit organization founded in 1987 as a resource for Jewish genealogy. Its website [www.jewishgen.org] serves as an international clearinghouse and resource center to assist individuals who are researching the history of their Jewish families and the places where they lived. JewishGen provides databases, facilitates discussion groups, and coordinates projects relating to Jewish genealogy and the history of the Jewish people. In 2003, JewishGen became an affiliate of the **Museum of Jewish Heritage - A Living Memorial to the Holocaust** in New York.

The **JewishGen Yizkor Book Project** was organized to make more widely known the existence of Yizkor (Memorial) Books written by survivors and former residents of various Jewish communities throughout the world. Later, volunteers connected to the different destroyed communities began cooperating to have these books translated from the original language—usually Hebrew or Yiddish—into English, thus enabling a wider audience to have access to the valuable information contained within them. As each chapter of these books was translated, it was posted on the JewishGen website and made available to the general public.

The **Yizkor-Books-in-Print Project** began in 2011 as an initiative to print and publish Yizkor Books that had been fully translated, so that hard copies would be available for purchase by the descendants of these communities and also by scholars, universities, synagogues, libraries, and museums.

These Yizkor books have been produced almost entirely through the volunteer effort of researchers from around the world, assisted by donations from private individuals. The books are printed and sold at near cost, so as to make them as affordable as possible. Our goal is to make this important genre of Jewish literature and history available in English in book form, so that people can have the personal histories of their ancestral towns on their bookshelves for themselves and for their children and grandchildren.

A list of all published translated Yizkor Books can be found at:
http://www.jewishgen.org/Yizkor/ybip.html

Lance Ackerfeld, Yizkor Book Project Manager

Joel Alpert, Yizkor-Book-in-Print Project Coordinator

JewishGen
Yizkor Book Project

This book is presented by the
Yizkor Books in Print Project
Project Coordinator: Joel Alpert

Part of the
Yizkor Books Project of JewishGen, Inc.
Project Manager: Lance Ackerfeld

These books have been produced solely through volunteer effort
of individuals from around the world. The books are printed and
sold at near cost, so as to make them as affordable as possible.

Our goal is to make this history and important genre of Jewish
literature available in English in book form so that people can have
the near-personal histories of their ancestral towns on their bookshelves for themselves and for their children and grandchildren.

Any donations to the Yizkor Books Project are appreciated.

Please send donations to:
Yizkor Book Project
JewishGen
36 Battery Place
New York, NY 10280

JewishGen, Inc. is an affiliate of the
Museum of Jewish Heritage
A Living Memorial to the Holocaust

Title Page of Original Yizkor Book

דוּבּוֹסַרי

ספר זכרון

זכור

Translation of the Title Page of Original Yizkor Book

Dubossary

Memorial Book

Title Pages of Original Yizkor Book in Hebrew

דובאסאר

יזכור־בוך

מי יתן ראשי מים ועיני מקור דמעה

ואבכה יומם ולילה את חללי בת־עמי   (ירמיהו ח׳, כג)

כל הזכויות שמורות לאירגון יוצאי דובוסרי בישראל

דפוס ישראל בע״מ, תל־אביב, טל. 441204

Translation of the previous page from the Original Yizkor Book

Dubossar

Yizkor Book

Oh that my head were waters, and mine eyes a fountain of tears, that I might weep day and night for the slain of the daughter of my people!   Jeremiah 8:23

Israel Press, Limited, Tel Aviv, Telephone, 441204

Foreword and Acknowledgements

About 15 years ago I found a request from the JewishGen's Yizkor Books Project to help translate Yizkor Books of Jewish communities that had been destroyed during the Shoah. These books memorialized the villages, towns and cities in Europe where Jewish communities had flourished for centuries until the onslaught of Bolshevism , civil war and finally the annihilation of almost all the inhabitants by the Nazis and their accomplices in World War II.

My family had the Yizkor book, "Dubossary," gifted to us by one of the editors, D.L. Granovsky of Tel Aviv –fellow activist and a long time friend of my father, Moishe Faerman who, unfortunately, did not live to see the book published. At the time, I did not consider myself sufficiently proficient in Yiddish to translate the book but I decided to translate and submit the table of contents so that the Yizkor Books Project would at least have a start with "Dubossary." However, the vivid, personal accounts of the authors were so gripping that with the help of two Yiddish/English dictionaries, I went on to translate most of the book. Several others offered their help long distance via email, the web, etc. Their names appear under the title of each story that they translated.

Dubossar (as we called it), as reflected in the following first-hand accounts, pulsates with the verve of this community of 10,000 Jewish souls. In the late 19th century, the traditional synagogue-based world of the Jews exploded into the many new modern ideas and "isms"– Bolshevism, Zionism, Bundists, followers of the Haskala (enlightenment) movement, Self Defense organizations, theatre troupes, etc. However, after the honeymoon period of the Bolshevik regime, D.L. Granovsky writes: "A flood of blood and fire descended upon the tents of Israel." This was written by a man, who in the opening words declares: "We are not writers but have done our best."

Many thanks to Lance Ackerfeld and Joyce Field, successive heads of the Yizkor Books Project who guided, participated and brought the translation of the book to fruition, and Joel Alpert, coordinator of the Yizkor-Books-In-Print Project, which produced this hardcover translation.

Sarah Faerman, Dubossary Translation Project Coordinator

About five or six years ago, I found out that I have a branch of my family from Dubossary. On a birth record of a brother of my great grandfather I found that he was a Dubossary Meschanin (registered in Dubossary Middle Class society). A year ago I created a KehilaLink website for Dubossary on the JewishGen.org web site. That turned out to be very interesting and rewarding work. I believe that this translation is going to help many people with connections to Dubossary. Please read carefully every page and every paragraph of this important book.

Yefim Kogan, KehilaLinks Website Coordinator

Dedication

This book is dedicated to all victims of the Shoah, to those who lie in Mass Graves in Dubossary, our brothers and sisters from many places in Moldova and Ukraine. It is also dedicated to current Jewish Community of Dubossary (about 100 people), who are doing what they can to keep and maintain the Holocaust Memorial in Dubossary and to Ozias Ukshteyn, directory of Jewish Community of Dubossary wrote: "Until we alive – it is our duty to perpetuate the memory of the past!"

Yefim Kogan, KehilaLinks Website Coordinator

Combined map of Bessarabia Gubernia, Russian Empire, as of end of 19th century with part of Transnistria region of Republic of Moldova in 21sy century with the town of Dubossary.

MAP OF UKRAINE IN 2014

Map of the Ukraine with Dubossary

Geopolitical Information:

Alternate names: Dubasari [Romanian, Moldovan], Dubossary [Russian, Ukrainian, דובאָסאַר (Dubasar) [Yiddish], Dubosary [Polish], Dobyasser, Dubosari, Dubosar, Dubassar

Period	Town	District	Province	Country
Before WWI (c. 1900):	Dubossary	Tiraspol	Kherson	Russian Empire
Between the wars (c. 1930):	Dubossary		Moldavian ASSR	Soviet Union
After WWII (c. 1950):	Dubossary			Soviet Union
Today (c. 2000):	Dubăsari			Moldova

Nearby Jewish Communities:

- Criuleni 4 miles SSW
- Masauti 8 miles W
- Grigoriopol 10 miles SE
- Corjova 12 miles S
- Ivancea 15 miles W
- Orhei 18 miles WNW
- Petrovca 20 miles SSW
- Krasni Okny, Ukraine 23 miles NE
- Chisinau 24 miles SW
- Vorotet 25 miles NW
- Straseni 27 miles WSW
- Frunzivka, Ukraine 28 miles E
- Discova 28 miles WNW
- Putintei 28 miles WNW
- Ofatinti 29 miles NNW

History and Governments

First mention of Dubossary is at the period of the Mongol invasion in the region, 1260-1360. The town was established in 15th century as a capital of one of the Tatar regions. The name Dubossary is from Turkic "Tembosary" or "Dembossary" meaning yellow hills.

From 1360 to 1385, Dubossary was part of the Grand Duchy of Lithuania; from 1385 to 1410, it was part of Poland, from 1410 to 1430; then it returned to the Grand Duchy of Lithuania. From the second part of the 15th century Dubossary belonged to Crimean Khan, and it was part of the Tatar region with several fortified towns which included Dubossary. In the 18th century, Dubossary was a center of a district with 41 localities in the district. At that time, Nogay tatars governed the region, but also living there were Velikorossy, Malorossy, Moldavians, Jews, Greeks, and Poles. Finally after the 1771 Russo-Turkish war it was included into the Russian Empire and became a district town with 13 smaller towns in Ochakov region, district of Kherson gubernia (principality).

The history of Dubossary was always influenced by neighboring Moldova. After 1812, when Russia annexed part of the Moldova Principality, which became Bessarabia, the strategic importance of the border town diminished, until 1918 when Romania annexed Bessarabia.

Starting in 1918 Dubossary became part of the Ukraine, Soviet Union. In 1924 the Soviet Union established the Moldavian Autonomous Soviet Socialist Republic inside the Ukraine Soviet Socialist Republic. The capital of that region was Balta, and later became Tiraspol. Though the majority in that region was not Romanian/Moldovans (only about 30%). The establishment of an autonomous republic was mostly political, in order to tell the world that the USSR did not recognize the annexation of Bessarabia by the Kingdom of Romania.

In 1939, the USSR and Nazi Germany signed a 10-year non-aggression treaty, the Molotov-Ribbentrop pact. Soon after that Germany occupied part of Poland, and USSR occupied Lithuania, Estonia and Latvia and in 1940 occupied Bessarabia. On August 2, 1940, Dubossary became part of the newly established Moldavian Soviet Socialist Republic, with the capital in Kishinev. During the World War II Dubossary, as all Moldova was occupied by German and Romanian armies. After the Second World War, Dubossary was part of Moldavskaya SSR in the Soviet Union and on September 2, 1990 Dubossary became part of unrecognized Pridnestrovskaya Moldavskaya Republic also named Transnistria Republic, a self-proclaimed territory.

History of Jews in Dubossary

The Jewish community of Dubossar and surrounding areas had existed for about 300 years, during which time a vibrant Jewish culture was developed. Jews were artisans, merchants in grain, wine, fruit; they also grew tobacco. In 1897, there were 5,220 Jews in Dubossary, 43% of the total population according to All Russia Census of 1897. At the beginning of the 20th century, the community operated a Talmud Torah, nine chederim, and four private schools. During the civil war in Russia of 1918–20 Jewish self-defense was organized in town and the community remained relatively free from the pogroms occurring at the time. Thousands of refugees making their way to Romania in 1920–22 passed through the town, and many from Dubossary itself also crossed the border to Romania, which was at that time Dniester River. There were 3,630 Jews in Dubossary in 1926 (81% of the total population), dropping to 2,198 (total population 4,250) in 1939.

From June 22 1941, when the German and Romanian armies started the war against the Soviet Union, only a small number of Jews from Dubossary were conscripted to the Soviet Army or evacuated to the East, and in the mid-July 1941 town of Dubossary was occupied by German and Romanian troops. With the capture of Dubassary, the Einsatzgruppe commandos gathered all the Jews from the district (about 18-20,000) into the town. Among them were Jews who had fled from Besssarabia and Bukovina, when the war started. At the end of August a ghetto was set up, and on September 1 the town was annexed to Romanian Transnistria administration. In Dubossary gathered Jews also from Tiraspol, Kishinev, Balta, Ananiev, Grigoriopol and other places, including villages. Jews had to wear yellow Star. They could not go out of the Ghetto and buy produce from the local people. Often many Jews were killed on the streets.

Between September 12 and 28, 1941 25 SS men from Einsatzgruppe 12 D with help of Romanian troops and others murdered 4,500 Jewish men, women and children. The execution was conducted publically; all local population was gathered to see it. Local administration and local police participated in the execution. 12 large pits were dug by Jews from ghetto and local people. During the executions many were wounded and buried alive. Murderers forced mothers to hold their babies during killings. By different estimations during this period from 6-8 thousand Jews were murdered. On January 4, 1942 only 228 Jews remained in town, and on January 9, 1943 there were only 13 Jews from Bukovina.

In the fall of 1943 a large number of Jews from Transnistria camps were brought to Dubossary region to work on railroad repair. Many Jews were from Yassy, Romania. Most of them died during 14-16 hours working day, or from typhus, or were killed when they try to escape.

After the liberation of Dubossary on August 14, 1944, the Soviet Commission for Investigation of Nazi Crimes found that about 18,000 Jewish victims were buried in mass graves near the town. Approximately 100 to 150 survivors returned after the war.

In 1956 at the site of Mass Graves a monument was erected without specifying Jewish identity of the most of the victims. In the beginning of the 21st century a new Holocaust Memorial complex to the Victims of fascism was built by sculptor Epelbaum N.E. and architect Shoykhet S. M.

The Jewish Community of Dubossary was able to gather 2984 names of people murdered in Dubossary. List of the Jews murdered in the autumn of 1941 and buried in the Mass Graves can be found at the Bessarabia SIG website at http://www.jewishgen.org/Bessarabia/files/holocaust/Dubossary-Memorial.pdf.

Gedenkstattenportal zu Orten der Erinnerung in Europa - Memorial portal to places of remembrance in Europe, Moldova, Dubossary

(http://www.memorialmuseums.org/denkmaeler/view/409/Dubossary-Holocaust-Memorial)

דאָ ליגן
פרידלעכע
איינוווינער
פון מאלדאווע
און אוקראינע.
מע האָט זיי
אלע
אומגעבראכט
נאר דערפאר
ווייל זיי
זיינער
געווען יידן.

Here lie
peaceful residents
of Moldova and Ukraine.
They were all
murdered by fascists
only because they
were Jews.

Fragment of the Memorial
Translated from Yiddish by Yefim Kogan

From the Commemoration of Jews killed in Dubossary, 2007

Sources:

1) Holocaust on the territory of USSR, Encyclopedia, Moscow, 2011
2) "Holocaust: FINAL REPORT of the International Commission on the Holocaust in Romania, November 2004. (http://czernowitz.ehpes.com/stories/chapter_05.pdf)
3) Gedenkstattenportal zu Orten der Erinnerung in Europa / Dubossary. (http://www.memorialmuseums.org/eng/staettens/view/409/Dubossary-Holocaust-Memorial)
4) Dubossary KehilaLinks website (http://kehilalinks.jewishgen.org/dubasari/)
5) Bessarabia SIG website (http://www.jewishgen.org/bessarabia)

Yefim Kogan

Bessarabia SIG Leader and Coordinator

www.jeiwshgen.org/bessarabia

yefimk@verizon.net

Dubossary Memorial Complex

Photograph by Ozias Ukshteyn, Director of Dubossary Jewish Community

Dubossary Memorial Complex

Photograph by Ozias Ukshteyn, Director of Dubossary Jewish Community

Dubossary Jewish Cemetery – Old Section

Photograph by Ozias Ukshteyn, Director of Dubossary Jewish Community

Notes to the Reader:

Within the text the reader will note "{34}" standing ahead of a paragraph. This indicates that the material translated below was on page 34 of the original book. However, when a paragraph was split between two pages in the original book, the marker is placed in this book after the end of the paragraph for ease of reading.

Also please note that all references within the text of the book to page numbers, refer to the page numbers of the original Yizkor Book.

An electronic version of this translation can be found at:

http://www.jewishgen.org/Yizkor/Dubossary/dub901.html

The original Yiddish Yizkor book can be found on-line at the New York Public Library site:

http://yizkor.nypl.org/index.php?id=1276

Table of Contents

Many of the articles in the original Yizkor Book appeared in both Yiddish and Hebrew. Since they are identical, only one verson appears in this translation.

Way of Life – Folklore and Legends

Jewish Doctors in Dubossar

In Their Eternal Memory

Family Notes

[Page 8]

Preface

Translated by Sarah Faerman

With holy trembling, we of Dubossar approached the task of compiling this yizkor book of our community which in its history has more than once been threatened by enemies of Israel whose goal was to obliterate us. Each time when waves of anti-Semitic hatred swept down from South Russia and bloody pogroms decimated the Jewish communities, Dubossar was a like a thorn in the eye of the attackers as the Jewish residents fought with might and courage and consistently repelled the bandits. Thus it was at the turn of the century when anti-Semitism engulfed Tzarist Russia reaching its zenith in the Kishinev Pogrom of 1903.

[Page9]

Again in 1918-20 Ukrainian bands of bandits brought destruction to countless Jewish towns. Thanks to the bravery and defiance of the Dubassarers, the hooligans were afraid to attack our community and those that did try were compelled to retreat in shame as is described in the pages of this book.

Only during the most terrible of all the catastrophes that befell our folk – World War II – was our community unable to withstand the bloodbath that destroyed 'Israel's House' in Europe. The heroic Dubassarers were cut down together with the thousands from all of the other Jewish settlements in Nazified Europe.

Years flew by. We were not at peace. There was the need to memorialize our dear ones who in their innocence were slaughtered, whose spilled blood cried out from every stone, from every field. There was also the need to preserve the 400 year history of Jewish Dubossar. Our task was formidable. In other countries there was the possibility of gathering documents and eye witness reports of what had occurred during the great catastrophe. Survivors who came to Israel could also bear witness to what they had lived through. However, Dubossar, within the confines of the Soviet Union was hermetically sealed in and not until the year 1962 did we hear one word about our town. Most of the Dubossarers that were now in Israel or in other countries in the world, had left Russia forty years earlier, in the 1920's. The task of reconstructing the history of the town was thus also hampered by the natural process of forgetfulness which increases with time. Luckily, 3 years ago (1962), a Dubossarer managed to escape the "iron curtain" and emigrated to Israel. This man, a high officer in the Soviet army, personally heard many first-hand accounts from Dubossar survivors and fighters at the front against the Nazis. Thanks to this man, we know many details about our martyrs and fighters who died heroic deaths on the various fronts – details which appear in this book.

[Page 10]

As none of us who compiled this book are actually writers, we did our best to gather memories, threads, chapters in an attempt to create a faithful reflection of the life of our town throughout the generations.

We would like to take this opportunity to mention everyone who helped us with this endeavour. First and foremost, we remember our dearly departed Moshe Feldman, a'h, who was the strength and inspiration behind the Dubossar Landsman organization in America along with Harry Scheer, reb Itzik Klezmer's son – a philanthropist and gentleman, refined and cultured and our dear friend Louis Levine. As well, our dear friend from Canada, Moishe Faerman, a'h – a dedicated and faithful comrade; our beloved friend Leml Rubin – reb Shmuel Dayan's son in Argentina who together with our landsleit (fellow townsmen) in Israel spared no amount of money or work to establish the following memorials: a forest in Israel in memory of the martyrs of Dubassar and surrounding areas, a plaque placed in Jerusalem to remember our martyrs of the Shoah and now this book to commemorate Dubossar and our dear ones.

Had we writers amongst us, the book would probably be fuller and richer. Yet, we believe that we have achieved our goal – for us and for the future generations – to preserve the name of our community; to pay tribute to our landsmen and to fulfill the command: "Remember what Amalek did to you." May this book be a small solace in our endless sorrow, a sign that the past will not be forgotten. May it serve as a bridge between the precious Jewish life that was so tragically cut off and the future whose rays of sunlight we see rising before our eyes.

This book has been written in both Yiddish and Hebrew so that every Dubossarer, be it in Israel or in other lands, will be able to read and remember our dear community which is no longer. May it also serve as an inspiration for our children and children's children who know of Dubossar only from family tales.

M. Bick, M. Bassin, D. L. Granovsky, Y. Kantor, A. Timor
The Editorial Committee

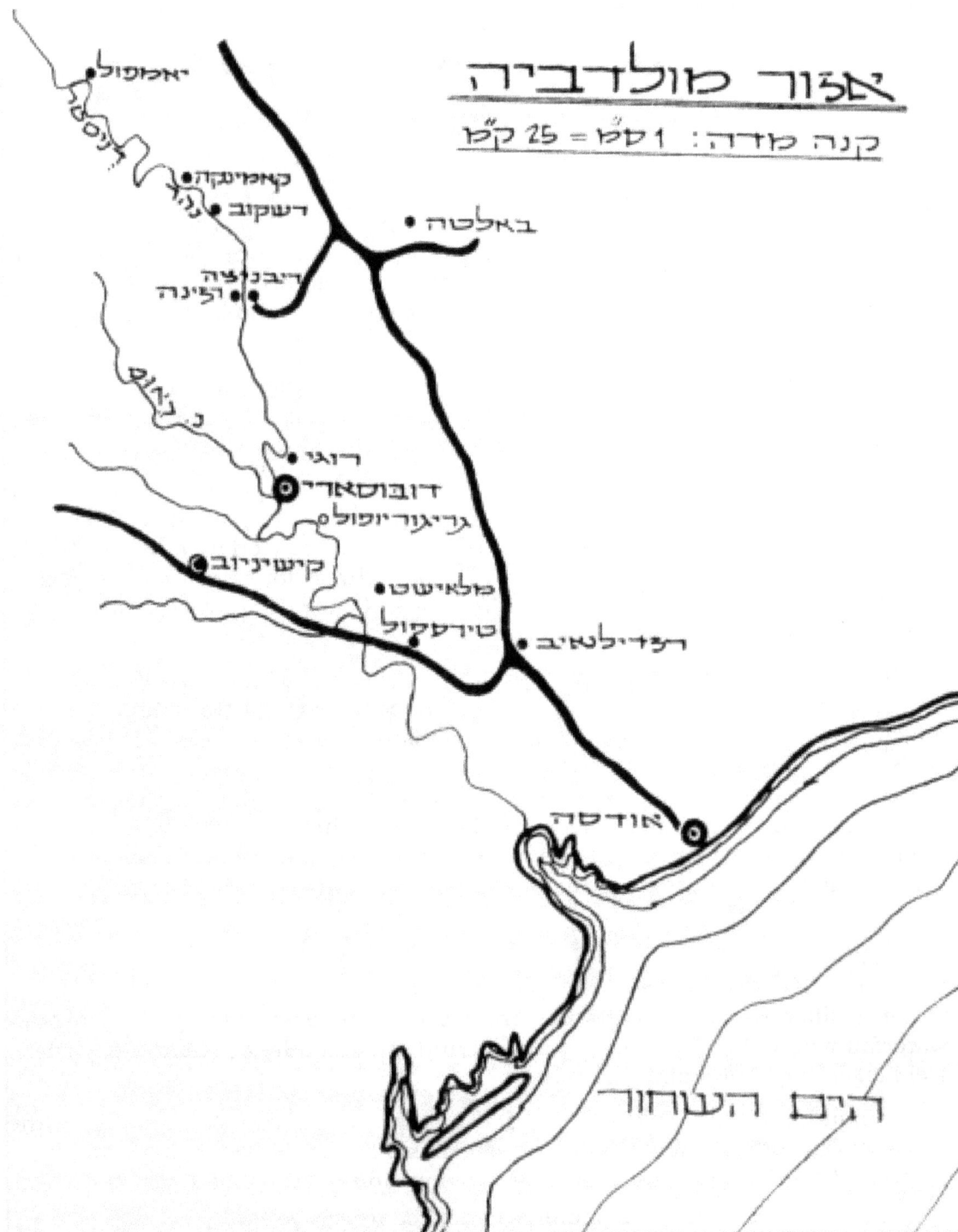

אזור מולדביה

קנה מדה: 1 ס"מ = 25 ק"מ

יאמפול

קאמיענקה

רשקוב

באלטה

ריבניצה

וקינה

רוגי

דובוסארי

גריגוריופול

קישינוב

מלאישטו

טירספול

רעזינה

תצילאיב

אודסה

הים השחור

Map of the Moldavian region.
At the bottom is Odessa and the Black Sea.
In the bottom quarter of the land mass by the big black dot in the centre is Dubossar.

[Page16]

An Overview of Dubossar

by Arkady Timor

Translated by Sarah Faerman

Moldavia

The sun in the south blazes. The aroma of wheat wafts over the fields and the vineyards ripen with deep crimson clusters of grapes. From the upper gardens there is the sharp scent of apples, white acacias and ancient wells. From a distance, the faint melody of the "Doina".

On the roads, wagon wheels scrape as long-horned oxen plod heavily on the dusty paths. At the side of the wagon strides a Moldavian. On his head is a pointy hat made of sheep's wool – certainly sewn by a Jewish cap maker.

Moldavia – not a large country – 350 kilometers from north to south and 220 kilometers west to east. In the middle, a small unimposing hill. On the horizon, beyond a shadowy grove of trees stretch the Kodari hills. Kodari in Moldavian means 'dense forest". In olden days, three- four hundred years ago, this land was covered with dense woods but now the woods have been transformed into gardens and vineyards.

To the north, the Belz steppe spreads out at the foot of the high Kodari hills. To the south is the Budjits steppe, surrounded by water with fields of wheat, maize and watermelons. Lengthwise across the way are scattered several wells. The villages are not very green and they nestle near the rivers and wells of the steppe where the treasured water is hidden. The hot dry air is laden with the gentle scent of melons. In the areas where the steppe cannot be ploughed, or where the earth lies fallow for a period of time, flocks of sheep wander hidden from the angry dogs and the quiet, pensive shepherds.

[Page17]

Quite a different scene greets one from the south east side by the Dniester waterfall where the river banks widened and created a lake. There the gardens yield legendary fruits and greens.

This small land had a colorful and rich history. In the very olden days, in the wooded Carpathian Mountains, dwelt Turkish and Slavic tribes. Moldavia evolved of these two tribes. Moldavia was first founded in 1359 although Jews inhabited the area since the end of the 12th century.

Historically, Moldavia was continuously under attack. From the north, Polish gentry would invade. From the west, the Hungarian king invaded. From the south-east, from the steppes by the Black Sea, expeditions of Mongolian Tatars would descend – and from the south – the Turks. One of Moldavia's national heroes – Stephen the Great battled many years attempting to safeguard his land. After his death, in 1513, Moldavia was vanquished by the Turkish Empire.

Stephen the Great was a statesman with great foresight and he had dealt in a positive manner with the Jewish community. In this atmosphere, Jews contributed greatly to the economy. They established various industries related to wood, leather, flour, milk and wine, among others.

In the 19th century, under the reign of Peter 1, Russia and Turkey had a severe and protracted battle on Moldavian land. On May 16, 1812, after 6 bloody years, a peace treaty was signed in Bucharest and Moldavia was annexed to Russia. This treaty was signed by Marshal Kotozov. January 1918, Romania grabbed a big section of Moldavia between the Dniester and Prut rivers and annexed the land.

From what remained, the autonomous republic of Moldavia was created as part of Ukraine by the left bank of the Dniester in 1924. Balta was the first capital city of the Moldavian republic and in 1928 the name was changed to Tyrospol. At the end of 1940, the Soviet Union demanded that Romania return the annexed land taken in 1918. This was returned at the end of the year and the area became the Soviet Moldavian republic with Kishinev as the capital city.

[Page18]

A few decades before Moldavia was freed from the Turks, Russia sent her south-eastern divisions to the Dniester. On the left bank, there was a narrow strip of land 8-20 kilometers wide. In those days there were many narrow rivers that flowed into the Dniester and tucked in around them were a number of villages that lived in fear of the Tatars who frequently attacked them. Near the Dniester,at the mouth of the river Garneh, was the village of Rivnitzeh. There, a bridge built in the olden times spanned the Dniester. The inhabitants of that area were hunters and fishers.

At the end of the 19th century, a train station was built at Rivnitzeh. The plan was to have the train go southward in order to link Dubossar, Grigoriopol and Tyrospol with Odessa. However, to this day (1965) the plan has not yet been realized. South of Rivnitzeh the Dniester curves around the village of Rogi, for a few kilometers and returns back to the north making another sharp turn southward. There woods filled with willow trees appear by the Dniester and alongside are the towns of Malobataya, Galergan and Kuchiery where Jews had lived for many years occupied with agriculture and the land.

Using the Dniester as a border, the Russians built fortresses at every intersection where ships sailed deep into Russia. Such fortresses were built in Grigoriopol and in the town of Farkan that was inhabited by Bulgarian refugees from the Turks in Tyrospol. This fortress was built to protect the district from the Turkish fortress at Bindera on the opposite bank of the river.

[Page19]

In ancient times, the Greeks named the Dniester "Tyros" and hence the town on its banks became Tyrospol. In time, soldiers who had finished their term of duty under the famous Russian General Savorov settled there. Tyrospol was of such vital military importance, it was considered the most important town in the entire south-easter region. Odessa for a time also belonged to the Tyrospol province.

Dubossar was one of the fortress towns on the Dniester. Dubossar – the town where we were born, the town where our childhood and youthful years flew by – was founded at the end of the 17th century.

Distance of Dubossar from the other towns:

North:	60 km.	from Rivnitzeh
North-East:	80 km.	from Balta
	80 km.	from Ananiev
	60 km.	from Katovsk (Birzola)
	35 km.	from Tchorny
	35 km.	from Krasni Okne
	40 km.	from Kishinev
South-West:	18 km.	from Grigoriopol
South-East:	60 km.	from Tyrospol
	150 km.	from Odessa

On the bank of the Dniester, where the willows grew higher than the water, the earth was elevated and a fortress built occupied by a military division. Some towns were closed off from the fortress. Five miles to the south, near the bridge, a (?Karantin?) was erected and that is how the town of Karantin got its name. The fortress didn't last long – only until 1820. Once it ceased to be a border, it had no further strategic importance.

Not far from the center of the old fortress there was a four sided square. In that square was Pipelshtein's drugstore. The central axis of the town is east of the square in the direction of the "small fountain". Jews lived in Dubossar since its founding. In a Moldavian folk song, there is the story of the Jewish blacksmith, Moishe Gazal who shod the soldiers' horses.

The purpose of this article is to portray the history and fate of Dubossar until 1922-24 – our days. (See further on "Under the Soviets and During the Holocaust").

[Page20]

Before I go further, I must pause to describe two characteristics of the Dubossar Jews which over the years shaped the character of our community and which influenced her fate both during good, peaceful periods as well as in days of terrible misfortune.

The first characteristic – which existed for generations from the very beginning until the mass exterminations – was the productivity and work orientation of Dubossar Jews. The expression "luft mentsch" was almost unknown in Dubossar. There was also nobody enslaved to strangers. The fate of each was in his own hands. The Dubossar Jews were bound to mother earth, to the orchards and vineyards. All were involved in truly physical work: the water carriers, the craftsmen, the stone masons; the goldsmiths, the millers, the farmers, the fishermen – all.

The second characteristic was the deep nationalistic (Jewish) bonding amongst the Dubossar Jews. Living among many ethnic groups – Russians, Moldavians, Ukrainians, Germans and Gypsies, the Jews maintained their pride in their own culture. They were also lucky to have upstanding and brave community leaders.

In all of Southern Russia during the worst periods of the revolution and bloody pogroms, the Jews stood fast and repulsed all enemy attacks. Their bravery was not only for themselves but also in aid of neighboring Jewish settlements that were threatened and in danger. It is no co-incidence that the pogrom in Kishinev did not start in Dubossar where the Jews were too strong and organized. Nor did the plot to incite hatred against the Jews succeed when a dead Christian child was 'planted' on Jewish land. The various attempts to wipe out the Dubossar Jewish community failed.

[Page26]

Reb Yakov Feldman (father of Moishe Feldman) and family

[Page28]

Reb Kalman Feinshil

[Page33]

Our Community Dubossar

by D. L. Granovsky
Translated by Sarah Faerman

A flood of blood and fire descended upon the tents of Israel in Europe. Thousands of communities were wiped off the earth. Millions were sent to the slaughter, burned and choked to death in gas chambers, buried alive. The lives of ten times one hundred thousand Jewish children were snuffed out. Ashmadai's rule reigned over Europe, cut down Jewish lives, extinguished fountains of wisdom and knowledge, destroying culturally vibrant Jewish communities while the rest of the world watched and did not stop the hand that raised the sword against the house of Jacob. Our lives are filled with sorrow and woe. The tragedy befell the entire house of Israel without exception. We mourn all our near and dear ones and we do not cease to weep.

Our community Dubossar was not spared. Our Dubossar that sat by the shores of the Dniester in South Russia across from Bessarabia. Close to 10,000 Jews lived in Dubossar and all but for a very few were wiped out, removed from the book of life when Ashmadai lifted his mighty axe.

We know very well when the folk of Israel in Dubossar were cut down but we know very little about the beginnings hundreds of years ago. The elders, from whom we might have learned something about our history, were destroyed with everyone else. Therefore, I will attempt to dip into my memories and to relate some episodes from my own life and from events that I heard from others, older than myself.

[Page34]

Together with others who will do likewise, we will erect in this book a monument to our town where we were born, grew up and later spread our wings to leave our warm nest – some to Israel and some to other countries thus escaping the frightful fate of our unfortunate brethren.

The City Dubossar

There are no documents available prior to mid 19th century. Our town was called "New Dubossar" and on the other side of the Dniester was "Old Dubossar" which in time withered into nothing more than a village. In my youth, I found a tombstone in the old Jewish cemetery with the date 1616. We had a legend that a bride and groom who both died on their wedding day were buried there. I still see before my eyes the ancient stone, moss covered and weather beaten for it made a big impression on me.

As mentioned, Dubossar was on the banks of the Dniester that served as a main highway for the many surrounding towns and villages like Tyraspol, Grigoriopol, Rivnitza, Rashkov, Yogarlik, Zvanitz and Kaminka. Ships, steamboats and barges sailed back and forth laden with wheat, produce and lumber. There was a big wooden bridge that united the two sides of the Dniester and which the Romanians burnt down when they captured Bessarabia. There was also a ferry that went back and forth between the two banks of the river. During the entire day the bridge and the ferry buzzed with activity. Peasants from the surrounding villages would pile on to the ferry with their wagons, sheep and cattle, traveling from one side to the other.

Dubossar was surrounded on three sides by villages, south, north and east and they contributed greatly to the economy of the town. The earth was fertile and there was a daily parade of farmers bringing the blessings of the earth – dairy products, honey, chickens, grapes, apples, pears, plums and an abundance of other fruits.

[Page35]

As it is written, a land flowing with milk and honey. The reputation of the fine wines and fruit reached as far as the distant provinces of Russia.

As with most of the Jews in Russia, Dubossar Jews were also involved in all the trades and businesses. They had factories and large as well as small shops. There were merchants of wheat, wine, fruit and especially dried fruit. There was also every variety of artisan and tradesperson. There was almost no trade in which Jews did not excel and these included tailors, hat makers, shoemakers, coppersmiths, painters, sheet metal workers, tinsmiths, bricklayers and so forth. Not only were trades and business in Jewish hands, there were also Jews who worked as laborers in the mills, in the oil factories, beer factories and in the huge tobacco plant "Lauffer's" that employed dozens of Jewish workers. Nor were Dubossar Jews strangers to field work. Many worked in the tobacco fields. Away they would go at dawn and return at dusk. This was Dubossar – a city humming with life and work; a city that supported with honor its inhabitants. Seldom did one hear a Dubossarer bemoan an inability to make a living.

Two springs gushed forth in our town – "the big fountain" and "the little fountain". Both, with their crystal clean water, would quench the thirst of man and beast. We also had many wells which not only provided water for drinking but had another mission as well – that of dousing fires which in Dubossar occurred frequently.

During winter, when the Dniester was frozen, wagons and sleighs would cross over the ice and the youth would skate. From the months of 'Shvat' to 'Tevet' –

the coldest months of the year – ice would be chopped off from the river for the hospitals and ice cellars. In the month of 'Adar' as the frosts diminished, the ice on the river Dniester began to heave, to stir and this river which had been solid, now began to crackle and foam. The water would flow over the banks and flood the town. The water reached up to the hill near the old *Beis Medrish* (study hall). The flood would extend several kilometers and then the only way one could reach Bessarabia would be by boat. Many a time there was the danger of a boat being smashed to pieces by the giant ice floes.

[Page36]

Granovsky family
Front row: Baruch and Malya, centre, Left – Tova, Malya's mother. Right – His brother Simcha's wife and their children.
Back row: Simcha, Shloime, Elka and Azriel.
(the above name Malya was corrected by hand in the book. The printed name was a mistake: Malka)

Deeply etched in my memory was this one time during just such weather conditions when the river seethed and threatened. It was in the month of 'Adar' 1911 – the month I became a Bar Mitzva. My father was on the other side of the Dniester in Bessarabia and because of the turbulent river and the floods, he was unable to return for my Shabbat Bar Mitzva. With great anticipation and anxiety we all waited and looked for my father's return but no great miracle occurred. The danger in crossing the stormy waters was too great. On that shabbat, my father remained on the other side and I became a Bar Mitzva boy without a feast and without a drasha (sermon).

From time to time our calm, routine lives were shaken due to either external or internal events. I was barely four years old when the pogrom in Kishinev broke out and this event remains deeply engraved in my memory.

[Page37]

The Dubossar Jews had a special reason for their great trepidation as the mob that had carried out the pogrom in Kishinev was emboldened by a 'blood libel' that was spread about the Jews in Dubossar by "The Black Hundred" in Russia. The incident began with the discovery of a murdered Christian boy in the garden of an important Jewish homeowner. The atmosphere was tense and on the verge of explosion. I recall how my parents paced back and forth in the house with panic stricken expressions. They hid every prized possession in the cellar but only during the night.

Immediately a Jewish self- defense group was organized and guards were placed at every corner of the town. They were on the lookout for any suspicious movement. This self-defense group was famous in the surrounding areas and the knowledge that they were there, cooled off the hundreds of predatory and bloodthirsty pogromchiks so that they did not dare to attack these Jewish folk. I would like to take this opportunity to fulfill a holy obligation and name those who were at the forefront of the self-defense organization. At the head was the outstanding power behind the organization – Abraham Isaac Yagalnitzer (Golani) who had started the first Hebrew school in Dubossar. His close collaborators were Pinchas Bassin, Shaul Sokai, Golack, Malchis and others. It later became known that the murder was committed by the boy's own uncle who was after the boy's inheritance. Once the truth was known, the story faded away.

The blood libel in Dubossar, the pogrom in Kishinev and incidents in the other towns in Southern Russia prompted many from our town to leave this land of woe for other countries. Therefore, a great exodus began at this time for America and other free countries. With the launching of 'Aliya Bet' (second migration to Palestine), many also chose the road to Eretz Yisrael.

* * *

World War I, the Russian Revolution and following this, the civil war, left deep scars in our town even though we did not experience such tragic events as in the other towns. "Only" here and there, at the outskirts of the town and in the surrounding areas hooligans managed to kill a number of Jews;

[Page38]

"Only" here and there did they rob a Jewish store, "Only" one Jew was killed by the "Denikintses" who fled from the Bolsheviks as they passed through Dubossar. They doused him with oil and set him on fire. "Only" one Jewish man and his wife were killed as three others were carried off and no-one knows what became of them. And yet, in comparison with other towns and villages where the frenzied pogromchiks of all stripes ran amuck, murdering, pillaging, destroying whole communities, Dubossar escaped with grace.

When the February, 1917 revolution broke out, a democratic election was held in Dubossar and a government was voted in that represented all the different groups in the town. The Jews elected Rabbi Abel and Joseph Visoky (who later lived in Israel) and they worked diligently on behalf of all the townspeople. These were the "spring" days of the Russian Revolution and we Jews, along with the other Russian ethnic groups. believed that the dawn of a new era had begun, leaving behind the hundreds of years of the despotic Czarist regimes. We believed that in the wake of the revolution, man had changed his character and a bright future awaited us where love, peace and brotherhood would reign. The honeymoon lasted only a few months. By October, the Bolsheviks grabbed power and everything was turned upside down. Our rosy expectations were obliterated and bitter disappointment took its place.

During the years 1920-21 starvation swept over Russia. Dubossar, which had always been a land of plenty now had inhabitants walking around like ghosts, swollen with hunger. The need was so great that people ate the bark off the trees and many collapsed from hunger in the middle of the street. In the courtyards of the hospitals lay many corpses as those whose duty it was to bury them, had no strength for the task.

The hunger, the civil war and the heavy hand of the Bolsheviks prompted those Jews who had any opportunity whatsoever, to cross the river Dniester to Bessarabia which was under Romanian rule. Masses streamed to the Dniester from all corners of the Ukraine. The river swallowed many and we also heard of many who drowned at the hands of the border smugglers. Those that were lucky enough to reach the other shore were attacked, robbed and left barefoot and naked. My wife and I also tried countless times to steal over the border without success. Once, during just such an attempt, hot coals were thrown at us that killed one woman but we miraculously were saved. We also were arrested during another one of our attempts.

[Page39]

I remember one episode from that period that nearly cost me my life. I was the secretary of a branch of the organization "Tzeirei Tzion" (Youth of Zion) in Dubossar. On a summer day in Tamuz 1922, my friend Yeshayahu Kantor's wife approached me and requested that I write a certificate for him, confirming that he was a member of our organization. (He was then preparing to cross the Dniester and make his way to Eretz Yisrael). Although I was ill, with a temperature of 39, I gathered my strength and wrote out two certificates #150; one for Kantor and one for my friend Rasch who was also planning to steal across the border. Rasch fell into the hands of 'Cheka' (Russian secret police) and was arrested. I shook with fear twofold: first, over the fate of Rasch and secondly, in fear that the certificate would fall into the hands of the communist police which would mean being stood up against a wall...

On the eve of Rosh Hashana, I was arrested for Zionist activities and with nine others was transported the next day... on Rosh Hashana... to Tyraspol. There a true miracle occurred. The certificate I had given Rasch did not fall into the hands of the 'Cheka'. If it had, I would not be able to write this memoir.

Dubossar Institutions

I would like to open up this chapter with mention of the oldest institution found in each and every Jewish community – the Shul (synagogue). There were many shuls in Dubossar but I will mention here only the most important and well known ones:

The Great Shul: The elders used to relate that the Baal Shem Tov, may his piety be remembered, laid the cornerstone with his own hands. If it has not been destroyed by hooligans, this shul would now be over 200 years old.

The Great Bais Medrish (study house): This one was also amongst the oldest institutions in Dubossar. Elders used to say that when the Bais Medrish was being built and the foundation excavated, they found such a large quantity of clay and building material, that they were able to complete the whole building from these materials alone. Many perceived this as a miracle. Sixty years ago (1905), the Bais Medrish was renovated and it was a very fine and spacious building.

[Page 40]

In addition to the above two, there were many small Klayzl (synagogues) belonging to the various societies and trades. Among these were the Talner and the Sadigorer about whom a pun was told. The story is that when they started to build their little shul, they threw into the foundation a jug of "yash" (brandy) so that when it was said that the synagogue stands on "YY'SH" (an acronym for fear of God), they would, God forbid, not be telling a lie.

Practically every type of artisan and trade had its own shul. We had a tailors' shul, a shoemakers' shul, coachmen's shul, the shamosim's (sextons) shul, etc. The shamosim had a "weakness" for cantors and every visiting cantor was obliged to come first to their shul. These shuls were too small to contain the overflow of people on the high holidays and especially on Simchat Torah. At such times, the Sefer Torahs would be taken out of doors and minyans (quorums for prayers) would be held in the neighbouring houses.

On Hashana Raba (7th day of Succot), ballot boxes were installed in the shuls and study houses and elections were held to vote in the new Gabbais (trustees of the synagogues). After the elections, there was some hearty drinking and the newly elected Gabais were paraded down the streets under a chupa. Crowds accompanied them, singing, dancing and carrying burning candles. The following tale is told about Israel Kalman, the son of Aaron: On Hashana Raba, his wife sent him to slaughter a hen for the holiday. On the way, he got caught up in one happy group of revellers after another until he finally came dancing home with the hen still tucked under his arm.

The main point is that Simchat Torah was a joyous occasion. After an Aliya to the Torah, the whole congregation would help themselves to some food and brandy and were soon drunk. They would then spill out into the streets to celebrate with the Torah. On Simchat Torah they gathered strength against the cold, grey winter days which were already creeping toward them.

In our town, we also had a Psalms Society that had been founded in 1840. Ordinary Jews belonged to this group and they would get together each Shabat afternoon to read aloud a chapter of the Psalms. There was pure magic in the reciting of the Psalms. The whole year they would pour out their hearts to the creator – those who understood the meaning of the words and those that didn't. The words of King David, may he rest in peace, were like a drop of sweetness in their bitter lives.

Six years after the establishment of this society, the members commissioned a new Sefer Torah to be created for their shul. In 1926 I had the great honor of bringing this Sefer Torah to Israel and installing it in the Nahalal shul. In 1853, the society had presented a crown for their Torah. It was made of silver and was a meter high.

[Page41]

41 1906 Folk Shule in Dubossar. Back row right Yishayahu Kantor

Decorated with golden bells and silver birds, it cost a fortune in those days – a thousand rubles. Because of its great value, the crown was kept in a private home and only on Shabbat and holidays was brought to the shul. It was considered a great honor to place the crown on the Torah. To this day it is not known what happened to the crown just as the whereabouts of many other valuables belonging to the Jewish communities is unknown following the great destruction, the Holocaust.

Educational and Cultural Institutions

There were many educational institutions in Dubossar starting with the "cheder" (small traditional religious class), the Talmud Torah (religious elementary school) and finally, a school that was attended by a mixed group of Jewish and non-Jewish children. The majority of Jewish children learned in a cheder and Talmud Torah from the very youngest age and up. There they learned Bible, Rashi (commentaries on Bible and Talmud), Prophets and Scripture as well as Gemara (commentary on Talmud and Mishna).

[Page42]

The teachers were more or less inspired in their profession yet in spite of their antiquated methods of teaching; they managed to stuff into the children a basic knowledge of Jewish customs, a love of our holy Torah, a love of the Jewish people and of Eretz Yisrael. During the whole day, from eight in the morning until eight at night, with very few breaks, Jewish children sat in cheder engrossed in prayers and studies. There was almost no time left for play. The children, however, found a way around this. Every time the teacher stepped out of the room, the class would erupt into fun and games. Truth to tell, although strict discipline was evident, there was no lack of childish joy in cheder. The winter nights were lovely when the group of children headed home with lanterns in hand to light the way.

At the turn of the century, in 1905, a new school was founded in Dubossar. This school was more suited to modern times and was directed by the famous pedagogue Yagolnitzer (Golani) who will be described elsewhere in this book. Yagolnitzer was the school director for only two years as he left for Eretz Yisrael in 1907.

Not far from the Boulevard State Garden, there was a Gymnasia (high school). The scholars of our town, headed by Rabbi Abel and Reb Yechiel Tzelnik, founded "The New Talmud Torah" in a large building, airy, well lit and on one of the nicest streets in town. The educational methods were new, synthesizing old and modern techniques. In the ensuing years there was a bitter battle between the fanatics of the older generation and the more progressive, younger one. Finally, the spirit of modern times won out, the new school became firmly established and many children there absorbed Jewish and general culture.

As mentioned before, there was a school for both Jews and gentiles under the direction of H. Karatenko. Special teachers would come to the school to teach religion. The most talented was Reb Yakov Feldman whom the pupils admired and loved. He was a dear Jew and a fine human being wholeheartedly devoted to his work. When his son, Nathan, drowned in the Dniester, we mourned for months together with the family exactly as if he had been our brother. Reb Yakov Feldman was also a journalist and during the time of the 'Blood Libel' he did his utmost to uncover the true facts about the child's murder.

Amongst the various cultural groups in our town, a special place was occupied the Kapelye (klezmer band) "Lyubiteles" which had been established in 1890.

[Page43]

Among the many musicians in the Kapelye, were Kalman Ben-Ami Feinshil (of Chabad), Yechiel Reznik (who lived for many years in Eretz Yisrael to the ripe old age of 93 in 1963), David Chochomovitch, Yitzchak Bider (murdered in a pogrom in the early 20's), Shmuel Yengaltz, Pinchas Bassin, Avraham Guzman and Yitzchak Shargaradsky. These were all talented musicians and they played at weddings to bring joy to the bride, groom and the mechotonim (family, in-laws). The money earned was donated to the Community Philanthropic Society that paid for the weddings of orphans and the poor. Those, whose sole income was from their klezmer music, later left the band. There were also musicians in the band who were not Jewish - such as Kapuchenko and Dyardeh the fiddler who would enchant people with his artistry. One of the Jewish players was dubbed 'Kol Mikdash' (everything holy). To this day I do not know why they called him that but I had the "pleasure" to feel his "playing" directly on my body. One day, when I was ten years old, I spotted him in the street and yelled out "Kol Mikdash". He was a tiny but swift Yidl. He grabbed me and let me have it. To my great luck a passerby noticed and rescued me from his hands.

At the turn of the century, a troupe of theatre aficionados launched performances in Weinstein's big hall. Many were the meetings and festivities celebrated in this hall. It was there that we heard Rabbi Abel deliver a report upon his return from the seventh Zionist conference that was held in St. Petersburg between the February and October Revolutions. In that same hall, not much later, we were forced to attend communist meetings where an atmosphere of hatred prevailed with a hefty amount of propaganda against everything that a nationalistic Jew holds dear and holy.

Dubossar was a town that loved cantorial music. Great cantors, world renowned, would seek out our town and bring great pleasure to the townspeople with their hearty, sweet cantorial pieces. Some of those who visited were: Reb Nissy Beltzer with his choir, Cantor Bialik (no relation to the poet), Chaim Steinberg, David Roytman, Icht Arbitman, Chaim Shwartz and more. We also had our own famous local cantor – Nachum Matenko – a renowned baritone, famous throughout Russia and beyond. Even today legends circulate about the deep impression he made on royalty including a princess of the Russian Czar's family.

[Page44]

It is told that she was totally enamored by his voice. He gave cantorial concerts in Odessa, Moscow, throughout Russia and other countries. He died in Milan. A rumor has been circulating to this day that Cantor Matenko did not die a natural death but was poisoned, the victim of jealousy.

As we are talking about cantors and talented musicians, it is worth mentioning that the renowned pianist Anton Rubinstein (1829-94) was born in Dubossar. Also the violinist Metz, famous throughout Russia, hailed from Dubossar. He lived in Rostov on the Don and earned his living by giving music lessons. On one occasion when he visited Dubossar, he gave a concert in Sribner's garden.

Dubossar Jews were not only fond of music, their souls were hungry for the spoken word and flocked to hear lectures, sermons, talks and recitations. Multitudes would come to hear speakers such as Rabbi Yevzarov (yhl'l), Chaim Greenberg, Joseph Vitkin, Moishe Shoichet, Jacob Rabinovitch, the orator Masliansky and others.

Zionism in Dubossar

From the days of "Chivat Zion"(organization "Lovers of Zion") and the first Zionist Congress, there were Zionists in Dubossar. Our town also contributed its share to the Second Aliya. Numerous youths settled in Eretz Yisrael from 1904-14. The biggest impetus toward Zionism occurred because of the 1913 Beilis trial. The terrible lies and incitements against Jews that were heard day in and day out and that were spread throughout Russia by the reactionary and anti-semitic press, trampled upon our holiest feelings and revealed before our very eyes the terrible abyss that awaited Russian Jewry. These terrible insults helped to forge a nationalistic Zionist consciousness, particularly among the youth. From the darkness that engulfed Russian Jewry a light was kindled that led the way to Eretz Yisrael.

Until the outbreak of World War II, "Kayleh Chaim Mordecai's Shul" served as the centre for Zionist activities in Dubossar. In those days, the greatest source of inspiration in the Zionist organization was (shu"b) Kalman Ben-Ami Faynshil, a descendant of (b"ch) Reb Yisroel Sirkish, the author of "A New House", one of the fundamental works on the literature pertaining to 'Poskim' (religious pronouncements).

[Page45]

Rabbi Kalman was a learned Torah scholar and well versed in the Hebrew language. He also published an important book "Against the Bible Critics" (Christian Bible). For us in Dubossar, he was the highest authority amongst the Lovers of Zion. Reb Kalman was an exceptional and tactful man, loved and respected by all who knew him. He "Made Aliya" in 1925 and settled in Nahalal where he lived to a ripe old age.

The home of Pinchas and Leah Bassin was a Zionist home in every sense. She was the daughter of the respected Filler family. Their house was home to the Council of Sages and the best youth in town would frequently gather there. Also, when a noted speaker or Zionist arrived in Dubossar, the Bassins would make a welcoming party at their home. As mentioned before, famous people frequently visited Dubossar. When Chaim Nachman Bialik and Pesach Auerbach came to Dubossar in 1903 in connection with the blood libel, they stayed with the Bassins.

"Hatchiya" (The Revival), another Zionist group primarily attended by the younger generation, was particularly active during World War I. "Hatchiya" also laid the foundation for the organization "Kadima Tzeirei Tzion" (Forward Zionist Youth) which was founded in 1917 after the February revolution. This organization was instrumental in spreading the Hebrew language and Zionist ideals among the youth. Thanks to this organization, hundreds of young people would gather at the end of the Sabbath for readings, debates, presentations and general entertainment.

With the advent of the Balfour declaration, in our naiveté, we awaited our 'Geula' (redemption) and prepared for a mass exodus to Eretz Yisrael. The following episode will illustrate the atmosphere of Geula that caught up the masses of Russian Jewry: At that time the noted Zionist Agronomist Zussman, may he rest in peace, was visiting our town and we consulted with him about making Aliya to Eretz Yisrael. Upon his suggestion, we began to make lists of the candidates who wished to make Aliya. Every evening scores of people wrote their names down on lists. An Aliya committee was elected whose task it was to screen out those that were suitable from those that were not. As a member of this committee, I had to carefully deal with one candidate whom the committee had considered unsuitable. He let out his full fury and wishes for revenge on me. Luckily, in the chaos of those days, he disappeared one day and we never saw him again.

That period of "Sturm and Drang" was also the most interesting and fruitful of our Zionist activity. We organized groups to learn Hebrew, to study Eretz Yisrael geography, etc. and the work was done with great enthusiasm.

[Page46]

With our help many young men and women studied the Hebrew language and the Hebrew word was heard daily in our town. After the October revolution, the Zionist activities were forced underground and many of our comrades were banished by the Bolsheviks to Siberia. After years of hard labour, the Soviet regime allowed some to leave Russia and emigrate to Eretz Yisrael. among those lucky few were our friends Yoseph Vargon and Elimelech Tcherkis – both residents of Rishon L'Tzion.

Dubossar Fires

As in other Jewish towns, fires were a frequent occurrence in Dubossar. We had a "Fire Brigade" and in the yard of the magistrate there were always wagons filled with barrels of water ready in case of a fire alarm. Frequently, however, when the alarm was sounded, the horses would be far away, grazing in the pasture or else the water would have frozen in winter or at other times, it would have dripped out entirely. Very often, by the time everything could be organized, the fire fighters would arrive too late to be of any use.

I remember many fires but the most frightening ones were those that happened during my childhood years. Perhaps because I was so young and impressionable these events are deeply etched in my memory.

The first great fire that I remember occurred when I was two and a half years old. My father carried me and my older brother who was five years old. He ran across the street looking for a safe spot to set us down. That fire broke out at nighttime in Laybe Rashe's Shul. I remember that the sky was as red as fire and from all sides one could hear the sounds of lamenting and wailing. There was the panic that the fire would spread to the many flammable items in his shul where he had benzene, alcohol, gasoline, resin, etc.

The second fire that I remember well was in the summer of 1908. Sitting in "cheder", we boys suddenly saw a torrent of black smoke pouring up to the sky. We ran like crazy with all our might from the cheder to the lake to hide in one of the caves that were there. This was one of the biggest fires ever in Dubossar. Approximately forty houses, including my parents' house, disappeared with the smoke. All our belongings turned to ash.

[Page47]

Speaking of the fires, I am reminded of the following tragi-comic event: A winter night. Outside is a terrible blizzard. The wind whistles and howls. The alarm bells are shivering in the air. In a house not far from Yosef Filler's mill, a fire broke out. In great confusion, the owner of the house ran outside screaming:"Reboynoy Shel Oylom" (Lord of the Universe) "Sweet Father. Where are you? Holy fathers Avraham, Belam, Jacob, Terach...Where are you?"

* * *

There were several medical institutions in our town. There was a government hospital that rather reluctantly took in Jewish patients who, from their standpoint, also had little desire to use these services. As opposed to this, the Jewish hospital fulfilled its mission with great dedication. We also had an organization called "Linat Hatzedek" (name of the benevolent society) comprised of volunteers – both men and women. If a member of this organization was sick for a lengthy period or severely ill, "Linat Hatzedek" would send over one of its volunteers to help care for the invalid thus lightening the burden of the family. In certain instances the help was also financial.

* * *

There were two cemeteries in Dubossar – the old cemetery and the new one. Already in my day there were no further burials in the old cemetery. Scholars and the righteous had been laid to their eternal rest there. Among them, Reb Mendele, a disciple of the author of the book "Pool of Living Waters" and a student of the Baal Shem Tov. In times of trouble people gathered at his graveside to throw notes into his mausoleum with prayers and the hope that by virtue of Reb Mendele's good deeds, the much needed help would be forthcoming. Near his grave was that of the "Baal Tshuva"(the penitent).It is told that one day, on Yom Kippur, near the time for Kol Nidre, an apostate drove by. He was an important Muscovite businessman. When he heard the mournful melody of the Kol Nidre, his heart filled with remorse and he vowed to return to his Jewish faith. He rid himself of his business, left his family and turned to Reb Mendele to guide him in his atonement. He became a very pious Jew. When he died and was buried in the old cemetery, Reb Mendele wrote in his will that he wished to be buried near the "Baal Tshuva". Recently we found out that the remains of Reb Mendele and the bride and groom were all re-interred in the new cemetery. As far as I recall, we only used the new cemetery for burials. There ordinary folk were interred alongside scholars and other important people.

[Page48]

Not many from our town are aware that in Dubossar there was a third cemetery behind Moishe Kantor's estate. That cemetery was used during a very tragic period when cholera swept through our area in 1851. The epidemic devoured many poor souls and within two years the cemetery was filled to capacity with room for no additional graves.

Dubossar Scholars and Hasidim

In the last generations, Dubossar was a town of scholars. Without a doubt, the greatest amongst them was Reb Shimon Rabinovitch. With great affection, the townspeople called him Reb Shimeleh Dayan (judge). Aside from his great mastery of the Torah, he was considered a 'Tzadik' (righteous man), very modest, with high standards and a fine character. Day and night he read Torah and studied.

Another famous scholar and genius, was Yerucham Hacohen, a descendant of sh"ch. In Dubossar he held the position of Rabbi and was on the Bet Din (judges of law according to the Torah). He was also the author of the books "The Tishbite" and "Brish Gali" – a commentary on the Hagada of Passover.

Dubossar was also a town filled with Chasidim (movement stressing pious devotion and ecstasy). This stemmed yet from the days of the Baal Shem Tov and the town elders would describe how Reb Yisroel Baal Shem Tov would often visit Dubossar and sit in 'Urka the Coachman's courtyard', under a tree and there discuss Chasidism with his friends and students. This tree was still standing in Urka's courtyard in my day also. Many a time we young lads would look at that tree and lost in our thoughts, would contemplate the path of the Baal Shem tov and the impact the Chasidic movement had on Jewish life.

In Dubossar the Chasidim would flock around a very pleasant rabbi, Reb Mordecai Morgolius. On Shabbat and holidays, he would host a "Tish" (the

Rabbi's Table) where Torah was discussed in the manner of the Chasidic rabbis. Well known Chasidic rabbis would come to visit the Dubossar Chasidim, among them The Talner Rabbi, The Olesker Rabbi and Reb Nachum Makarever.

A distinguished and beloved scholar was Reb Chaim David Dayan. They would tell how, on Fridays, when the gentile hawkers would see Reb Chaim David walking to shul for Mincha prayers, they would immediately put away their merchandise "to prepare for shabbes". Reb Shmuel Dayan, Reb Shimeleh's son, was a scholarly, spiritual and modest man beloved by everyone. He carefully handled the community money and with zeal guarded every penny. He was also a member of the Rabbinic Council for many years.

[Page49]

P. 49 Families Puchis (?) and Volovsky of Yagorlik. Bluma Volovsky, Menky Puchis, Zalman Puchis, their children Moishe and Natan, Fruma Granovsky (nee Volovksy), Israel and Sara Volovsky and daughter Rasya. and daughter Rasya.

(Yagorlik was corrected by hand in the book as printed name was a mistake. These corrections were made by D.L.Granovsky one of the authors and a friend of our family).

In remembering Dubossar personalities, I am obliged to mention both Jews and Christians who excelled in their humanitarian deeds and were exceptional people. First of all, I must mention Dr. Layb Polnikovsky, the son of a well known rabbinic family. He was a very good doctor and had a golden heart. He was also a modest and humble person. When he was called to a sickbed, he would immediately set forth either by foot or by wagon. Many a time, when he would see that the family lived in poverty, he would refuse to accept a fee and would leave them money to buy medicine. The simple folk did not grasp his great humanity. His unpretentious and warm approach to young and old led to their undervaluing him and this resulted in their withholding from him the respect that he deserved.

I would like to mention Zisha Yaffo who was one of the feldshers (barber-surgeon). He was a dedicated Zionist and already in 1911 he sent his four children, a son and three daughters, to Eretz Yisrael to study at the "Herzlia" high school.

Moshe and Golda Granovsky and children. Vanished without a trace.

[Page50]

Among the Christians, I would like to mention the feldsher Frakafenko who was an expert in the medical field and because of his goodness and warm heart, was beloved by everyone. He was always ready to help the needy regardless of their religious background.

Also to be remembered in a positive light is the priest Trentavsky of the New Market Church. He was a dear man who faithfully followed the commandment to love his fellow beings. With his good deeds and fiery sermons, he more than once mediated and dampened the excesses of his people against the Jews in Dubossar.

* * *

In erecting this monument to our Jewish community in Dubossar, I have the moral and holy duty to dedicate a few words to the town of Yagorlik – our closest neighbor. Yagorlik was small but simmering with Jewish life and content. It will sound like a legend when I tell you that as early as the beginning of the 1900's almost everyone in Yagorlik spoke Hebrew. For this they could thank Gad Layb Rechev whose love of Zion and the Hebrew language was so great that he dedicated his whole life to teaching Hebrew to the Yagorlik inhabitants, in particular the young.

[Page51]

In 1906 he made Aliya to Eretz Yisrael and thus served as an example to his many friends and students. The Yagorlik Jews were honest and hardworking. They viewed their town as a transit station to Eretz Yisrael. Because of their great love of the land of their forefathers, many did achieve their goal of settling in Eretz Yisrael. Among others, I would like to mention David Puchis z'l, who emigrated with the second aliya and who, with his bare hands, dug into the earth of the motherland as he was one of the founders of Ein Ganim where he lived to the end of his days. In the War of Independence, his son Isaac, a teacher and a poet, sacrificed his life on the altar of the motherland. Yagorlik was wiped out along with the other towns and villages in Eastern Europe when the enemy of the Jews lowered his axe over our Jewish communities.

* * *

These are the memories that I managed to rescue from oblivion. On many a sleepless night, people and places from the past flit by my eyes and once again I relive these incidents exactly as if they occurred only today. This is how one town, one of many, lived and labored, experienced joy and pain. This is how one town continued the thread of tradition and added a brick to the old fortress of the house of Israel in the Russian exile until the enemy, the devil, came and cut off the memory of the Dubossar community in Nazified Europe. In one day 18,500 Jews were wiped out, martyrs and innocents from Dubossar and the surrounding areas. H"y"ch.

יוסף וחיה פילר, סבא וסבתא של ברוך בסין

Yosef and Chaya Filler, grandparents of Baruch Bassin

[Page54]

What Once Was

by I. Dunayevsky, z"l

Translated by Sophia (Ostrowsky-Warshavsky) Adler

In glowing memory of my in-laws,
Shmuel and Nekhama Kharton, z"

More than sixty years have passed by since the day I last saw Dubossar. And yet the characteristics of that Shtetl are as sharply etched in my memory as if it were only yesterday that I left it.

A little old town was Dubossar, on the shore of the Dniester River that winds past as it rushes on its course. True, the town itself was not so pretty. Yet, perhaps for that very reason, God blessed her with truly enchanting surroundings. Dubossar lies in the embrace of a wonderfully lovely landscape, among rolling forests and plains interwoven in a heavenly unity.

Excepting for the beautiful countryside surrounding the town, the exterior of Dubossar was no different from most other Jewish towns in Southern Russia. From the outside the houses were small and low; from the inside modest and chaste. Mostly the roofs were covered with aged wooden shingles, over which hung the sense of generations long past. Outside of the main road in the town, the streets were not paved, and few had sidewalks. In summer, when a wagon passed by, clouds of dust were raised, and in autumn one must wade through marshy mud.

Thus would Dubossar have appeared at first glance in the eyes of strangers. But quite differently she appeared in the eyes of natives and those who knew her intimately. Much charm and inner beauty lay hidden in Jewish Dubossar. Of her one might with justice turn to the old Talmudic saying "Judge not the vessel by its outer appearance, but rather note the quality of its contents." And in the "vessel" Dubossar there was much worthy of note.

The small town had Mazl (good luck):

Encircled by the Creator with blessed surroundings from which fertile farms and gardens yielded God's abundance, Dubossar Jewry evolved a broad-branched commerce which extended over wide distances of greater Russia.

True, there was no great wealth in Dubossar. But most of her inhabitants were folk of good substance and had abundant Parnossah (means of income).

And where there is Parnossah, one does not begrudge the other and jealousy gains no power. So it is no wonder that in Dubossar life flowed on tranquilly and peacefully and one person did not creep under the skill of another. Each person was absorbed in his own work or business and there was no need to pursue sharp competition, because there were abundant sources of opportunity.

I will here outline the main sources of livelihood. The major enterprise was the trade in grains from which most Dubossar Jews drew their livelihood. Ships and barges loaded with grain would depart from Dubossar on the Dniester River toward the Black Sea to reach the great Russian port of Odessa. Among the big grain merchants from our town, the largest were considered to have been Joseph Zeev Katz, Shmuel Yitzhak Nissenboim and Yitzhak Lufalaver.

The branch of "parnossah" second in importance was the wine trade. There were many vineyards in our area, and when the time came for harvesting the grapes and treading out the juice, then the courtyards and even the streets of the town, were flooded with thousands of casks of wine, that had been brought to Dubossar in fermented state. It would become very lively in our town with the arrival of those casks of wine. People would be going in and out of the wine cellars, some to buy, others to sell, and some as connoisseurs in order to taste and render judgment on the wines. Many Dubossar Jews drew their livelihood from the wine trade because wines from our region were sold both for wholesale and also for taverns and restaurants.

A respectable place in the Dubossar economy was occupied by the tobacco industry which gave employment to a large part of the population. As it is well-known, the tobacco industry demands much physical labor and specialized abilities, from the growing to the selling. Tobacco goes through many processes until it is ready to go up in smoke. And every stage from the growing, drying, sorting and packing, demand special skills. Only after the tobacco has been sorted and packed according to its special qualities, is it ready to be sold. Dubossar was a center for the tobacco industry and from afar there used to come the buyers' representatives for the cigarette makers to buy our tobacco. The largest tobacco warehouse was owned by "Lofers" whose manager was Chayim Finkelstein of Petersburg.

Another important branch of enterprise was in sheep-pelts. The pelts, bought when they were still moist, had first to be dried. Artisans might then work them to flexibility. In either form the pelts were shipped off to the great Annual Fair at Balta.

Beside the above-mentioned four main branches of livelihood, in Dubossar as in all other Jewish towns and shtetlakh there were many shops that provided a good livelihood for Jewish families. There were spice shops, haberdashery establishments, shops of crockery, work tools, etc. Most of the shops were concentrated at the Market Place, where the deep mud was up to ones knees on rainy days, but did not deter Jews and others from energetically doing business. In our town there were also many Jewish craftsmen and artisans:

metal workers, coopers, smiths and hot-tar workers, tailors and shoemakers, hat-makers and cap-makers that served the entire area, the farm-folk as well as the townsfolk, who earned their living one from the other.

Concern over livelihood did not prevent Dubossar Jews from devoting themselves to community matters, which included many domains. Most of our folk were traditionalists, faithful to Yiddishkayt. Many did not see any contradiction between cherishing Judaism and giving their children a worldly education. Among the families where Torah and general education lived in peace, I would particularly like to honor the memory of: Isaac Roshkovsky, Shmuel Kharton Katz and especially Rabbi Joseph Filler, who between his sons and grandchildren, were among those who called themselves Maskilim (the enlightened), people of modern impulse.

In our town there had come forward a number of earnest folk who enthusiastically devoted themselves to culture, the social order, and Zionist concepts, which by the beginning of the century had captured a significant portion of the Jewish folk, especially the youth.

As though alive before my eyes, I remember the Sabbath gatherings in the home of my now deceased friend, Mordechai Rosenberg, where we used to perform Readings and also conduct Discussions on literature and timely events. Perhaps compared with later experience, our flaming discussions might today appear naive or childish, but one must not forget that in the conditions in which Russian Jews lived during the first decade of the century, Utopian themes were of tremendous importance.

I wish to mention the names of a few individuals whose activities were especially notable among the Jewish Dubossar community, and who left a lasting influence. They are: Mordechai Rosenberg, Pinhas Bassin, Lipeh Sirotzki, Yitzhak Bider and Joseph Peretz Visoki.

* * *

The wheel of life turns... Memories of the entire community from out of the deep past appear before me in every detail, pressing forward one after the other. Dear and beloved they are to me. They are part of my life. Suddenly the scroll of memory is violently ripped away. A black raging storm carrying murder and butchery laid waste the House of Israel. The Hand of Satah descended upon the Jewish communities in Europe, tearing them out by their roots. Great was the fracture, and the wounds incurable. Torn apart were the links in the chain.

P. 56 Yankelevitch family.

Standing from Right to Left: Nisan Yankelevitch and wife (drowned with the sinking of the ship Struma).
Standing from Left: Azriel Yankelevitch (died in Israel), his daughter Ethel (also drowned with ship Struma).

**P. 61   Family of Pinchas and Leah Bassin, daughters of
Joseph Filler (father of Leah Bassin) their daughters and husbands.**

Standing L-R: Bracha Shochet, Emanuel Finbron, Sara Bassin, Rivka Shochet,
Miriam Filler, Rosa Perlshtein, Lyuba Filler, R. Finbron.
Seated L-R: Tila Filbron, Pinchas Bassin, his wife Leah, Chana Finbron, Rachel
Finbron, Aaron Finbron. Children: R. Finbron, Hinda Bassin, Bella Finbron, Meron
Finbron, Shulamit Finbron.

התמונה לקוחה מתעודת הספר הזהב של הקרן
הקיימת והזורע הוא איש דובוסרי, אהרן
הורוזיץ ז"ל, שעלה לארץ בשנת 1900.

**This picture which was taken from the Keren Kayemet
(Jewish National Fund) golden book is of Aaron Horvitz z"l.**

[Page65]

Memories of the past

by Baruch Bassin

Translated by Sarah Faerman

My Zaide's house

It is already fifty years that day in, day out, I am flooded with the light of Eretz Yisrael – out eternal homeland; a light that I dreamed of and that my soul yearned for since my early childhood days. Yet, it is enough that I just close my eyes for a while and my imagination soars on wings to carry me to my town Dubossar of fifty, sixty years ago. Then, other lights from my childhood satisfy my soul as with the blessings of raindrops. It is a great wonder – every year that I get older, the lights shine stronger and brighter and their effect on me becomes sharper and more penetrating. My fantasies and memories are pervaded with great longing and bring me back to my early childhood, to the enchanted Dubossar with her dazzling nature that encompassed all the vivid colors of the rainbow; where I absorbed the very atmosphere and where my very first impressions were formed.

On the shores of the Dniester, on its very border, a little town totaling only 10,000 souls, sprung up – a colorful, small world which, like a single drop of water from the sea, mirrored the surrounding areas. Dubossar spread out like a circle within a circle. In the center, in the heart of the town, there lived a lively, colorful Jewish world whose customs and practices had evolved over a period of hundreds of years of an inner autonomy. All around, like an encircling shawl wrapped around her, was a different world, a strange Christian one which was at times, hostile and at times indifferent. And when, in the course of their daily activities, the two worlds did interact while dealing with business and parnosse (making a living), the contact was a superficial one, not from the heart and each of the two worlds lived their lives separately and within their own circle. The Jewish community was like a solitary island in the great sea, living as behind a walled fortress. Her physical horizons were narrow and limited. Her soul, however, soared above and within her, enriching with grace, charm and spiritual beauty, the environment.

* * *

To my great joy, I was privileged, in my childhood years, to be part of that rich and bountiful tradition that one generation passed on to the next. My mother's parents – Yossl and Chaya Filler, may they rest in peace, guarded these traditions zealously and with love and passed them on to my parents' house and to my generation.

Yossl Filler, one of the finest men in Dubossar, was a fervent Chasid and it didn't prevent him from also being a learned and modern, liberal person - unlike my Zaide (grandfather) on my father's side who was a zealot and a misnogid (opposed to Chasidism). Aside from the fact that Yossl Filler was a very busy man, thanks to his many businesses, he always made time for learning. He was fluent in Russian (as a child he finished at a state school) and every day he read the Russian newspaper so that he would know what was happening in the wide world. He loved order. He organized his day in a strict routine and every task was done at its appointed time. He would get up quite early in the morning and because of his many pursuits, he would say his Shacharit prayers alone at home. On the Sabbath and on holidays he would pray with others in his own shul, the synagogue that he inherited from his father Reb Dovid Yenkl, may he rest in peace. Because of his many businesses (I alone remember nine of them aside from one that Bobbe (grandmother) handled) he was away most of the week. However on Shabat and on holidays he always made certain to be home. For many years he was a member of the town council, although the only Jew. Many years later, close to the time of the revolution, my mother, may she rest in peace, was elected to this same position and on her initiative and with the help of the councilman Lipe Siradsky, a Jewish Gymnasia (high school) was founded. Under the Soviet regime the authorities became the heads of the Gymnasia and insisted on their ideology.

Yossl Filler's house was a gathering place for the prominent Jews of Dubossar. My Zaide's friends and comrades would often gather in the afternoons for a friendly visit and a glass of wine. In mentioning some of my Zaide's friends, I will start with Yossl Duboner who lived across the street from. On the high holy days and on Passover, Shavuot and Succot, he would pray at the Pravizorisher synagogue that was in his courtyard. He was Reb Chaim Finkelstein's father, a sage, a Zionist, a respected homeowner in Dubossar and the representative of the big Tobacco factory " Lofers". Among others, there were Shmuel Novaset and Shmuel Charitan – Reb Yeshaya Dinayevsky's son-in-law – who just recently passed away at a ripe old age in Haifa, z". When this group of friends would get together, my Zaide would call his clerk, Reb Shmuel Charabastian and say: "Shmiyel – Tzap!" Shmuel, who was the overseer of my grandfather's wine cellar, without saying a word, would go down to the cellar and bring up a couple of bottles of good Bessarabian wine. The friends would sit for a few hours in pleasant conversation with wine and nuts – another of my Zaide's businesses.

My Zaide, Reb Yossl Filler was also imbued with a deep pedagogic sense. My mother would relate that when she was a child, he would go in the morning to the school and would gather the children together (he had four sons and six daughters). He would then tell them wonderful tales about the Rambam (philosopher and scholar, Maimonides) who had also been famous as a great physician and about whom many legends were told by the Jewish folk. My Zaide spun stories of other great ones of Israel in order to plant in the children's hearts, a love and interest in these Jewish personalities. Also from my childhood, engraved in my memory are the Jewish holidays that were celebrated in my Zaide's house with great tradition and splendor.

Looking back, from a distance of fifty years, I see that my Zaide's house was a synthesis of two worlds – the old and the new. My Zaide and Bobbe were religious people. They strictly upheld the rules and commandments but at the same time, their ears were open to catch the sound of modern times. It is a wonder that in their house, both worlds lived in peace whereas in many other homes, they clashed. Their home was open for young and old, including the friends of the grandchildren who were raised by my Zaide after their parents were murdered. Not only Jewish folk but Christians also would come to his house and my Zaide treated them with great friendliness.

In reminiscing about my Zaide's house, I feel impelled to mention two weddings that were held in his house and that illustrate the extensive ties Reb Yossl Filler had with various circles of both the Jewish and Christian communities. One wedding was of his daughter, Aunty Feinbrun (the mother of Prof. Naomi Feinbrun) who died two years ago in Tel Aviv and the second was the wedding of his granddaughter, the oldest orphan that was raised in his house. Both weddings were celebrated lavishly and among the guests were the cream of both the Jewish and the Christian societies. His strict adherence to the Jewish customs in no way diminished the Christians' esteem for him.

As already mentioned, my Zaide saw no conflict in following both the pious Jewish path and having a worldly education. Two of his children, a son and a daughter (the youngest) were given a higher education. His son studied to be an engineer in Munich and in Petersburg and worked in his profession. His daughter studied to be a dentist. He also enabled two of his grandchildren to obtain a higher education.

With the above description, I aimed to paint a picture of my Zaide's home and to emphasize that Reb Yossl Filler's house was not extraordinary in our town. The spirit that was there was the general spirit that reigned in Jewish Dubossar. In that very garden, my parents' generation, as well as my own, grew up. In that very atmosphere that was suffused with Jewish and general humanist values, we breathed and drank into our blood, standards, aspirations and hopes. We can attribute much to that environment – our faithfulness to Judaism and our modern outlook. Thanks to it we found the synthesis between traditional yiddishkeit and general humanistic values.

Bringing up these memories of "my Zaide's house" I would also like to dedicate a few lines to my father's parents, of whom, to my great sorrow, I do not have many memories as they lived in Balta where my father, may he rest in peace, was born and raised. From my childhood, I remember two times when my Zaide, Reb Moishe Bassin visited my parents' home in Dubossar.

My Zaide, Reb Moishe was a very devout Jew and in the middle of the night he would get up for midnight prayers. I remember the first time that I woke up in the middle of the night and saw my old Zaide sitting on a footstool by a small candle, chanting in a mournful melody lamentations on the destruction of the Holy Temple of Jerusalem. That picture made an exceptionally strong impression on me. Once, I recall, he brought me a present – a winter outer garment of brown material and a velvet hat. He always hoped that I would be a Rabbi when I grew up. That was his greatest desire. I don't know if I should regret that I did not become a Rabbi. It seems that I was not suited for that. My Zaide's wish was not realized but memories of both my Bobbe and Zaide are dear and warm.

Dubossar my childhood years

In spite of the fact that I spent most of my Gymnasia (high school) years (from 11 years old to eighteen) in Kishinev where I studied at the Reali middle-school, I have very vivid recollections of events that occurred in Dubossar during that period. I believe that the reason for this is that although Dubossar was a small town, it lived through the many upheavals of that time: the Russian- Japanese war, the 1905 revolution, the pogroms, the waves of liberalism that flooded the vast land after the years of 'Reactzia' (reactionary forces) and finally the national and social awakening that gripped the largest Jewish population in the world – six million – with no less intensity than in the large centers with greater populations.

Capricious fate played a role in those tragic times that the Russian Jews had to live through at the beginning of the twentieth century. The Kishinev pogrom in 1903 had its roots in my Zaide Yossl Filler's garden by the banks of the Dniester where the body of a murdered Christian boy, Ribalenko, was found. This "discovery", as quick as lightening, became the pretext for a "blood libel" against the Dubossar Jewish community. It sounds like a paradox: the libel that the Dubossar Jews killed a Christian boy for ritual purposes was the direct cause of the Kishinev pogrom. Yet these same Dubossar Jews, the supposed perpetrators of the crime, were able to avoid the slaughter that was prepared for them by the frenzied pogromists thanks to their lightening swift organization of Self-Defense groups. The Jewish youth of Dubossar proved worthy inheritors of those Jews from the previous century who for 80 years also fought off with great courage the pogroms that swept over Southern Russia.

This blood libel immediately thrust Dubossar into the spotlight of both Jewish and Russian societies, including the highest government echelons. Famous activists, renowned jurists as well as known anti-semites – foremost among the M. Sabarine, the editor of the reactionary newspaper "Novaya Vremya" (New Times) – descended upon Dubossar to investigate the blood libel. Understandably, great Jewish personalities and activists did not remain silent and did their utmost to find out the truth to exonerate the Dubossar Jews of this shameful libel. Also our own Dubossar activists were involved with Yakov Feldman and Dovid'l Chochomovitch at the head, devoting days and night to uncovering the truth. They hunted and investigated; took testimonies of dozens of people, gathered volumes of material relating to murder and libels; ceaselessly laboring to uncover the truth. I see before my eyes a picture as real as if in the present – that of Chaim Nachman Bialik and the teacher Averbach (they came specifically because of the blood libel) sitting in my parents' home. Dovid'l Chochomovitch personally handed over to Bialik a written report of the investigation that our local people had carried out here.

For a whole year we lived in a pogrom-like atmosphere and like Damocles Sword, the blood libel hung over our heads until the Czarist regime, that was very skilled at instigating pogroms and hate campaigns against Jews as well as stopping them when they had served its political purposes, finally decided to clear up the foul stench and sent to Dubossar an investigator who knew Yiddish. In no time he named the murderer of the boy. It turned out that the boy had inherited considerable wealth from his deceased parents and his uncle, hoping to lay his hands on these assets, had murdered the boy. In order to remove himself from suspicion, the uncle had thrown the dead body into my Zaide's garden. The murderer was promptly arrested and sentenced thus exonerating the Jews of Dubossar of all blame.

1905, the year of the first Russian revolution. We, the young Jewish students who were enthusiastically caught up in the tempest of the revolution, lived through bitter disappointments and many high hopes were dashed in the waves of pogroms that swept through the vast land after the collapse of the revolution. My summer vacations were spent at my parents' house and until today, I clearly remember the strained and anxious atmosphere that the Dubossar Jews lived through at that time.

The gentiles from the suburbs and surrounding villages ground their teeth but didn't dare to show their faces in our town out of fear of our Jewish Self-Defense groups. At that time the Self-Defense was very well organized. There was a Jewish militia equipped with live ammunition, revolvers and rifles. The Self-Defense also had a mounted division. The militia received a salary and food from the Citizens' committee which was under the control of the defense command.

The main task of the militia was to hold vigil at night. I remember an episode from that time that left a deep impression. My father, may he rest in peace, was an active member of the Self-Defense and every night he would come home after midnight. One night he was out later than usual. The clock on the wall struck two and he had not yet returned; it struck three and he still was not home. My mother, may she rest in peace, and we children were awake the whole night and we didn't know what to think. Finally, with the first rays of sunshine we heard the horse's hoof beats and father stumbled into the house, dead tired.

What was the reason that he came home so late? The espionage section of the Self-Defense found out that a big pogrom was being planned against the Jews of Dubossar for that night. They were planning to come from the other side of the Dniester river. The armed Self-Defense units and the mounted militia stationed themselves by the banks of the Dniester all night. It turned out that the information was correct and at one hour past midnight, barges could be seen drifting closer to our shore. The commander of the mounted police yelled over to them and warned them to go back to where they came from. The leader of their band, seeing that the Jewish Self-Defense was ready and waiting for them ordered his men to leave this place and go further.

In general, relations between the leaders of the Self-Defense and the local police was a civil one. The police noted the courage and dedication of the Jewish men and did not interfere with the militia and its goal to protect the Jewish community from the rampaging hooligans. Once, though, something happened that for a time spoiled these good relations. Actually, the ones to blame were a couple of men from our militia who were generally comprised of common youth – butchers, coachmen and so on. They were fellows who all year were accustomed to arguing and fighting and not infrequently, their altercations ended up with terrible blows. Many of these men were eagerly waiting for the opportunity to meet up with the hooligans, to give them a lesson that Jewish young men are able to protect their Jewish honour, lives and property. One night, a couple of them could no longer restrain themselves and in the midst of rough-housing, shot their rifles several times into the air. A panic broke out in the town and the regular police sprang into action. The militia men argued that they had been shooting only to frighten away a band of hooligans that were trying to smuggle themselves into town. The Defense committee had to work very hard to mollify the local police and the incident ended with a sharp reproof from the chief of police.

In conjunction with the tradition of bravery of the Dubossar Jews, I heard the following story from Dubossar landsmen (fellow countrymen) from America who came to Israel for the planting of the forest in memory of the martyrs of our town who were murdered by the Nazis. They related that they heard a rumor from the other side of the "Iron Curtain" (Soviet Union). Apparently when Hitler's hordes invaded Russia and the advance guard of Nazis entered Dubossar, the local Jews surrounded them and killed sixty German soldiers. Later when the Germans conquered the city and its environs, all the local Jews and from surrounding areas were herded to a location outside of town where they were shot. This story, which apparently contains a kernel of truth, is a continuation of the Jewish Dubossar tradition of standing up to the enemy even though the possibility of success was nil.

* * *

In reminiscing about my childhood years in Dubossar, I find it necessary to mention the wonderful period of the Zionist renaissance in our town and the people who stood at the head of the movement exerting such a great influence on the younger generation. I mentioned before, the visit to our town of Chaim Nachman Bialik and Pesach Averbach. There were other people – community activists and writers who came to our town and gave us great pleasure with their instructive words. Of note, was the teacher Yagolnitzer (Golani) who was in Dubossar for two years as director of our Hebrew school. He was among the main founders of the Self-Defense organization in Dubossar and on his initiative, a Tzeirei Tzion (Young Zion) movement was organized and was very active. It was in our town that Chaim Greenberg together with Yagolnitzer created the Tzeirei Tzion program that became a prototype for all the other Tzeirei Tzion groups in other locations. It was henceforth known as the "Dubossar Program". In the year 1907 Yagolnitzer settled in Eretz Yisroel and was a role model for all the Dubossar youth that later followed him.

P. 73 Zionist group in Dubossar before WW. 1

First row R-L: Leml Shmuel ?Dayan's? (Rubin), Zelig Berkovitch, Abraham Koifman, Moishe Feldman, Yoel Gurevitch, Yosef . Manshnyager.
Middle row: Joseph Tzelnik, Israel Greenspan, Joseph Visoki.

[Page74]

Blood libel in Dubossar

by Yosef Visoki (Ram) z"l

Translated by Sam Blatt

In spring 1902, the socialist-revolutionaries assassinated the Minister of the Interior, Sufiagin, and in his place Czar Nicholas II nominated Count Fleveh who excelled in his tyrannical and cruel campaign against the Freedom Movement in Czarist Russia.

At about the same time, in the month of January 1903, the body of a Russian boy, Ribolenko, was found stabbed to death and lying in the garden of a Jewish resident of Dubossar. The newspaper "Bessarabitz", organ of the "Black One Hundred" of Bessarabia that was published in Kishinev and supported by the government, latched on to the story. On a daily basis the paper was filled with inflammatory articles claiming that the Jews murdered the boy for ritual purposes, namely to obtain Christian blood in order to bake matzos for the coming holiday of Passover. The paper went even further, inciting pogroms against the Jews as revenge for the "Spilling of Christian blood".

The Christian population of Dubossar and environs, especially the rural population on the other side of the Dniester, was influenced by the daily inciting propaganda for a pogrom. The chutzpa of both the inciters and incited was without limits and open. With no fear, they threatened the Jewish population with revenge for the "spilled Christian blood". They were certain that the government would support them and that no one would prevent them from carrying out their diabolic plan.

A sense of dread took hold of the Jewish population that each day expected the outbreak of the storm. That does not mean, however, that the Jews of Dubossar were sitting with arms folded, waiting passively for the pogromists. Under the initiative of the Zionist youth and under its leadership, a self-defense group was organized with lightening speed to thwart any attack in the event of an assault on the Jewish population. At the request of the self-defense command, Jewish men of various ages volunteered and all were prepared for the excesses which might break out any day.

One particular day, a few weeks before Passover, in the early morning hours, unusual movements were noted of Christians heading toward the direction of the river. There they were to meet the farmers from the other side of the Dniester to take part in the pogrom that was to take place in our town that day.

The self-defense group, armed with all manner of weapons, spread out in groups occupying positions at the entrance to the city in the direction of the Dniester. When the pogromists neared the city in order to slip into the Jewish neighborhoods, one heard a single shot pierce the air. That was the signal of the self-defense group to attack the enemy from all sides. When the pogromists realized that the city was defended and that the Jews were prepared for a heavy battle, they reconsidered and retreated in great haste to the Dniester.

On that day there was no pogrom in Dubossar. Not on that day and not any other day. The reputation of the Dubossar Jewish self-defense force spread all over Russia and whenever a band of bandits happened to be in the area of Dubossar, they always tried to avoid the city in order not to meet up with the heroic young men of Dubossar.

[Page78]

Additional facts about the Blood Libel in Dubossar

by L. Rubin (B. Iris)

Translated by Sarah Faerman

In early spring, 1903, by the river Dniester, in the garden of a Jewish homeowner, the body of a murdered Christian boy was discovered. The boy's wounds appeared to show signs associated with ritual murder. That was enough for rumors to spread like wildfire that the Jews had killed the boy for ritual purposes. The owner of the garden was arrested along with another couple of Jews who, due to business, were often seen by the shores of the river. Following strenuous interventions on their behalf each of the arrested was provisionally released.

The next day, the hooligan, Krushevan, in his Pogromist newspaper, "Besarabetz" which was published in Kishenev, demanded that all Christians take revenge on the Jews for the spilled Christian blood. A few Jews, local people from Dubossar, on their own initiative launched an investigation uncovering clues that led to the identity of the actual murderer. They immediately alerted Kherson, the capital city of the province, and the governor himself arrived in Dubossar with a Commission to investigate the matter on the spot. A Jewish delegation headed by the judges Reb Yerucham and Reb Shmuel,z" (the father of the author of these words) holding Torahs in their arms, met the Governor and his retinue.

The next day the judges were summoned to the governor to give evidence.

The judges explained Jewish law to the Commission. They quoted from the book of Deuteronomy that prohibited the ingesting of blood. "... No blood is to be eaten... as the blood is the soul... " According to Jewish law, every piece of meat must be salted and soaked before it could be used in order that there would not remain even one drop of blood. This alone, they argued, should indicate how Jews take special pains not to use any blood. The judges also described various other aspects associated with the laws of slaughter and making food Kosher.

The hearing was a friendly one and the details of the private Jewish investigation were conveyed to the Commission. The Commission sent an undercover agent, disguised as common laborer, to the village where the suspect was living. He worked there for a few days and did find out the identity of the actual murderer. It turned out that it was the boy's own uncle whose motive had been the boy's inheritance.

And that is how the case was solved-exonerating the Jews. However, this did not slake the appetite for Pogrom that had been aroused in the local population and it caused days of worry and panic for the Jews in the area.

The Jewish youth organized a self-defense cadre that day and night manned strategic sites and vigilantly remained on the look-out for troublemakers. Jewish horsemen were prepared to torch the villages of the Pogromists if they tried to attack. Those "heroes", seeing that the Jews would defend themselves and fight back, decided to drop their devilish plans altogether.

Krushevan, with his filthy newspaper in Kishenev and the Duma deputy Purishekevitch, another foe of the Jewish people, poured out their venom on the Kishinev Jews (Spring 1903). The Jewish workers, tradesmen and butchers tried to form a resistance but they were disarmed by the police and the army who assisted the pogromists in fulfilling their bloody work.

1906 Tzeirei |Tzion Org., Dubossar 1906.

Standing R-L: Yosef Visoki-Ram, Yosef Grinblat, Chaim Kornfeld, Tzvi Rosentzvit, Baruch Bassin, Chernivsky, Yosef Feinshil (Ben Ami).

Seated centre: Miss Bernstein, Boris Sapir, Leah Bassin, Yitzchak Yogalnitzer (Golani),Rivka Shocket, Moishe Faygis.

First row: Sara Bassin, Hinda Bassin, Zaidl Spector.

[Page82]

My Dubossar Years

by A. Y. Golani, z"l

Translated by Sam Blatt

In the year 1905, the struggle between the "Zion Zionists" (those wanting to settle in Eretz Yisrael) and the "Uganda-ists" (those willing to settle in Uganda) became stronger. Dr. Ben-Zion Mosenson and Dr. Chaim Bograshov visited southern Russia in the name of the "Zion Zionists", and Dr. Mosenson's visit to Bessarabia turned into a triumphant move. In Argeyev he silenced our strongest opponents. The triumph of the Zion Zionists was a complete one. In Kishinev, in the "Tzeirei Tzion" (organization called Zionist Youth) circles, a new star shone – Chaim Greenberg. The Zionist Youth movement blossomed, taking on the character of a working national movement, close in ideology to the Russian-Socialist-Revolutionaries. At that time we, a group of the Tzeirei Tzion from Argeyev, after great deliberations adopted a decision to begin spreading the ideas of the movement with our own efforts. We visited many shtetlekh and Jewish colonies (in Khersaner Gubernieh), bringing the word of the movement to the youth.

On one of these trips I arrived at the shtetl Dubossar, near the Dniester, and settled there for two years. I put in a lot of energy and effort into this town, reaching the peak of my galut Zionist activity. The Jewish population of Dubossar was composed of not wealthy, but well established merchants, tobacco planters, tobacco workers, various trades-people and workers on the ships which traveled on the Dniester. The Jews of Dubossar also had a reputation of being fearless fighters and this cast a fear on the non-Jewish population of the entire region. They were plain people, naïve in their beliefs, proud Jews, and not overly religious.

In this town, there was a Zionist organization which decided to found a Zionist school, acknowledged by the government and with the name "Talmud Torah". The city leaders searched for a director for the school, which was just about to open and they also required that the director be a Zionist. At exactly that time I was sent to Dubossar to conduct Zionist "propaganda", and to repel the attacks of a few young men close to the Russian S.D. party and the Bund. In the course of 2 –3 evenings of stormy debate I was successful in winning over the opponents of Zionism and on this opportunity I formed a branch of the Tzeirei Tzion organization to which most of the youth of the town signed up, and even some of the previous opponents of Zionism. When the Zionist leadership of Dubossar became aware that I was a graduate teacher, they invited me to accept the post of director for the new school which they were in the process of founding.

At that time I was already seriously considering the idea of aliya to Israel, and I was interested in saving a bit of money for expenses for the trip. I accepted the invitation, and later, when the confirmation arrived from the government, I opened the school. Aside from Russian, we taught Hebrew, Tanakh, and other Jewish subjects. The subjects were taught according to the "Ivrit B'Ivrit" (speaking only Hebrew) method, and after a short time, Hebrew became a living, spoken language for the students.

After opening the school, I threw myself energetically into Zionist activity. I organized the Zionist youth into groups, in order to teach them the foundations of Zionism. The lectures were held a few times during the week, and on Saturdays we had larger meetings, where we explained general Zionist and Jewish issues. During the winter months we held the meetings in the Zionist school, and during the summer we gathered outside the city, in the shade of nut-tree forests. There we would read the newspapers about Jewish life, events of the day and primarily about Zionism.

After a few months of intensive explanatory work, we decided, after weighty deliberations, to officially join up with the Tzeirei Tzion movement. To accomplish this goal, we turned to the Tzeirei Tzion movement in Kishinev, who sent us the young, barely 19 year-old Chaim Greenberg. In the course of a week's time, Greenberg conducted numerous educational sessions for the Jewish masses. He made presentations in the large schools and the large halls. During his stay in Dubossar he wrote up, with my participation, the program and goals of the Tzeirei Tzion, composed of 16 paragraphs. This, I believe is the only published document of this type of that time. The program was accepted at a general meeting, and published on January 1906 in Russian in the weekly "Chronicle of Jewish Life". Then, when the program was ratified, I explained its various parts to the members, when we held meetings.

I also visited the shtetl Yagorlik to explain and clarify the program. The Zionist Agudah (federation) that was founded there had in the meantime joined up with the Tzeirei Tzion organization. In the summer of 1906 and 1907, during my summer vacation, I visited all the Bessarabian shtetlakh along the length of the Dniester, and the Zionist associations that existed there joined up with the Tzeirei Tzion movement in agreement with the program drawn up in Dubossar. Aside from the cultural and explanatory work, we developed multi-faceted practical Zionist activities, such as working for Keren Kayemeth (Jewish National Fund), selling shekels, and more. All these works took first priority at that time in my Zionist and cultural efforts.

Self Defense and Zionist Conferences

Fall of 1905. With the outbreak of pogroms in the Jewish towns in southern Russia, our organization took a decisive role in organizing self-defense. I was elected to the leadership of the self-defense and together with Pinchas Bassman and Shaul Sukai led the self-defense with a strong hand. We had enough weapons, and organized patrols which were posted in all corners of the town. The nerve center of the self-defense was in the shul. In the Aron Kodesh (Holy Ark), near the Torah scrolls, we kept the weapons, and from there we sent the patrols out over the city. We had riders on horses, who acted as the communicators between the various defense and lookout posts. And in reality, thanks to the heroic and well organized self-defense, Dubossar was shielded from a pogrom. The farmers from the surrounding villages simply feared coming into the city.

I want to take this opportunity to acknowledge the S.R. movement in Kishinev, which sent us several members to scout out the surrounding villages. Through them we were aware of what the farmers were preparing to do.

In order to gather as much weaponry as possible, I and a friend visited Kishinev, Tirospol, and Benderi, and we were successful in assembling a cache of guns, revolvers, and bullets. More than once, we two Jews traveling alone on the trains, were faced with serious danger amongst a riled up mob.

Summer 1906. On the recommendation of Z.K. of Tzeirei Tzion in Kishinev, I was invited to participate in an important Zionist conference in Odessa, called together by M. Ussishkin. In Chanuka 1906 the Tzeirei Tzion movement sent me as a delegate to the well known Zionist conference in Helsinki, Finland. At both conferences the Tzeirei Tzion delegates appeared as an organized caucus. Our caucus was composed of the following members: Yosef Shprintzak, Chaim Greenberg, Yaacov Efter, Yisroel Drachler, Chaim Vaisudler, Aryeh Feldman, and this writer.

After successful Zionist activity over a period of two years I decided to leave my excellent position, my friends to whom I was closely tied, and make Aliya to Israel. Other friends from Dubossar also decided to make Aliya, and today many of them are farmers in the villages and workers in the cities.

In the summer of 1907 I was elected through the Dubossar Tzeirei Tzion movement and the Argeyev Zionists, as a delegate to the 8th Zionist Congress held in The Hague. At the congress, the Zionist Youth caucus made contact with Hapoel Hatzair organization from Israel, and the "Hatkhiya" movement. Also there was born the idea to call a conference of all the Zionist youth groups.

After the congress I traveled to Dubossar to give an accounting of the Congress and to bid farewell to my friends, prior to my leaving for Israel. At a joyous goodbye-party which my friends arranged, they inscribed me in the "Golden Book" of Keren Kayemeth (Jewish National Fund). That was the best reward for my Zionist activities in Dubossar. In that year I made Aliya to Israel.

[Page87]

Zionist group (names not legible – handwritten)

A Sabbath in Yagorlik

by A. Y. Golani, z"l

Translated by Sarah Faerman

During the years of 1904-1906 Zionist activity in Russia was at a standstill. The state of extreme social fermentation that reached its peak during the revolution of 1905, caught up the best of the intellectuals amongst the Jewish youth in the ranks of the radical Socialist movements: The Socialist Revolutionaries, the Social Democrats (this group split into the Mencheviks and the Bolsheviks), and the Bund that ruled over the Jewish street. Yet, there were also young intellectuals in those years that were not mesmerized by the above-mentioned organizations and in their quest for new paths they attempted to create a synthesis between Zionism and Socialism.

From these circles in Russia, there arose the "Poalei Zion" (Workers of Zion) party and other radical Zionist groups, such as "Hatchia" (Renewal), "Hashachar" (Dawn) and "Tzeirei Tzion" (Zionist Youth). These particular organizations were based on a combination of Zionism and folk socialism by the Tzeirei Tzion who was ideologically close to the Social Revolutionaries and the Poalei Tzion, who, as Marxists, were close to the Social Democrats.

New branches of the Tzeirei Tzion organization would sprout up daily in the towns and villages of South Russia. Its centre was in Kishinev under the leadership of Yosef Shprintzak who had a great influence on the young Jewish students. He involved the best with their youthful vigor in the activities of the organization. Among others, there were: Chaim Greenberg, Yisrael Garfinkel (Guri), Yakov Epter, Yosef Baratz, Nachum Tversky and Chaim Vaisodler. Later these same young men would play a distinguished role in the Zionist movement and in the building up of Eretz Yisrael.

When sending speakers to the towns and villages to spread the concept of a National Jewish Revival, a typical tactic of Tzeirei Tzion was to utilize local talents side by side with the "imported" lecturers. I also was given this task during the period when I was the Director of the Hebrew/Russian school in the town of Dubossar by the shores of the Dniester River. In the winter of 1906, the Dubossar Tzeirei Tzion group invited Chaim Greenbers (he was then 19 years old) to come to Dubossar and within one week we worked out a program consisting of 16 points that reflected the ideological foundation of the movement. This very program is recognized in the history of the Zionist movement by the name of "The Dubossar Tzeirei Tzion Program".

After the program was ratified by the Central Committee of Tzeirei Tzion, I was invited by G.L.Rachev of our neighbouring town, Yagorlik, to visit them to report on this newly created program and to influence the local youth to join the Tzeirei Tzion movement. One Friday night that winter, accompanied by another member of our Dubossar organization, I made the visit to Yagorlik.

Yagorlik was a tiny town with a small Jewish population that, like all other similar little towns, earned their living as tradesmen, craftsmen and small handlers. In one aspect, however, Yagorlik differed from the other towns. Practically all of their youth, including the girls, could speak Hebrew and were infused with Zionist convictions. They admired their leader and teacher Gad'l Layb Rachev who spared no effort in educating the youth in Yiddish, Hebrew and Zionism.

That Friday night, until after midnight as well as the next day – 18 hours in all – discussions, explanations, arguments and education took place. The Dubossar program was dissected point by point and clarifications made until, finally, the assembled in Yagorlik accepted the program and decided to officially join the Tzeirei Tzion movement.

The main principles of the Dubossar program were as follows: Nationalism; Transforming the Hebrew language into a living, spoken language; Practical work in the Diaspora; Aliya (immigration to Eretz Yisrael); Actualizing the ideals via physical labour, particularly farming; Helping to create a just society in Eretz Yisrael with membership in the Socialist Movement. Which brand of Socialism was covered by the point :"Only when we will be in Eretz Yisrael as workers or farmers will we decide which Socialist party to join – the Socialist Revolutionaries or the Socialist Democrats.

Not too many years went by – 2 or 3 at the most – and the majority of the Yagorlik Tzeirei Tzion members, with their leader Chaver (comrade) Rachlev, emigrated to Eretz Yisrael, concentrating mainly in Moshav Ein Ganim which was the forerunner of Moshav Ovdim. Most of them planted deep roots in the land and realized with their lives and bodies the "Torah" of Labour Zionism. Sorrowfully, Rachev's students did not have much time with their respected and beloved teacher. he died one year after his arrival in Yisrael. However, to this day, the name of Gad'l Layb Rachev is heard on their lips with great love and esteem.

May his name be honored.

[Page90]

Images and Memories from my Town Dubossary

by Moshe son of Yakov and Rachel-Lea Feldman (Haklay) z"l
Translated by Yocheved Klausner

In Moldavia, by the Dniester, lies my town Dubossary.

Years ago, it was called Dumbissar.
It was in old, old times,
When, from a very far country
The Turks ruled over Moldavia.
The ruins of a castle are still to be seen,
Cut into the rock on the "Calanter" Mountain.
The name was changed in the time of Empress Ekaterina.

Dubossary… my shtetl, where I was born,
You are alive and fresh in my memory.
Your magical exotic landscapes
Are hovering before my eyes;
A dream and a mirage
Are woven together.
As in a mist, you are wrapped
In an enchanted panorama;
As through a silky transparent veil
Your skies are shining, at night as in the day;
Spread over mountain and valley,
Encircled by a long chain of gardens,
Orchards and vineyards,
Watered by the Great Dniester River.
Berries of all kinds are growing there,
And fruits – grapes, apples and pears, and melons.
Around you are forests, villages and plains,
Where tall stalks of corn are rocked by the wind
And sheaves of wheat are gathered, replete with heavy seeds.

Dubossary! … It is there that I saw the world for the first time.
There my childhood passed, happy and free of worry.
I miss your long, wide streets,

[Page 91]

Your narrow, crooked alleys,
Your spacious courtyards, houses with ornate balconies,
That hovered proudly
Over the small poor houses with roofs of straw,
Surrounded by pits and muddy holes
That even in the summer did not dry out.
In the shade of the large, ramified acacia trees,
Through rows of blooming lavender
Young noblemen would ride
While the fragrance of the flowers and trees
Would fill the air with sweet aroma and magic

And on the mountain, far from the town's horizon,
Among picturesque landscapes that caught the eye
The silhouettes of winged windmills
Rose thoughtfully, standing in watch
Around the clear water from the springs.
The water carriers, bent under the load
Of heavy jugs on their backs
Would deliver water to the houses,
Filling the water containers for a few pennies.
When the town was dry and suffocating from heat,
The water would quench the thirst
Revive, refresh and invigorate the drinker.
And when the sun would burn and bake the air
The shtetl would run to the Dniester to bathe,
Or to Itzik Hertzes, the attendant of the Mikve,
To cool off in the water, to dip, to play.

The young men and the coquette young girls
Would go sailing on the Dniester in small boats,
Managing the oars and having competitions
All the way to the Bessarabia shore
Where they would visit the villages
And rest in the shade of the magic forest.

The Dniester streamed idyllic and silent,
A light wind would blow, caressing the velvety coolness.

[Page92]

Night came, the sky darkened,
A star was shining and sparkling,
As if reminding the unconcerned youth:
Enough of frolicking – it is time to go home.

From the Dniester, the road back home
Is winding through romantic gardens.
Silent is the night, only the echo remains
Of joyous songs and melancholic longing.
A peasant woman is singing somewhere
A sad folksong about green leaves –
Just like the leaves, the longing bride will wither,
Waiting for the soldier, her fiancé.

My little town, the happy Dubossary! ...
Along your beautiful, graceful boulevard
Young people, brave, golden young people
Are taking secret walks toward the Mountain
That smelled of sweet cinnamon and other spices
Reviving in their hearts sweet feelings and dreams...
The youth was captivated by the new "renaissance":
During illegal meetings
Every night in a different home,
Where Hershel the Zionist watched for the police –
They exchanged ideas, opinions
In intense and passionate discussions.

The youth of Dubossary was courageous and defiant,
Brave Jews, with bold Maccabean flame in their hearts;
They have organized self defense
To protect Dubossary and surroundings when pogrom comes.

I remember from my childhood the terrible measles epidemic:
Life was in danger in the entire town.
I remember also, in a frosty winter night
A fire broke out and brought disaster and chaos.

[Page 93]

All types of Jews in Dubossary: rich, strong, distinguished, honest,
Charitable, righteous, pious simple folk;
Also scholars, learned people, geniuses,
Some with imposing appearance, like our Patriarchs.
They would sit in the Bet Hamidrash, in the Kloiz and other synagogues,
Study Talmud and rabbinic books, or reading from the Psalms.
We had also educated people, part of the Enlightenment Movement,
Immersed in discussion or research
Reading new Russian and Hebrew newspapers, as Hatzefira.

I remember a snowy, freezing, stormy winter day,
All Dubossary was weeping in sorrow.
On that day the rabbi, the judge, the great scholar,
The Tzadik R'Yerucham the Kohen died.
All houses were locked by locks and bolts,
All, young and old, filled the streets.
Students from the Talmud Torah, group after group,
Walked with the funeral.
The sad and grief-stricken procession
Stopped at the gate of the cemetery,
Waiting for the son of the deceased to arrive from Kishinev.
Meanwhile, when they dug the grave, I fell asleep.
Late at night, long after the funeral was over,
The cold woke me and I stood up terrified.
Alone among graves and dead people,
I burst into bitter tears.
The watchman, hearing my cries,
Came running, trembling with fear,
Not knowing what had happened.
Astonished and scared he looked around,
Until he spotted me.
He brought me home, a weeping child,
Whose parents were sick with worry and suffering.
The entire town had been in havoc –
Who knows? Perhaps, God forbid, he was kidnapped by gypsies? ...
Since that day, the world had gone through trouble and tribulation,
Generations passed away and new generations came,
And still the fright at R'Yerucham's funeral was remembered.

[Page 94]

I remember the night of Simchat Torah [rejoicing with the
Torah]:
In the small synagogue, in the yard of Keile Chaim
Mordechai's,
The members of the Chovevei-Zion movement danced.
Some respected Jews of Dubossary
Decided to "have a good time:"
Drunken, they stormed through the rich houses
Looking for the holiday delicious dishes
That the housewives had hidden, in time,
Under lock and key, in a safe, cool place.
But they broke all the locks,
And brought out dishes of fine holiday food – ducklings
and cake.
In the morning, the empty pots and pans
Hung on the fences like so many crowns.

I remember the weddings, in Hershel Chaikel's Hall,
Where R'Avraham "Potato" [Kartofle], the matchmaker
and community gossip,
Personally served the "wedding families" the festive meal,
And Itzik the Klezmer played his heartfelt tunes.
Young and old, hearing the music,
Would run to the place, to look, to listen,
And secretly enjoy the happy moments of their fellow Jews.

From one end of town to the meadow at the other end
All along the bank of the Dniester,
Through the New Cemetery, by the old army barracks,
The road stretches through all of Dubossary,
Past the steam-driven flour mill
Then by R'Zalman Rikles' warehouses.
Climbing a little on the hill, you'll find the legendary Old
Cemetery,
Where trees grow beyond the fence – the beginning of the
woods.
Ancient tombstones, hundreds of years old,
Of holy Tzadikim, which are hidden
In crooked little huts and tents.
One of the Tzadikim – so legend says –
Was the miracle-worker R'Mendel.
He was a scholar, a Cabbalist, a genius, a sharp mind,
A disciple and friend of the Baal-Shem-Tov.

[Page 95]

Miraculous stories were told about him,
And he protected Dubossary from sickness and trouble.

But... no miracle protected the town of Dubossary
When disaster and horror struck
In the dark days, not many years ago,
When the Jewish community was destroyed.

Empty and ruined are the courtyards, deserted the streets,
No more warm and affectionate people.
The remaining little houses are sunken into the ground,
Like orphans they stand, seemingly flickering
And simmering like an eternal memorial light.

Looking... here in the valley Dubossary lies in ruins,
And on the mountain, 18,500 martyrs lie in the large pits –
These are our brothers lying there in heaps
Our brothers from the destroyed community.
Silently they lie in eternal peace...

You run... and suddenly you stop and look back,
You cannot tear yourself away – one more glance...
Inside you, your heart is in a fog, cold and frozen,
As if you are yourself in the ground,
Buried together with all the martyrs.

[Page96]

Reb Naftali Ish Horvitz (father of Bernardo Gurevitch, Argentina)

A Memorial Candle for My Town Dubossar

by Bernardo Gorevitch

(Dov, son of Naftali Halevi Horovitz, z"l)

Translated by Sarah Faerman

Dubossar, where I was born, is located in Moldavia by the shores of the Dniester River, between Kamenietz Poldolsk and Bessarabia and forty viorst from Kishenev. Let it be remembered that following the Kishinev pogrom of 1903, some of the orphans of that massacre were brought to Argentina – a tradition that would be repeated years later following the 1918-1920 Ukrainian pogroms. Dozens of orphans were then brought over by the Jewish community and placed in the Buenos Aires Jewish orphanage.

In the olden days, Dubossar was under the Turkish regime and later under Moldavian rule.

In the 18th century, the Russian Czar annexed the land. It has been noted in various records and also on old tombstones that the Jewish community in Dubossar dates back to the 17th century.

I see Dubossar before my eyes – vibrant and alive as it was during my childhood. Calm and peaceful, she lay by the Dniester River where barges and steamboats would pass by on their journey to the Black Sea. Colorful fruit orchards and wheat fields adorned the entire area and clear and sweet water cascaded down from the adjacent mountains. A sip of water from the springs during the heat of summer was deliciously thirst quenching. In the meadows, the animals would graze; calves and lambs would cavort and leap. One could hear the warbling of birds in the trees while the Acacia trees perfumed the air with a delicate fragrance. Lovely and bright were the moonlit evenings in Dubossar. The blessings of the earth and the beauty of nature filled every heart with a desire and lust for life.

There, in that earthly paradise were our cradles. Can we then forget this? Can we believe that all this has been wiped out, destroyed? That thousands and thousands of our nearest and dearest were annihilated at the hands of murderers? And yet, it is true and the reality is much more horrifying than one could even imagine.

Being unable to eulogize the thousands of the martyrs of our town, I would like to mention some who are engraved in my mind. On the way to the second, old cemetery, going toward the meadow, lies the grave site of the Tzadik (Pious man) Reb Mendele, a student of the Baal Shem Tov, as well as graves of other saintly men, may they rest in peace. In the new cemetery, which we all remember, I would like to mention the graves of the Dubossarer Rabbi and Reb Chaim David Dayan, z'tz"l. These two great scholars would be summoned to all the surrounding areas when there was a need to make a very difficult Torah judgment. Also at their eternal rest there were: the Rabbinic judge, the Tzadik Reb Chaim Shimon son of Menachem; Nachum Levi; Isaac Rabinovitch and his son Reb Shmuel Dayan – the father of our friend Leml Rubin, long may he live. There also lies the great scholar Reb Yerucham Dayan and the ritual slaughterers, Israel Layb Farnshul and Reb Efraim Greenblat.

I remember them from my childhood years and they actually appear before my eyes. I also would like to mention Reb Nachum Shotek (the Quiet One) – we would call him Nachum Aronke's. He was silent and he always studied. All week he would go from house to house collecting donations for Sabbath Kiddush or Havdala for the poor. And Reb Yosef, the trustee of the Talner Rabbi's synagogue, z'tz"l, the father of the famous cantor Nachum Matenka, who would, at the 'Three Sabbath Meals' dance with great devotion: "A day of rest and holiness You gave to our people."

I also wish to name these wonderful men – Isaac Rashkavski; Yosef Filler; my grandfather Mordecai Layb Ish Horovitz, of the lineage of Isaiah Horovitz ,the holy one , h'sh'l'h (author of Shnei Luchot Habrit); his father Reb Naftali; Reb Pinchas, son of Yosef Melech Finkelshtein; David Zalmina, son of Moishe Horovitz; Motl Chazan; Eliezer Bendersky , sh'tz; Reb Motl Cohen; Israel Tzelnik; Chaim Tzvi Tzelnik; Layb Batalsky; Yechiel Tzelnik, Rabbiner (Rabbi) Layb Pitchiniuk; Moishe Bronfman; Yosef Ben Naftali Horovitz, Guteh Molavyatisky; Krasnavetz; Feldsher (medical aide) Yeshpe, Yosef Rofeh (doctor); Abraham Baruch; Isaac Vaisman; my brother Yosef Horovitz, his wife and their daughter who died of hunger; Doody Jacob, son of Mordecai Layb Gurevitch and wife Rayzl; Doody Elkana Gurevitch; Doody Abraham Jacob Piltchikov and wife Raizy; Reb David Lifshin; Chanan Kipnis, Yudl Filler, Jacob Feldman; Simcha Vaisman; Nachum Cohen; Zalman Korpirst and many more that I cannot remember.

Their blessed memory and that of the thousands of Dubossar martyrs that were killed in World War II will always remain before our eyes. May their names live on forever in this Yizkor book.

Kantor family – Parents: Moishe and Nechama,
Son Yosef was killed in the war while serving in the Red Army.

Seated: Avraham Fishgold, active member of Hagana.
Standing – his good friend Hershl Shargarodsky who lives in America.
1910

[Page110]

Self-Defense in Dubossar

by Yehayahu Kantor
Translated by Sarah Faerman

Like most of the Jewish communities in Russia, the Jewish community in Dubossar by the Dniester River, over many years wove its own distinctive ways and patterns. Dubossar served as a center for the outlying towns and villages. The murderous Nazi axe that descended on the head of Jewish Europe and wiped out one third of our folk during the Second World War also cut down the Jewish lives in our town. After the war, trusted witnesses described to us how the Nazis herded almost all of the Jews of Dubossar and the surrounding towns to one of the hills nearby and in the thoroughly bestial manner that only the Germans are capable of, massacred all of them.

Along with the holy ones from all of the Jewish communities that were annihilated during World War II, we remember with love and honor the heroes of our town that heroically fought off aggressors of all stripes, pogromists and hooligans who attempted to attack our town during the stormy period of World War I and during the difficult days of the revolution and counter-revolution, defending with courage and dedication Jewish lives and Jewish honour.

In the following sentences I will attempt to draw out from the depths of my memory some of the finest chapters that have been woven with golden threads into the history of the Dubossar community.

* * *

For the first nine years of my life, I lived in a village four kilometers from Dubossar. From my carefree childhood years, I remember wonderful stories that the local Jews and gentiles would tell about the Jewish Dubossar heroes. (One of the legends that circulated about the Dubossar heroes was that each one of them was capable of killing a whole village of gentiles). Dubossar was a city that provided shelter for Jews that were hiding from the powers that be, for refugees fleeing pogroms – an oft repeated occurrence in Czarist Russia. I heard many stories about these heroes during my childhood and their names are vivid in my memory. The most famous were: Aaron Shmuel's son, Chaim Isser's son, Laybele Dishovke, Mendele Patran, Shaul Sakai (the knife), Yidele Katrazhan, Yosele Bezh, Laybele Katzap and many others. Any Jew who could claim to be a relative of one of this famous group could be sure that no hooligan would dare to lay a hand on him. So great was the terror that they cast on the enemies of Israel in the whole district, that it was enough to remind them that in 1902, other enemies of Israel fabricated a "blood libel "blaming the Dubossar Jews of murdering a Christian boy in order to use his blood for a Passover ritual. At the time, the whole area was inflamed by hate propaganda and lies, yet the pogromists did not dare to assault the Dubossar Jews.

The young heroes were not learned men nor did they have much education. However, they were simple and honest people. They did not differentiate between Jew and gentile. However, when a Jew was wronged because he was a Jew, then their national pride would ignite and the need for revenge would burn like a fire. Jewish honor was very important to them. That is the secret behind the heroism of the Dubossar Jews throughout the many years until the day when the Nazi murderers annihilated out town along with hundreds of other Jewish communities that were slaughtered and wiped out in Nazi occupied Europe.

After the defeat of the first Russian revolution in 1905, a stronger mood favouring pogroms prevailed. In response, a "Self-Defense" group was organized headed by the teacher, Golani (Yagolnitzer), Pinye Bassin (Baruch Bassin's father) and Shaul Sakai (Tzvi Sakai's father). Legends abounded regarding the bravery of Shaul. Of the three, Shaul evoked the greatest terror amongst the local gentiles. It happened that a relative of his (Mendele Patran's uncle) was attacked and beaten by the gentiles. One day, Mendele told Shaul that he had invited these same hooligans to his house for a glass of brandy. Of course, on the way to Mendele's house, they had to pass the home of Shaul. Mendele and Shaul made a plan to make sure the two visitor would receive a "warm welcome". And so it was on the appointed day. As the hooligans came closer to Shaul's house, he was ready and waiting for them. They were soon lying on the ground, bloody and beaten until one of them managed to pry himself loose and 'hendus pendus' ran to Mendele's for help. Until he reached Mendele's house and until Mendele made his way over to Shaul's house, Shaul had finished off the troublemakers and even the police refrained from interfering when Shaul was thus "occupied". He put a halt to his "holy work" when Mendele ran up and "begged for mercy", pleading that Shaul should release his "friends" who were coming to his house as guests.

Such episodes and similar ones did not occur infrequently in Dubossar and generally would end with a "sulcha" (forgiveness) and pardon. Following such incidents, the reputation of the Jewish heroes of Dubossar traveled far and wide. On the other side of the Dniester, eight kilometers from Dubossar, is the town of Moshkovtzi where 80 Jewish families lived. At the beginning of the 20th century, when the air was thick with hatred toward Jews, hooligans of that town made a pogrom against the Jews and robbed them of their possessions. When the people of Dubossar heard the news about the pogrom, the sons of Aaron Shmuel and Chaim Isser (two sons each) decided to pay a visit to Moshkovtzi and to teach the hooligans that Jewish property is not free for the taking.

When the inhabitants of the town became aware of the "visit" that was awaiting them, they became very frightened and a delegation, including the head of the town (chief) himself, arrived in Dubossar bearing a letter to Rabbi Abel from the village priest. The chief pleaded with the Rabbi to influence the four young men to cancel their plans and vowed to return the stolen property to the Jews. They also promised that this would not occur again in their town.

News of this and similar incidents would spread as quickly as lightening among the towns, far and near, and prevented many a hot-head from starting up with the Dubossar gang. Dr. Bernstein-Cohen, in his memoir "Dubossar," mentions several times the "Self-Defense" organization in Southern Russia. I will quote the following fragment:

"Not only in Kishinev but also in Dubossar did the Jews with their own strength put a stop to the pogroms. The government listened to the advice of the Moldavians and sent in the local militia on a robbing "action" in the Jewish community. That night however, they were bitterly cut off. In the military report it was reported that 16 soldiers "disappeared", intimating desertion. A week later, near the border, the Dniester River spit up their dead bodies. In Dubossar there were no further pogroms – not that year and not later even though waves of pogroms continued to flood the whole South West of Russia. Needless to say, the entire Jewish population of Dubossar was overjoyed and for years after, praised with gratitude the heroes and their families who had resorted to the only possible, logical tactic."

The Dubossar police chief would rein in his police and prevent them from confronting the 'gang' (Self-Defense) for whom, it appears, he actually felt sympathy. There was a story about one of Chaim Isser's sons (Nachum, a mechanic by profession) who dealt such hefty blows to two gentile attackers that their souls departed on the spot. The police chief gave Nachum a wink and Nachum took the hint, immediately fleeing over the border. The Dubossarers and in particular, "the gang" couldn't reconcile themselves to the absence of such a treasure as Nachum.

* * *

During the years 1917-20 in our district, one government followed another and various marauding bands raged undisturbed. The greatest panic was generated by the bands that were led by the sword brandishing Cossack chiefs: Zabalotny, Titiniuk, Zheliane, Grigoriev, Popov and others. None of them had a political agenda but all were anti-semites and robbing and murdering Jews was a daily activity for them. In many towns and villages in Ukraine, Jewish blood flowed like water but they did not dare to set foot in Dubossar. And if it did happen that one of the bands did try to advance toward our town, they had the good sense to retreat at the last moment. Sometimes, however, there were incidents that had the distinct appearance of government approval. At times it was the Bolsheviks and at other times, the Petlyura or the Denikin rulers. Later several of these incidents will be described.

During the First World War, the Russian military built a bridge over the Dniester River for the purposes of war. At the beginning of the war, as the soldiers were closing in on the Romanian front, the Jews used this opportunity to do some business with them. With the outbreak of the Revolution, when the front started to crumble and the Czar's soldiers retreated in a state of great disorganization, many soldiers formed themselves into bands in order to rob and murder. The main path of retreat from the front was over the bridge near Dubossar and our town was therefore often the target of these marauders. To protect our town from their attacks, a "Self-Defense" organization was formed. Unfortunately, they had very few weapons.

In those days, the well known adventuress Mishke Yapantchik organized a Jewish regiment in Odessa, assembled primarily with fellows from the underworld. Their goal was to protect the Jewish community and to teach a lesson to the pogromists. Not only did they defend Odessa's Jews but they also sent help to the nearby communities. Dubossar's Self-Defense group appealed to them for help and the commander sent over a unit of 30 men under the leadership of officer Korlandsky. Many Dubossar young men joined up with this unit. They obtained weapons and after a short while Dubossar became a power to be reckoned with – one that could hold its own against a regular military regiment.

A winter night. From the eastern part of town, shots were heard. A significant sized group of retreating soldiers were quartered there and proclaimed that they were now the Red Army, heading toward Central Russia. These particular "Red Army" soldiers however, did not mind a little robbing and killing on the side. That night, a group of them attacked a house at the edge of town and murdered a father and son. The shots and screams spread a panic amongst both the Jews and the soldiers. The Jewish commander Korlandsky and his men mounted their horses and rode off to headquarters to find out what had happened. They were arrested on the spot and badly beaten with the excuse that the Jews had killed 2 soldiers. In the meantime, the volume of gunshots had accelerated and both sides appeared to preparing for a slaughter. The city council, comprised of 40 men, half of them Jewish and led by Rabbi Abel and Yosef Visoky Ram (who died 3 years ago in Jerusalem), seeing that Kolandsky and his men had not returned, quickly convened an emergency meeting.

The shooting went on throughout all this time and we even increased the fire with the hope that it would frighten off the other side. I was in my position and lying next to me was Averbuch, one of the Odessa group. Suddenly I noticed a stranger crawling closer to us. Before I even had a chance to tell Averbuch, the stranger was already at our side and requested that two from our side accompany him. He was striding in the direction of the pogromists and telling them to hold their fire. Our men also stopped shooting. Averbuch ran after the stranger. He had recognized his voice.

When the pogromists saw two men approaching, some of them went to meet them. One thrust the butt end of his gun on Averbuch who, with an acrobatic jump, deflected the blow. The man accompanying him grabbed one of the pogromists by the arm and yelled into his face: "Don't you recognize me?" In one second the situation changed. The other gave a command to his men to cease firing while Averbuch gave the same order to our people. Both went off to the City Council to meet with the pogromists.

In the meantime I received a message that I should immediately go home. My family lived near the "small fountain", in a suburb in north Dubossar and the 'front' that night was in the eastern part of town. In the suburb Lunka, every bit of unexpected news caused worry and panic. I didn't waste any time and went directly home. However, on the way, near the City Council House, I met my parents. They told me that soldiers had forced themselves onto our farm and my parents had run for their lives. I calmed down somewhat and went closer to the City Council House to find out what had happened in the meantime at the meeting.

A big crowd was gathered around the City Council House. I looked in through the window and saw the stranger who had insinuated himself into our position. He was talking to the City Council and Averbuch stood next to him. Suddenly my father whispered into my ear that he knew that man. He was the leader of a robber band and my father, along with other Jews who had been traveling to Kishinev, had been attacked and robbed of all their money by this band. The coachman of the wagon that was robbed, was Yosele Bezh and it appears that he was a partner in this "business". Sometime later, my father was summoned to court to identify the robber. At the last moment my father decided not to identify him. On the other hand, Israel Rampal, who had 259 Rubles stolen, did identify him and his name was Kotavsky.

I returned to the Council House just when the meeting ended with a peace pact between the "Red Army" and the Jews of Dubossar. At the end of the meeting, Kotavsky approached Rampal and invited himself over for the evening meal. Rampal pretended that he was very pleased at the honour and invited him home. The guest brought Averbuch along. At the meal, the guest asked Rampal if he remembered him. Reliable witnesses later said that if Kotavsky hadn't reassured him on the spot than nothing would happen to him, Rampal would have fainted on the spot. At the end of the meal, the guest thanked his host and quickly ran off.

Nobody knows how Kotavsky managed to get out of town. Korlandsky and his assistant came back severely wounded from the blows they had received from the "Red Army" and it took a while for them to recover. For a long time after that night people in town did not cease bringing up Kotavsky's name and crediting him with saving Dubossar from a pogrom.

At this opportunity, I would like to provide a few details about this Kotavsky in order to explain what kind of a man he was. He came from a refined family and he had a higher education. Ideologically he considered himself an anarchist and in keeping with this, he formed a band that "worked" in the Bessarabian forests. He would attack the passing coaches to rob the rich in order to distribute their money to the poor. It is told of him that one day he met a peasant riding by in a broken down wagon pulled by two worn out old horses. Kotavsky gave the peasant a sum of money to buy two good horses. Upon parting, Kotavsky called out after the peasant: "Don't let me see you again with those two carcasses!"

His name rang out over the whole district and the governors offered a cash reward for his capture. Kotavsky, however, had many friends – even among his victims – because he always acted in a friendly manner with everyone. Also they knew that his robberies were not motivated by self-gain but for the poor and needy. Finally he was captured by the regime but even then they did not treat him as an ordinary criminal. When the Revolution broke out, he was serving time in the Odessa jail. When they set him free, he joined up with the Bolsheviks where he performed many courageous deeds. After his death, the Soviets memorialized him in various ways, among them a film that was even seen in Israel.

* * *

During the whole period of the military retreat, we were under constant tension and had to keep constant vigil on the army. In the meantime, the Odessa group became bored with remaining in Dubossar. They were used to more action in the big city and they decided to return to Odessa. To sweeten the pill, they told us that we were now sufficiently experienced and capable of defending our town on our own. The true reason, however, was their desire for greater adventures. Later, we found out that on their way home to Odessa, they tried to 'settle accounts with our previous attackers, as they deserved. Exactly how this action worked out, we do not know to this day.

We would have been able to brag that in the history of Dubossar, not one pogrom took place were it not for one tragic time when the gentiles in the surrounding areas decided to join forces with a large regiment of soldiers retreating from the front. On a certain day there appeared in our town a group of Cossacks known by the name of "The Wild Division". They had organized the peasants from the surrounding areas and together planted themselves in the center of town in order to disrupt our defense units. The pogromists entered Dubossar with their wagons in which they were intending to load Jewish property and goods. The Cossacks, in the meantime, stood guard so that no harm, God forbid, would befall them while the peasants looted and plundered from the Jewish shops. To celebrate their "victory", the Cossacks got drunk (there was no lack of strong liquor as this had been stolen from the shops). They stationed someone to guard over the stolen goods and off they went to drink. In order to frighten the townspeople, they periodically shot into the air. The shots became fainter as more and more Cossacks passed out.

When we were certain that only a small number of Cossacks were awake, we attacked. The pogromists awoke in a panic and began to flee, leaving behind their loot. The drunken soldiers, also frightened, fled behind them. The cost to us was one victim, Pinchas Sirkin, who died protecting his shop against the pogromists. The next day at his funeral, not one gentile from all of the surrounding areas, showed his face in town.

Later, the commander of the division came to the City Hall and apologized for the tragic event. He proposed that he would withdraw his soldiers from Dubossar if we signed a statement that they had peacefully passed through our town. The Mayor signed the statement thus averting an even greater tragedy. The division left town in military formation, their flags fluttering in the wind displaying the words. "Kill the Jews. Save Russia".

After "The Wild Division" left Dubossar, the Mayor contacted the governors in Tyraspol and Kishinev and requested help from them. The next day, a Ukrainian squadron came from Tyraspol and a Bolshevik one from Kishinev. Soon they were arguing over which group should remain in Dubossar. In actual fact, neither side could be trusted as they were cut from the same cloth as the pogromists. We were happy when we rid ourselves of both groups' "favors". Only then did we begin to search thoroughly in the local gentile homes where we recovered most of the plundered goods and we returned these to their Jewish owners. Many of the gentiles expressed regret that they had allowed themselves to be swept along in the pogrom. After that time, I do not recall that any of the local gentiles participated in any further attacks against the Jewish community.

The army division left and they were in any case milder than the previous military presence. There was reason to hope that the situation was improving. In order to give the youth some relief from the tension of the last few months, plans were made for a big party with dancing. In the midst of preparations for this event, notification arrived from Kishinev that General Semyanov with his White Guards were seen heading in the direction of Dubossar. This particular group was constituted mainly of officers and no less anti-semitic than the previous pogromists. The only distinction was that they were disciplined military soldiers. They were also better equipped with all types of weapons. Semyanov's plan was to join up with Denikin's army that was in the process of getting reorganized with officers who had been in the Crimea and the Caucasus.

Once the military group entered town, the thought was to cancel the party. When the commandant became aware of this, he insisted that the event proceed as planned and in fact many officers attended as well. Understandably, this was not the type of evening we had desired but we had no choice and carried on with it. Suddenly, before the party was over, the officers received a command to leave the hall. This seemed very suspicious to us and we all left to take up our positions. To our great joy, nothing sinister happened. The unit had simply received notification to leave town.

After that, no further organized divisions of the disintegrated Czarist army came to Dubossar. From time to time, individual soldiers would show up trying to sell their weapons or horses in order to make some money for their journey homeward. For a few months, there was relative quiet.

* * *

After the capitulation of Kaiser Wilhelm in Germany there was once again a stormy period of unrest. The German army left Russian and every type of gang surfaced and started to organize into new marauding bands. Once again there was no stable governing power. Whoever could organize a band, ruled. Governments arose like mushrooms after a rain; there were many peripheral battles and the lack of a central ruling power made it possible for every type of band to wreak havoc all over Russia. Often they didn't use their own names and it wasn't always clear with whom one was dealing. The Jewish Self-Defense had no alternative but to once again take up arms.

One fine morning, a brigade of 100 men showed up in Dubossar. They presented themselves as the vanguard of the Red Army that was out to conquer all of Russia. They let us know that the staff of the Bolshevik Army was located 100 kilometer from Dubossar and their task was a technical one – to prepare for the advance of the Red Army. Not more than a couple of hours passed when the "vanguard" advised Rabbi Abel, z'l, that in the name of the Red Army, he expected a contribution from the local Jewish population of one million rubles as well as 49 pairs of boots. This sum of money and the boots were to be delivered within a few hours. With this command, the officer admitted that he was representing only himself; otherwise the command would have fallen on all of the local inhabitants, not only the Jews.

By nightfall, when it became apparent that the command would not be fulfilled, an order was given forbidding all the Jews from leaving their homes. We were prepared for that and the whole community was confined to their yards. All except Mendl Batalsky. He paid no attention to the command and went out into the street. Immediately two armed soldiers apprehended him and headed over to the commandant's office. On the way, walking between the two of them, Mendl grabbed the head of one with his right hand, the head of the other with the second hand and with great strength, banged their heads together until they were both sprawled out on the ground. He quickly disappeared into a side street.

Not far from there, near an opening of a cellar, was Froikele the thief, who had been watching the whole 'spectacle'. When he noticed that the two soldiers got up and started to run to the commandant, he lost no time, ran over to a church and began to ring the church bells -this being the accepted alarm signal. Immediately, a volley of bullets went flying into the yard of the commandant. When the commandant staff saw the two bloodied soldiers and heard the shots, they panicked and these "heroes" ran off as fast they could from the scene. Our people went out into the street to cut off their retreat but no-one could be found except for the two that Mendel had taken care of and who were hiding in the hospital. This piece of business was completed in the Dniester River.

A thorough search of the town led to the discovery of Jacob Fishman's entire family tied up. When they were freed from the "vanguard" 's bonds, we found there sacks of goods and property that the soldiers were intending to steal. Nothing was missing. In their panic, they had left everything behind.

Fleeing the scene, on the road the soldiers met Motl Nitzkaner driving two wagon fulls of sugar. They "bought" his entire stock and told him to demand from Rabbi Abel the payment for his goods from the million rubles that were coming to them. For a long time people in town joked about Motl's "business deal. " However, heal so was relieved that the encounter had ended with the loss of money only.

One after the other, different armed units started to show up, each claiming to represent the vanguard of this or that army. One day, one such group appeared and taking advantage of the fact that the whole police force was concentrated at the Magistrate's Halldue to an important hearing, they captured all of the police, the chief of police, the magistrate and the city councilmen, proclaiming a curfew in town. In the notices that they put up, they announced that they were the deputies of the Petlyura Central Government.

The whole night, the whole town was wrapped in suspense. In the morning, when it became apparent that the whole "occupation army" consisted of only one small unit, we decided to free all the prisoners from their captors. The band sensed that we did not fear them and began negotiations with the Mayor. They agreed to free all the prisoners except for the chief of police because he was of the "White Army", namely, a criminal and all such as he must be handed over to Central Command. In the meantime, we were preparing to liberate the town by force in the event that the negotiations fell through. When the leader of the band became aware of our intentions, he and his friends fled.

On this occasion there was total understanding between the Jews and the gentiles. The leaders of the Christian community admitted that the stance that the Jews had taken had been logical and brave. Thanks to this action, the chief of police had been saved from a certain death.

The next morning, we received the information that the same band had carried out a pogrom in the town of Okna, 40 kilometers from Dubossar. At this, no-one doubted any longer that the land was now totally plunged in chaos and anarchy and that we must stand guard against every band that advanced toward Dubossar.

* * *

In winter of 1919, Petlyura reigned over Ukraine and founded the Independent Ukraine Republic. In order to win the backing of the Jewish population, he created a Jewish ministry in his government under the leadership of the known businessman A. Revatzky. Actually though, he gave a free hand to the anti-semites and pogromists that had infiltrated into his army and they had no restraints in their persecution of the Jewish population.

That winter we had to stand on guard duty many nights. We were also unable to change our clothes for a week at a time. Those who were in the Self-Defense organization were prepared for every and any eventuality. Approximately two weeks before Passover, standing at my post while on patrol duty outside of town, I noticed a suspicious movement beneath a hill. Through one of our collaterals, I sent word immediately to our commander of the Self-Defense.

As usual in situations like this, all the inhabitants of the town – big and small – went out into the streets dressed in their holiday finery in order " to make a good impression". Very soon, my suspicions were confirmed. A large, armed unit of 200 men on horseback advanced toward our town. From the blood-thirsty anti-semitic songs that they were singing, we knew that they were part of the professional pogromists in Pelyura's army. Coming into town, they were startled by the festive reception we had prepared for them. They stood still in the Market place and the whole situation appeared very suspicious to them. They had heard that they must be very careful in Dubossar; that Dubossar was not like the other towns. Usually when they would enter a town, the streets would be empty, the horses and yards locked and barricaded while here, to the contrary, even the shops were open, the people were all in the streets and even the children gazed at their horses without fear. "Never mind", said several of them, "we'll grind them into dust".

While the Magistrate was assigning the soldiers to various houses where they could sleep overnight, the unit received an order from their commandant to head out to the German farm that was situated 4 kilometers from Dubossar. They had discovered in the cellar, barrels of wine and feed for the horses.

When they were gone, the town quickly changed its appearance. The streets cleared out and the youth began to prepare for the imminent attack that was sure to occur. Spies were sent out to ascertain how well equipped the band was and what weapons they had, in order to assess what we were up against. The spies sent back word that there were at least 200 wagons carrying food and they were already 2-3 kilometers from Dubossar. The Christian population organized 70 men under the command of Officer Kozlovitch, who suggested that the Jewish Self-Defense unite with them to fight off the attack of Petlyura's men. The strategy of the Christian group was to capture the wagons and to hide them in Loffer's huge tobacco warehouses.

The night passed in feverish activity. The gentile group, as planned, captured the food supplies as well as the Chief of the local militia, an ex officer, who was given an ultimatum to put himself at the service of the town's defense. By the way, in Dubossar, the militia was comprised of 30 men, half of whom were Jews.

The whole night, the Petlyura men "celebrated" their anticipated victory in drunken revelry. The next day at dawn, in military formation, they marched into town. The Self-Defense was prepared for them and as soon as the Petlyura unit was spotted, an alarm signal was set off. The bells of all the churches started to ring and the Self-Defense sprang forth for the assault. Our boys took the few weapons that they had with some rounds of ammunition and went forth to meet the enemy. Our first victim was the rider at the head of their column. The battle was of short duration. The pogromists, seeing that they had serious opponents, began to flee, leaving behind on the road a considerable amount of weapons and supplies. Some of them fell in battle and others tried to swim across the Dniester to the Romanian side. All day we pursued them and only in the evening did we head back home where a superb reception awaited us. The whole night we dance in the streets to celebrate our victory. Among the goods that we had recaptured from them, were boxes of Matzot, clothing, Talitim, Tefilim and other holy articles.

In spite of our victory, we were not at peace. Our unrest proved to be valid. A few days went by and our intelligence people informed us that a huge military battalion was advancing toward Dubossar. The Christian townspeople that had collaborated with the Jewish Self-Defense in the previous battle knew that their position was already compromised so they energetically joined us in preparing for the next assault. This time the pogromists sent their supply wagons by a different route and with increased manpower entered our town. The Mayor quietly sent them a warning to get out of town if they didn't want to have a "brilliant victory" like their friends had. The band understood the hint and were driven off.

In the meantime, the holiday of Passover was getting closer. We hoped that after these two victories we would be left in peace to celebrate our beloved holiday. The first Seder went by peacefully. The next day, however, going to shul, my father and I were informed that a telegram had arrived from Plosk stating: "KOZOVSKY IS GOING FROM TYROSPOL TO DUBOSSAR. SEND HELP IMMEDIATELY." The telegram had been sent to Rabbi Abel who was already in Shul. As soon as he received the telegram, he hurried off to the market. He got up on a table and warned the town to go out and meet the enemy.

The news descended on the town like thunder on a sunny day. The synagogues all emptied out and all the worshipers gathered in the market square. With the speed of lightning, the defense was organized. Horses and wagons were mobilized to carry men and provisions to Plosk. Eighteen horseback riders and several dozen wagons loaded with courageous youth, weapons and ammunition left that night to meet the pogromists. A unit accompanied them that would carry provisions. I would like to mention here the good Dr. Laybele Polinkovsky who assembled students from the higher classes of the Gymnasia and instructed them how to administer first aid.

This time the attitude of the Christians was different than before. Some time earlier, they had been secretly informed about Kozovsky's "visit" with the recommendation they be prepared to rob the Jews after his men were through with the pogrom. This time the gentiles stood to the side and made fun of the "Zhides" who were playing at being soldiers. They were certain that Kozovsky's assault on the town would demolish the Jewish defense.

The next day, the second day of Passover, the Dubossar men arrived at the front. A battle erupted between Petlyura's rear guard army who numbered in the thousands under Kozovsky's command and against our men together with the Plosk peasants. Against the resistance of the combined forces of Plosk and Dubossar, Kozovsky had no alternative but to give up his plan of revenge in Dubossar. He ordered his men to retreat to the Dniester.

This was the last attempt of Petlyura's men to attempt pogroms in our district. Thanks to the brave young men of Dubossar and the Plosk peasants, Dubossar was spared the horrors of a pogrom.

At this opportunity, I would like to mention a few details about Plosk. Plosk was a big village of several thousand families, all Russian. In our district we called them "Katzapes". Not one Jew lived there nor did anyone of any other nationality. After the revolution, the people from Plosk refused to recognize any of the regimes that were constantly supplanting the others. They established their own autonomous government as well as a local army consisting of their own village residents. They were wealthy peasants and were powerful both materially and militarily; thus they were able to withstand pressure for a long time. More than once did they bravely repulse armies that were sent in to take over their town until the Bolsheviks sent in a division named 'Marusia' (named after the commander) with the order to conquer Plosk no matter what the cost. Here also the village fought with great courage and the revolt ended after the leaders of the village were allowed to cross over the river to Romania.

The village of Plosk is linked to a tragic event in which ten innocent young men lost their lives. When Denikin came into power after the defeat of Petlyura's army, all young men of military age were conscripted. We and the young men from Grigoriopiol set out for the conscription center in the capital city of Tyraspol. We, the Dubossar group, presented ourselves at noontime and those that were released immediately set off for home by foot, not waiting for those from Grigoriopol who were behind us. Dubossar is 60 kilometers from Tyraspol, 18 kilometers further than Grigoriopol.

That day Plosk revolted against the Denikin Army and by evening they had occupied Malayeshty, 15 kilometers from Tyraspol in order to cut off communication between Tyraspol and Dubossar. When we arrived at Malayeshty, the Ploskers allowed us to continue. However when the Grigariopolers arrived after us once they had completed their registration for conscription, the Ploskers captured them and brought them to their commandant who sentenced them to death on the spot. This was carried out that very night. We had been allowed to go free because the Dubossar people were known to be anti-Bolshevik. The Grigoriopolers were executed because they were believed to be "Red".

During the time that General Denikin ruled in Ukraine, there were two opposing forces in our region – the Bolsheviks and the Denikinsts. After Denikin's armies suffered a great defeat near Kharkov and they began to retreat from the entire front, we realized that it was the end of these inner battles and that the Bolsheviks had emerged victorious. The Jews were very happy with this outcome because in Denikin's army, in spite of his liberal political program, there were many pogromists who slaughtered Jews and the General could not control them.

The Denikinsts retreated to three areas -Caucasus, Crimea and Romania. On the way, they had to cross the Dniester River from Dubossar to Bendery. At the last hour, the Romanians did not allow them to enter and so the Denikin Army of approximately 120,000 men had to turn around and head northward.

One Friday, at the beginning of 1920, the entire Denikin army entered Dubossar and like a swarm of locusts, covering the town. There was no house, no warehouse, no stable that didn't contain soldiers. For 24 hours we could not cross over from one yard to the next and we were totally cut off from each other. The problem was that amongst the soldiers was the Cossack "Wild Division". This time, we thought, will be the end for us. Suddenly a miracle occurred. Two o'clock in the afternoon we heard the rat-at-tat of machine guns. When the sounds of shooting came closer, the soldiers panicked and started to run in every direction. All night we heard the sound of machine guns and the thunder of cannons.

In the morning, only when the sounds of shooting had ended, did we dare to go outside. The streets were empty. As we approached the Market, we saw from far away soldiers with red flags. This was the Bolshevik Army. This ends the story of the valor and courage of the Jewish Self-Defense in Dubossar. From here on a new era began of "fearful days" and a new reality.

———————

Everything related here is no more than a few of the details of the heroic chapter of the Self-Defense history of Russian Jewry in which our town Dubossar holds a place of honor among the other Jewish communities that were annihilated between the two world wars. The historians that will write of this period will surely find interest in this chapter of bravery recorded by the Dubossar Jews who faced mortal danger in defending the honor and the lives of their fellow Jews and their Jewish life.

May Their Memory Be Honored

Moishe Kantor near his wife's grave. She was murdered by the Nazis.

[Page 128]

Characters in the Dubossar Self-Defense

by Baruch Bassin

as told by A. Y. Golani

Translated by Sarah Faerman

Yosele Bezh was a coach man by profession in Dubossar but outside of our town he had other 'pursuits' as well. He was the head of a band that would rob merchants and other travelers on the country roads. To his credit, it must be stated that he never plied his trade around the vicinity of Dubossar.

One day, when the Pogroms were raging throughout south Russia, Yosele approached the head of the Jewish Self-Defense organization in Dubossar and said to him in these words: "Listen here, I will not tell you where my men are but we have decided to give you two weeks of our time. Whatever you would like us to do, we will do."

Golani, as leader of the Self-Defense, listened to the offer and gave Yosele several barrels of benzene with the following strict instructions: "You will use these barrels of benzene to set fire to those villages that the pogromists come from – but only in the event that they are attempting to attack Dubossar. I warn you not to cause any provocation."

Yosele solemnly promised to obey Golani's command. Not even three days went by before Golani was summoned to the police station. The Chief of Police, who was knowledgeable about the Jewish Self-Defense organization and supportive of it, gave a sharp reproof to Golani. It turned out that Yosele could not control himself and had set fire to one of the close by villages.

* * *

Yidele Golyak was a thin little Jew but he possessed an iron strong courage. By nature he was quick to anger and was constantly involved in one brawl or another.

One day, Golani told me: "I was standing by the shore of the river where a passenger ship was anchored. Suddenly I heard a commotion that had erupted on the ship. Gentiles had grabbed hold of a Jew and were beating him up. All of a sudden, I see a little Yidl running 'hendus pendus' and quick like a cat, he springs onto the bridge of the ship and begins to deliver punches right and left. Immediately the brawl on the ship died down. "When Yidele stepped down from the ship", continued Golani, "I went up to him and asked: Tell me Yidele, how do you happen to be so fearless?" Yidele immediately answered: "I have a corn that is called 'Dos Pintele Yid' (expression: the essence of a Jew) and when someone steps on my corn, I become wild and distribute blows to everyone who has it coming."

[Page 131]

The First Jewish Commune in Russia

Moishe Faerman z"l

Translated by Sarah Faerman

It happened in the year 1919, in the month of April. The Bolsheviks occupied Ukraine for the second time; the first time being after the outbreak of the October Revolution at the end of 1917. It must be stated that it was not without joy that the Jews greeted them – especially those from the villages on the banks of the river Dniester who were in great danger of being massacred by the passing hordes of Denikinsts, Petlurists and other lesser bands on their way to the borders of Poland and Romania. Yells of celebration accompanied the Bolsheviks' rifle shots as they sped after the retreating bands through our town Dubossar that lies in a valley very close to the banks of the Dniester.

The joy did not last long. The honey moon was soon over as the new regime tightened its grip on every part of the land instituting the well known militaristic Communism. The regime leaned heavily on the farmer who was already impoverished from the war with the Germans and Austrians. Greater though, was the oppression of the Jews as they were barred from all economic pursuits. As heavy as that burden was, an additional financial misfortune was imposed: "contributions" were demanded from which the other populations were exempt.

The following episode will serve as a small example of the tragic circumstances of the Jewish folk. The regime imposed a mobilization of the youth for the Red Army. Members of various families were conscripted into the army and in our family alone, three brothers were taken in one day. That was apparently not enough as the parents and the Jewish community were also forced to provide the horses and wagons to transport the conscripts to their military posts. It did not help to complain that the Jews did not own wagons and horses; that quite often not even a piece of dry bread was found in their homes and certainly they could not afford to hire wagons. More than a few young men were obliged to go to their military billets leaving behind parents who were arrested solely for the sin of being unable to provide the stipulated wagons.

In those days of unheard of desolation, after having just escaped with our lives from the Petlurists, the Denikinsts and the other bands, we were now surrounded by a sea of militant Communists. In spite of this, the youth did not lose their heads and did not give in to despair. On the contrary, they thought clearly and earnestly about their predicament, seeking solutions to untangle themselves from this terrible situation. The answer was clear: to become productive workers. However, how does one become a productive worker if there is no work to be found? Industry was totally ruined, the land was aflame because of the civil war and yet, one must live. I, affiliated with Poalei Zion (Labour Zionist organization) but not officially for well known reasons and my friend David Layb Granovsky, the secretary of Tzeirei Tzion (Zionist Youth organization) unofficially held a quick consultation and decided to organize a Kvutza (Communal farm) and become field workers with the permission of the authorities. We would work and serve no-one. Communist principles – yes. Communism – no.

Immediately, a larger group than we had expected joined us. At first there were fifteen young people but due to circumstances this number, in time, shrunk. Aside from us two, the others in the group were Natan Tshereshna, a wise, older man. He was a tobacco farmer, experienced in agriculture; David Gurovsky; Simcha Granovsky; Moishe Granovsky; Motl Netzkaner – a teacher; Yudl Schwartz (went to America); his brother who later joined a well established collective in the Crimea; A. Litman (also went to America) and others.

After the group was formed, we worked at formulating guidelines to regulate our communal living arrangements. One rule was that if someone was called up to serve in the army, he would not lose his rights and his share in the venture. (The writer of these words did actually have to serve in the military later). We immediately went out to find a suitable piece of land and farm equipment, both items being very scarce in these times.

By then it was quite late in the spring. Thirty-five viorst from Dubossar and ten viorst from the village Okneh, in the Podalya province, we quietly rented a small piece of land in a secret deal.

On an open field, far from any habitation, there was the neglected house of a German colonist who had been shot after the Germans left. The walls bore the marks of bullet holes and on the floor were still bloodstains – reminders of the murder. We feared no danger. Even later, when we had to sleep outside, spread out, some in the field, some in pits – all in hiding from marauding bandits who roamed the surrounding villages killing Jews – even then we applied ourselves to our work.

The greatest difficulty was in obtaining the necessary animals and farm equipment. The small amount of money we put together was worth very little. Aside from some food, we bought seven horses at a fair. With our horses harnessed to two wagons, we drove happily to our new "kingdom" were we were about to begin a new chapter in our lives. However, it was our 'luck' that just as we were leaving the fair, the sky darkened and suddenly rain, like a flood, poured down upon us. Half alive, we arrived to our land the next morning with only six horses.

We gave the horses one day to rest up. On the second day we went out to our work. As there were only six horses and two people worked with one horse, there were several of us without work. It was with some envy that we saw how proficiently some of our comrades could plough straight furrows walking behind the horse and plough on the fresh, soft earth. Many a time we would remember (much later, in 1921, when I was already in Canada and working alone with six horses harnessed to a plough on the fields of the "Montefiore Colony" in Alberta) when the playful and naive David Layb Granovsky suggested that we, who had been 'left over' with no horses to work with should take our shovels and dig the earth and if not – plough with our noses. And we young fellows jumped at the idea and began digging at the hill, from bottom up trying to dig out the whole hill.

We were not lacking in courage and idealism. Not a little self-sacrifice was bound to the principle of working on the land in our isolated kvutza at a time when all around us pogromists were raging. We heard rumors that in Elizabethgrad, Gregoriov rose up against the Bolsheviks. Machna and others were also skulking in our area. All this did not frighten or discourage us. We were determined not to leave our new home.

The following episode was characteristic of our group: as pioneers and Zionists, we decided that our day of rest would be Saturday and not Sunday. Unfortunately our neighbors under no circumstances would allow us to work in the fields on Sundays. They also refused to believe that we were working according to Communist principles. They couldn't believe that a Communist would work on his own with no-one over him. In their view, a Communist was one that plundered and confiscated.

Our endeavor did not have a very happy ending. After all of the hardships, troubles and work we had invested, the land re-paid us with a good crop. However we did not benefit from this. Exactly at threshing time, in the middle of August, The Denikinsts captured Odessa and the wheat that we gathered from the fields remained unthreshed. During the winter, the wheat was requisitioned and confiscated.

Thus, all the hard labor of the first group of chalutzim in Ukraine was for naught. Still, the kernel that was planted was not in vain. Our attempt and our success in overcoming so many obstacles encouraged thousands of others who came in our place.

A group of active Zionists in Dubossar.

Members of the Zionist Organization ' Tzeirei Tzion', 1918

[Page140]

Memories of my town Dubossar

by Leon Rubin
Translated by Sarah Faerman

In the days of the Baylis Trial

In the year 1913 the famous Baylis trial took place in Kiev. The group "The Black Hundred" that had great influence in Czarist Russia, had accused a Jewish man, Mendl Baylis, of murdering a young Christian boy in order to use his blood for ritual purposes. Prominent liberal lawyers – Jews and Gentiles – like Gruzenberg, Moklakov and Korabchevsky took up the defense of the accused Baylis and with scorn rebutted this outrageous blood libel. Pious Jews were not satisfied with the arguments and parries of the jurists and experts alone and they used other means. They flocked to the graves of the Tzadikim (the Holy ones) praying for their intercession in the battle for justice and the Jewish reputation. I would like to describe one event connected to our town Dubossar that psychologically bolstered the courage of a certain segment of Jews who prayed for a just outcome of the process.

In the old Dubossar cemetery was the mausoleum of the Tzadik, Reb Mendele, the Baal Shem Tov's nephew who had been sent to live in Dubossar to fulfill an important mission that only the initiates of the Kabala could understand. Reb Mendele had made it known that in times of woe for Jews, they should come to his grave and he would intercede for justice on their behalf.

I remember one day in the morning, two middle aged, well dressed men came to see my father in the Bet Din (court of law). They presented themselves as emissaries of the Kiev community. In reply to my father's questioning as to the purpose of the visit, they replied that they were sent to visit the grave of Reb Mendele so that he would intercede for justice for the Jews in the trial of the innocent Mendl Baylis. My father quickly gathered a minyan (quorum of Jews for prayer) and hurried off with them to the old cemetery to the grave of the Tzadik Reb Mendele. When the trial was over and Mendl Baylis was exonerated, there were many Jews who firmly believed that it was thanks to Reb Mendele in his appeal to The Almighty that the trial was concluded in favour of the Jews.

My first community endeavors and my father's slaps

The "Sturm and Drang" that enveloped Russia at the turn of the century did not by-pass our town. The youth were divided along the whole spectrum of "isms" and were heatedly engaged in all manner of arguments and debates in closed quarters or out in the fresh air. Summertime, on Sabbath in the afternoon, while our parents were taking a rest, we would go off to the stalls of the old market and there we would discuss and dispute Jewish and worldly issues. My involvement there was of a very brief duration for the following reason: One Sabbath whilst at prayers in the synagogue, my father, in front of all the others, asked me if it was true that during a discussion in the market place I had uttered atheistic ideas. My father did not wait for my answer that some antagonists of mine were slandering me. Instead, he lifted his hand and delivered a couple of resounding slaps on my cheeks. Henceforth he did not permit me to go out of the house on Sabbath afternoons.

When I was older, I started to work in the newly established "Savings and Loan Fund" established by JOINT (Jewish charitable organization) with the goal of improving the conditions for small grocery and business owners in establishing credit, etc., utilizing liberal and fair terms. While describing this co-operative institution, it is my duty to mention the dedicated and honest community activist, Velvl Bendersky, who held the office of director of the co-operative for a period of time. He was always an advocate for the poor, made allowances for those who were late in repaying their loans and also would cover the promissory notes from Kishinev for the grocers. He worried about them defaulting on their loans and thereby damaging their credit. He personally went to the storekeepers to remind them to keep their accounts up to date and would borrow from some to cover others' debts allowing them enough time to pay out what they owed.

I worked in the "Savings and Loan" together with my friends Joseph Mishniger (who died in Syracuse) and Velvl Vaynberg. Together we organized the group "Hatchiya"(Revival) whose goal it was to present nationalist and cultural activities to the Jewish youth. Many were the numbers of boys and girls who would attend our cultural events every Sabbath afternoon where we would read and analyze the works of our classics of both languages – Yiddish and Hebrew. We organized our own cultural evenings presenting renowned speakers, both local and from other places. Of the former, the following presented papers: Yosef Visoky (Ram), Tzvi Kris (who lives in New York) and Laybl, Berl Shochet's son. When Chaim Greenberg organized a branch of the "Tzeirei Tzion" (Young Zion) movement in Dubossar, most of the members of "Hatchiya" joined up with that Zionist folk party.

The Tzeirei Tzion party did not involve itself exclusively with Zionist work but also took part in local issues in the surrounding communities. We were the initiators and organizers of elections to ensure a democratically elected leadership of the community that would put an end to the regime of those who would put taxes on kosher meat and who ruled with an iron fist over the Jewish community in other areas as well. We visited schools and synagogues, explaining the principles of a democratically elected leadership and its importance for our society. The party nominated four candidates of which three were elected: Yosef Visoky, Misha Diner and the author of these lines. Although our candidates comprised not more than 20% of the councilmen, together with the general Zionists and with Rabbi Abel at the head, we were able to influence many aspects in the governing our community.

The members of the Tzeirei Tzion youth movement were the pioneers in practical Zionist work. We distributed Keren Kayemet (Jewish National Fund established for buying land and trees in Eretz Yisrael) collection boxes and emptied them out periodically; every Friday, we would go to the Jewish houses and sell Zionist stamps; on the eve of Rosh Hashana (New Years) we organized our own "Post Office" and delivered Rosh Hashana cards, which incidentally, also had its Zionist educational aspects.

We founded a club that attracted many youth each evening. There we held many lectures, discussions and concerts. We also frequently invited th gifted brothers, Velvl and Faivel Kazatzker, of the Socialist group (not Zionist) for talks as it was a pleasure to have discussions with them.

When the Bolshevik regime prohibited any and all Zionist activity and in Odessa the Zionist Centre was liquidated, the main activity was transferred to Berlin. We were the conduit for smuggled Zionist literature via Romania to Odessa and back. Thanks to us, the contact with the other side of the border was maintained for a long time.

Women's activities

The women in Dubossar were very active in a wide variety of community affairs and institutions. In particular, there was a group of women heavily involved in philanthropic causes. These women – Sarah Bendersky, Rachel Kazatzker, Rosa Rosenberg, Malka Katz, Mindl Polaver, etc. made sure that nothing would be lacking for newborns whose parents could barely afford the necessities. For the poor children that went to the Talmud Torah schools, they prepared hot meals and in general supervised their health. For working girls, they organized classes in the evening to teach them to read, write and other elementary subjects. These classes were held in the private school of Rivka Shochat, Yosef Feller's granddaughter, the future wife of Raphael Sverdlov, a teacher in the Herzlia Gymnasia (high school). Of great importance was their work on behalf of the Jewish hospital.

I would like to relate the following episode: When we were preparing for the elections of the community leaders, the women who had voting privileges decided that they would like to present to the community their own separate 'Women's List'. We men became very frightened. We feared that the women, who worked so energetically for the community, could conceivably gain more votes than the men and we would end up with a "Female" community... That's all we needed! We hastily started to negotiate with them and convinced them to join us on one candidate list. At first they refused but eventually they agreed not to present their own list.

In the days of the revolution and Civil War

Since the turn of the century, Dubossar was famous for its Self-Defense organization. This became particularly apparent during the Civil War when many diverse bands raged throughout Ukraine sowing terror in the Jewish settlements. In those days when Jewish life was worth nothing, Dubossar was relatively quiet. True, bands did sweep through our town demanding 'contributions' but there were almost no human sacrifices.

In the year 1918 there were bloody slaughters between the Bolsheviks and the Denikinists. The latter were forced to retreat and they fled to the Dniester River in order to cross over to the Bessarabian shore which was part of Romania. Rumor had it that among the Denikinists was a division called "The Black Death". This division left death and destruction in every place they entered.

On a certain Friday, word came that eighteen Jews in the neighboring town of Grigoriopol had been murdered and that the perpetrators were on their way to Dubossar which is right next to the River Dniester. Outside there was a bitter frost and the new fallen snow hindered one in hunting for a place to hide. I, my fiancée and her parents, Velvl and Sarah Bendersky, decided not to wait passively for our death and instead fled out of town to a Gentile acquaintance where we hid out in his garden. With fear and trepidation we strained to hear what sounds we could from the town in order to figure out what was happening. Thus, we sat anxiously the whole night. At dawn we heard a huge tumult, wheels turning, horses hooves, people shouting. "What did this mean?" The Gentile went off to town to find out and soon came back with the happy news: The Denikinists who had settled themselves overnight in the Jewish houses preparing to launch a pogrom the next day, were themselves forced to flee lightning fast, as the Bolsheviks who had been pursuing them were hot on their heels. In great haste, leaving behind all of the pillaged loot, the Denikinists made their way to the Dniester and on to Bessarabia. That time Dubossar was saved by a miracle.

When I, my bride and her parents fled out of town, my parents remained as they did not want to abandon their house. They relied on miracles. They told us that the two soldiers who had stayed with them in their house treated them with great courtesy. The soldiers heated the stove for them; they took the candlesticks off of the table and warmed up water for them to make glasses of tea. They weren't people, they were angels...

As mentioned, this time the Jewish folk were saved by a miracle. The Denekinists army was too big and powerful for the Dubossar Self-Defense organization to grapple with. However in those days there were very many other occasions where, thanks to the Self-Defense, the slaughter of the Dubossar Jews was prevented. I will describe one such event.

One night, two of Petlyura's men rode up on horseback. They circulated around the magistrate's office to survey the town. In a suburb called Lunke, there were another 120 riders, Petlyura's men, waiting for the signal to attack. The two riders chatted amiably with the people who were gathered in the street and then they rode off to Lunke. We were suspicious of them and prepared ourselves to greet them. All night we stood guard, waiting. In the morning, very early, the Gentile owner of the flour mill came running, calling out: "Jews! Save yourselves! A squadron of riders is on their way into town." He ran to the church and started to ring the bells – a signal to mobilize against the attack. The Self-Defense sprang into action and stationed themselves on the main road leading in from Lunke to head off the pogrom.

They had barely placed themselves in strategic places when the Petlyurists galloped in and were immediately peppered with rifle shots. Bewildered by the sudden onslaught, they tried to turn away into the other narrower street but there also were they greeted with heavy fire. They tried to push their way through. One of the Self-Defense men, Yosl Barbarash, decided the outcome of the battle. He leapt toward one of the riders that was shooting to the right and to the left with a machine gun. Hitting him over the head with the butt of his gun, he dragged him off the horse, grabbed his machine gun and proceeded to fire at the Petlyurists. Amidst great confusion, the Petlyurists made a hasty escape leaving behind two dead.

* * *

When the Bolsheviks gained power, their first action was to "make order" of all the economic institutions. The "Savings and Loan" where I was working was shut down. In its place they established a huge co-operative with merchandise that serviced all the surrounding areas. The farmers were obliged to send in their produce as 'taxes' that were required for covering various expenses.

I worked in this new co-op as the bookkeeper for starvation wages which often were not paid. The hunger as well as my opposition to the new regime made me realize that I should leave this Communist "paradise" as soon as possible. Leaving behind my wife and year old child with her parents, I stole across the border to Bessarabia. Not long after, my wife and child joined me and we made our way to Argentina where we found a warm and happy home.

[Page156]

חיים פינקעלשטיין, אומגעקומען דורך די
נאצים.

חיים פינקלשטין, נספה בידי הנאצים

Chaim Finkelshtein. Murdered by the Nazis.

Dubossar 1920-1922

by Yeshayahu Kantor
Translated by Sarah Faerman

The First Years of the Revolution

After two years of the Civil War, in the winter of 1920, the Bolsheviks strengthened their grip in our area and established a stable government. The Jewish community breathed a sigh of relief. They hoped that finally things would quiet down and life would return to normal. Many even exhibited a keen interest in the new regime and its revolutionary slogans. The illusion did not last long. After only a short period, all of the wishful thinking turned to naught and those who at the beginning had been drawn to the new regime soon realized that there would be no peace for Israel under the Communist rule. Whoever had the slightest possibility began to consider fleeing from Russia altogether. And, if to flee, there was only one way – to the other side of the Dniester River to Bessarabia.

Whoever had his assets in cash, lost it entirely. Because of the rise and fall of the various regimes and governments, the ruble no longer had any value. Those that possessed various types of goods or agricultural products such as nuts, dried prunes ,etc. believed, in the beginning, that they would at least be able to save some of their resources. Their hopes were also dashed before long.

During the first "honeymoon" days of the new regime, the Bolshevik victors were busy hunting down deserters of the Denikinst army. Every day they would herd groups of these ex-soldiers, supposedly to interrogate them and these "interrogations" usually ended up with them being stood up against a wall. The Jews were not frightened by this particular "sentencing" as the Denikinst army had been "Judenrein".

When the civil government began to get organized, their first project was "Collectivization", that is to relieve owners of all their private, "extra" property. True, this was carried out by the lower echelons of the Communist regime – many who were irresponsible, provocateurs, rabid anti-semites and even past pogromists that had weaseled their way into the new ruling power and some were even able to climb to the highest levels.

Even worse than they, were the communists who were B'nei Israel – our brothers- who, to prove that they were holier than the pope, acted with exaggerated severity toward any Jew who was suspected of withholding any of his property. The main point: Jews had to endure woes from both sides at the beginning of the Soviet regime, – a time when the gentile population was relatively free from suffering.

Units of the Red Army would go from house to house confiscating whatever they could lay their hands on, rarely giving a receipt, which in any case, had little worth. After this type of "Socialist" action, many families were left without blankets and cushions and on top of this, they were accused of hiding valuable items. After this first action, came the second operation – to make lists of the "surplus" food and provisions and to transfer same to the central warehouses. This time, the evil decree included the gentile peasants as well. In the beginning, when people still had some faith in the new rule, many delivered their goods and received a statement that indicated how much they would be paid according to government prices. Later however, when it became apparent that both the promises and the receipts were worth nothing, the goods started to vanish.

There were frequent raids at the homes of the rich where thorough searches were made for jewelry and other valuables. I, myself was a witness at one of these raids that lasted around the clock. On a Friday night, a group of local agents accompanied by Red Army soldiers surrounded the home of Isaac Rosenfeld – a man of high standing in Dubossar. He had no children and lived modestly. He also was not considered one of the wealthy ones in the community. Suddenly it was rumored that Rosenfeld was hiding a treasure in his house. A Red Army unit cordoned off the surrounding streets and three local agents entered the home demanding of Rosenfeld and his wife that they should, with good will, hand over all of their hidden diamonds and jewelry. When Rosenfeld told them that he had neither diamonds nor jewelry, the search began.

They searched furiously. Soon the soldiers came in to help. They actually did the hard work – breaking up the floors, tearing out cupboards, pulling doors off their hinges, breaking down walls and when late at night, they found nothing; they dragged Rosenfeld down to the cellar. They spread him out on the ground and covered him with a pile of stones, threatening that if he did not disclose the whereabouts of the "treasure", they would keep him there until he died. Rosenfeld, who by nature was a quiet man, did not answer. His silence infuriated them and they began to torture him. In spite of the fact that these "Soldiers of Justice" had closed the doors, the cries of Rosenfeld were heard outside.

Immediately the whole town knew what was happening in Rosenfeld's cellar and from every direction people ran to the house. The soldiers tried to chase them away but with no success. When the local agents saw that this could end with many casualties and after all their hunting, no treasures had been found, they finally decided, on Saturday night, to free Rosenfeld and to leave. True, Rosenfeld had a "victory" but he paid a heavy price. His health quickly deteriorated and after a short period of time, he passed away in terrible agony.

The Rosenfeld case did not deter the new authorities and they continued on with this method, which in some instances, yielded results for them. Coinciding with these raids which were primarily carried out by the CHEKA

(Soviet secret police), the government demanded "contributions" of the well to do according to a list of names that they had. Belonging to a group of youth close to government circles, we were privy to some information that was hidden from the majority of the citizens. In this way, I discovered that my father was on this list and that he would be requested to hand over 15,000 rubles – an impossibility for him to raise on his income. I immediately ran home to advise my father to disappear from town, to flee to Odessa until this black cloud would pass. The next morning, a letter addressed to my father arrived at the house from the Citizens' Executive Committee demanding the payment of 15,000 rubles within 24 hours. The town was in confusion. It was clear that any organized efforts to counter this edict had no chance of succeeding and everyone, therefore, tried to figure out a way to privately bargain with the CHEKA.

At the end of the 24 hour time limit, I appeared instead of my father at the headquarters. Participating in the hearing of this case was a friend of mine who whispered into my ear in Yiddish that he would be forced to arrest me if I did not have the money. I was soon informed that I was under arrest and was taken to the second floor of the big "Loffers" warehouse. Slowly more people were added, Jewish and gentile, who like me had not provided the money, demanded of them.

The first two days passed without incident. I felt easy enough, thanks to the ties I had with some of the soldiers who were guarding us. On the third day, I and one of the soldiers stood in a nearby room looking out of the window into the yard. A soldier that was standing in the yard, picked up his gun for fun and pointed it at us. Suddenly a shot rang out and the soldier who had been standing next to me, fell to the ground, dead.

Such incidents in those days did not cause any great reaction especially if it was the result of an accident and not intentional. Nobody investigated the accident and nobody took an interest in it. I, however, who had been a witness to that tragic event, could not calm myself and in my heart, vowed to bring this matter to the authorities. First of all, however, I had to be freed. I sent a note to my friend who had arrested me, asking that he summon me to one of the CHEKA sessions. I was summoned. At the session, I declared that I have no money but that I would commit myself to provide them with 3 tons of tobacco. They accepted my offer and set me free. At home I described the incident of the soldier's death and my intention to bring it up with the authorities. My family became very frightened and made me swear not to do this: "Enough that you were in danger for your life and came out safely! Instead of looking for justice from the Bolsheviks, better that you should recite the 'Goiml' prayer". (for escaping peril).

The next day, all the prisoners were sent out for forced labor: some to clean streets, some to repair damaged houses, some for field work. Each had to work a determined number of days to pay back the amount of "contributions" they had neglected to hand over. Forced labor was handed out to those that the Bolsheviks considered "soft". The physically unfit and the middle aged were not spared from this.

I remember one episode of forced labor that made me especially sad. Chaim Finkelstein, the director of the huge warehouse "Loffers" was a very fine and upstanding person in Dubossar society. He was a learned man, a Zionist and a philanthropist. He showed respect to each and every person – to all of his workers, Jews and gentiles. One day, as I passed by the Gypsy street, I came upon a group of Jews who were cleaning the street while soldiers stood guard over them. To my great astonishment, I saw Chaim Finkelstein among them. I went up to the oldest of the soldiers and told him who Finkelstein was. His answer was a laconic: "He is a bourgeois, a bloodsucker".

I went to my friend in the CHEKA and begged him to do something. He deplored the treatment that Finkelstein was subjected to but he did not want to mix in. In truth, he disliked everything that was happening around him but he believed it was all temporary and that soon the situation would improve. "We have to be patient", he would tell me, "until this transition period is over." Not long after, he paid dearly for his belief in the new regime.

My friend came from a prestigious family. He was a fervent Communist but not a renegade. One day, he and other party members were invited to a Party purge. The custom at these purges was for each member to relate biographical details of his personal past history up to the time of his membership in the Communist Party and also to describe present activities as a Party member. In addition, the Party members were obliged to answer all questions put to them by the others. At that purge, my friend stumbled when he was asked if he goes to synagogue. In his honesty, he admitted that he attends synagogue two times a year – on Yom Kippur and on the anniversary of his father's death – in order to fulfill his father's will. For that 'sin' he was expelled from the Communist Party.

In the transition period which stretched out over a long period of time, the highest positions in the local government were held by ignorant and coarse individuals who during the Revolution had clawed their way to the top. I remember one such person who was sent to us as the local Military Chief. On a certain day, some unknown person killed a CHEKA agent. The authorities declared the day of his funeral a day of sorrow and prepared a funeral fit for royalty which included a burial in the City Garden. Among the people delivering eulogies was the aforementioned Military Chief. When it was his turn to speak, there was at first a moment of absolute silence as a sign of honor for the man who had held a very important position. Then the Chief approached the grave and said: "Be well, dear friend. Sleep peacefully." It was no easy task to control oneself from bursting out in laughter.

Days of Hunger

Under the pretense that there could be no emergency food or produce near the border, the authorities confiscated all the area's food, crops and produce and sent them to Central Russia. After a short period, the entire region experienced a shortage of food and produce. The little that people had been able to hide was soon grabbed away by the many raids and searches of the authorities. In order to frighten the population, many who were discovered hiding food were sentenced to death.

One of the tricks that the officials used in acquiring staples, especially packaged tobacco, was the official 'purchase'. A delegation would arrive from Central Office issuing an order that whoever was in possession of tobacco was obliged to sell it to the government who would pay them with material. Needless to say, whoever possibly could, did his utmost to hide at least a portion of his tobacco. Unfortunately, the raids and searches were very thorough and whoever was caught with hidden tobacco was severely punished. Even the peasants could not avoid the regime's long arm. They "bought" from the peasants all that they possessed: wine, barley, dried fruit, horses, pigs, etc. They were given promissory notes indicating that they would soon be paid. These expropriations caused great bitterness. The severe punishments did not deter hoarding, however, and the black market flourished. Many paid with their lives for these "economic sins" and those that were not caught, lived in constant fear.

When even the emergency food and products were emptied out, the Jews, whose main occupations were trade and crafts, were left totally without the means to make a living. The peasants did not plough and did not plant because in any case their produce would fall into the hands of the confiscators. Soon, hunger began to rage among the population. Divine Providence, however, did not forsake Dubossar and help came from an unexpected source. At that time, there would appear in our town, guests from foreign places whose aim it was to reach the Dniester River. Not the river per se, but rather as a means of reaching the other side to Bessarabia which was in Romania. Soon these foreigners became a source of income for some of the locals. Thanks to them, a new industry was born - stealing across the border. The first to latch on to this opportunity were the men of the underworld, quickly followed by other residents, not excluding high government officials.

The good news that one could cross the Dniester via Dubossar spread as swiftly as on wings and from far-off distances, masses of people streamed into Dubossar as this could no longer be kept secret. On certain days, the police showed up in force, gathered up all the foreign people they found in Dubossar and sent them back to wherever they came from. Those who had jewelry were arrested. Still it was difficult to maintain all the throngs of people who were seeking to rid themselves of the Soviet 'Paradise'. In spite of all the danger and the casualties suffered by those who were caught, the flow of refugees did not abate. Each had only one goal: to cross the Dniester at any price.

In the meantime the Soviet Regime consolidated its power and in town, various institutions were created - economic, military and political. The Central Command sent trusted individuals, faithful Bolsheviks to direct these institutions. A miracle would happen and most of the directors of these high institutions would suddenly disappear. As soon as one of these important people escaped, another would immediately take his place and usually this devoted person would soon follow in the footsteps of his predecessor.

Up until the Revolution, our family owned a large business specializing in milk products. When the terrible events broke out, the business closed down. When the Soviets occupied the town, they registered every past business and among them, ours. They decided to re-open our business and appointed me as foreman. A couple of days later, they sent down two officials (both Jews) from Odessa – one as director and the other as his assistant. The two spent the next few days wandering around the yard, planning how to expand the enterprise. They planned for so long until they both disappeared as if the river had swallowed them both up. Two others were sent to replace them and they also followed the same pattern.

The CHEKA imposed terrible punishments on anyone who attempted to escape and people were frightened to death of them. Nevertheless the numbers of people who disappeared increased from day to day. The numbers managing to steal over the border reached astronomical proportions. High ranking Communists would often explain that the officials who had disappeared had actually been re-located to other posts but nobody believed them. It was an open secret what was really going on.

At the head of CHEKA in Dubossar, was a young man from Odessa – Kaminsky. He chose an assistant from the local men – Yuvika Gurevitch. Under their leadership, the CHEKA in our town reached new heights of cruelty. When Kaminsky was seen in the street, people immediately made themselves scarce in order not to cross paths with him. I, however, as a "faithful Soviet laborer" was not afraid of him. One evening, he and his assistant showed up in our yard. I invited them into the house and served them tea. All of a sudden a few fellows wearing CHEKA hats, showed up and invited my guests to accompany them. Kaminsky and Gurevitch parted with me in a friendly manner saying that they hoped to meet again soon. A couple of days later, we found out that these "faithful" Bolsheviks managed to get to Kishinev where they were arrested. Until today, I have no idea what happened to them.

Thanks to our proximity to the Dniester River, we were often privileged to see famous Cantors and entertainers – among them the renowned Cantor David Roitman z"l. They came to perform for the people of Dubossar but another reason was because we were close to the border. One day we received the wonderful news that the Moscow State Theatre was arriving to perform in Dubossar. On the first night, the troupe performed Andreyev's "The Days of Our Lives" and the hall was overflowing. Before the curtain was raised, an official of the Central Committee of the Communist Party, with great passion told the audience that this government of the Workers and Peasants was providing the opportunity for those who toil and are unable to come to Moscow, to see, in this their own town, the great Moscow Theatre. He greeted the actors and wished them a good beginning in their mission to bring pleasure to the laboring masses in far flung corners. On the second night, they performed the piece: "Sylva" and after the show, instead of going to the hotel, the artists quietly crept away to the Dniester River to cross over to the bourgeois side.

The hunger increased from day to day. The black market flourished although there was practically nothing to buy or sell. Thin pieces of bread went for fantastic prices. The main dish was a porridge of corn-meal flour called "zhandre". This dish was made of corn- meal flour, mixed with water and cooked without salt or sugar. At that time, salt was three times as expensive as sugar and very few could afford this. It wasn't long before even the wealthy were going hungry. These newly poor went from door to door – not to beg for charity, but rather for a few spoonfuls of warm "zhandre" just to keep the soul alive. Soon these unfortunates numbered in the hundreds every day. In spite of the fact that we lived outside of the town and it was not easy to make their way to us, our door was never shut to them as so many made their way to us. There were times when we did not look them in the face as we did not wish to shame them.

One misfortune brought another. There was another new food – oil cakes. This was the offal and left over oil that was used for feed for the animals. When the hunger was overwhelming, this was often the only food in some homes. This product caused stomach typhus and whoever became ill from it, did not recover.

The greatest hardship was in the winter of 1921-22. All the work animals – cows, sheep, and chickens – were either eaten or died of hunger. In order not to have to witness the suffering of the horses, the farmers would drive them away to far off fields. There was also a shortage of heating materials and people fell like flies from hunger and the cold. Every day, scores of people died in Dubossar. The militia would gather together the corpses and would mobilize the 'supposed' healthy ones to transport them for burial.

One evening, my father sent me to fetch two pounds of corn-meal flour in order to cook a "zhandre" for the needy who came to our door. On the main street I saw a little girl, ten years old, who was leading her father. I was a few feet ahead of them when I heard the screams of the little girl. I turned around to see what had happened and saw that her father was slowly sinking down to the ground. The little girl tried to pick him up but it was useless. At home, I told them about the incident and I ate myself up because I had not gone to help the man. My parents tried to comfort me by saying that in any case I could not have helped him.

At home, father gave the strictest attention to the distribution of our food so that we would not be overcome with hunger. If not for father's strict control we would not have lived through those bitter times. In the morning, each of us would receive a thin piece of bread and two dried prunes for our tea as a substitute for sugar. My younger brother, Joseph, who later disappeared without a trace in the Siberian tundra, would hide his portion of bread from morning until the afternoon in order to eat two slices at once and thus to quiet somewhat his pangs of hunger. For lunch, we had a cooked prune soup and "zhandre". We actually did not lack for wood as near our house was a large orchard and vineyard. We would uproot the trees and have wood for the oven. Compared to others we were among the fortunate ones.

Many of those who wandered toward the North in their search for food, perished on the way. This also was the fate of our good neighbor, the gentile Ivan Mazor. One day he told us that he had decided to go to Mogiliov – in the Poldolsk region, 200 kilometers away – where he hoped to find some feed for his horses that he was trying so hard to save. He offered to bring something back for us. My father, z"l. was happy with the thought of enlarging our food supplies and gave him a big, fur coat to trade. On his way there, one horse died and on the way back, his second horse and then he himself, perished. Jews and Gentiles risked their very lives to cross over the border to bring back a loaf or two of bread. Finally in 1922, the Soviet regime allowed in food from America via JOINT (Jewish relief organization). Large quantities of food packages began to appear and our people were saved from a certain death from hunger.

Perilous Escape Attempts

The woes in escaping from Soviet Russia did not begin nor did they end on the night that one crossed over the Dniester. In truth, the plan began with the thought to leave Russia and ended with leaving Romania as well unless the fugitive intended to settle in Bessarabia.

In the winter of 1921 I disclosed to my parents, wife and active friends of the Zionist organization in Dubossar, my secret plan of making my way to Eretz Yisroel. Visoky at that time was already on the other side of the border and the dentist Misha Diner was one of the prominent activists in town. I began to liquidate everything that I could possibly sell in order to raise money for the journey. I kept only the most necessary belongings for me, my wife and three month old child to take on the journey and on a Friday we left for Yagorlik in a wagon. We went to the home of Raphael Rampel (who was murdered only a couple of months later by the CHEKA), as had been planned earlier. We put down our belongings and went to visit my relative Shmuel Pochis, David Pochis' brother from Ein Ganim. During our evening meal, Leah Reznick (she now lives in Eretz Yisroel) came in to warn us that men from CHEKA had burst into Rampel's house and we had to disappear. Rampel was arrested and we hid for 3 weeks at the home of a man called Alter. When Rampel was freed he came to us and told us that for now, we must return to Dubossar. I decided that I alone would return. On the way back, I found out that two Jewish families were murdered in their attempt to cross the Dniester – Jacob Pilchokov's daughters and their husbands, Bershodsky and Jacob Grossman. Only one boy of ten years survived.

This terrible tragedy had a great impact in town and some of my family members vehemently opposed my plan to cross the border. The situation in Russia, however, was worsening from day to day and gradually the horror of what had happened to the Grossmans and Bershadskys faded away. Rampel was arrested a second time and they transferred him to the central CHEKA headquarters. In spite of the terrible danger that accompanied crossing the border, my resolve to leave Russia became stronger each day. I made arrangements with a Moldavian gentile who was known as an honest and trustworthy "smuggler" to deliver me, my family, my cousin Mayer Rash with his younger sister (now living in Rishon L'Tzion) and their little brother.

One day, the "smuggler" came to me and asked if we were ready to cross the border that night. I was not prepared and requested that he postpone the event for another night. My cousin and his group refused to consider postponement and they left with him that same night. To their great misfortune, somebody informed on them to the CHEKA and they sent out agents to intercept the attempt. When the boat was a short distance from shore, the agents began to shoot at them and they were forced to return. All in the boat were arrested except for the "smuggler" who managed to escape by swimming over to the other shore.

The CHEKA agents were disappointed when they did not find me among the arrested. This alerted me to the fact that CHEKA was spying on me and I had to be more careful. During the day I ran away to Groselova, 50 kilometers from Dubossar. A week later, I secretly came back and my neighbor, who worked for the CHEKA told me that my references were not good and he advised me that the sooner I crossed the border, the better. He offered to take me himself. We decided on a night that he had to cross the border anyway in order to bring back military documents. A few other people were included in the operation and when it became dark, we made our way to a hill where we spread out on the ground to await the boat.

From the other side of the Dniester on the Bessarabian shore, we could see the town Golkarni. We could see the lights from houses and from far off, we could hear the songs of the local young peasant men and women. In the silence of the night, we could make out the conversations of the townspeople as well as the barking of dogs and mooing of the cows. On our side, not far from the hill where we were waiting was the town of Kutchiyer where I had grown up until my ninth birthday. The town was enveloped in silence. There was no barking from a dog, no neighing from a horse, no mooing from a cow. A melancholy sorrow hung over the town. The distance between the two towns was a mere 200-300 meters, yet these were two totally different worlds. With great longing, the heart yearned for the other side – the well lit side – and great was the desire to reach that shore.

The boat didn't come and we all went home with our belongings. The border crossing attempt was postponed for a few days. Finally, on the specified day, another person joined our group - Moishe Tchaplik, the oldest son of the famous Chaim Isser. This time we were sure we would succeed because Eliezer, Tchapnik's son, was with the CHEKA and he was standing guard for us. As soon as it was dark, our whole caravan gathered at the border. The smuggler told me that twenty people were waiting to cross the river but the boat had room for only five. However, he said, I would be the first one on. When I was already sitting in the boat, Moishe Tchaplik came over to me and ordered me out of the boat. The reason was that he, his wife and daughter as well as a couple of brothers must be the first ones into the boat. Because of his great prestige (namely, his son from CHEKA) I understood that there was no room for discussion and I disembarked.

Hardly five minutes passed when we heard a suspicious noise and then stifled screams. The boat turned over and everyone in the boat was pitched into the river. Those of us who were standing on shore, disappeared immediately so as not to fall into the hands of the border police. I ran breathlessly not even aware of where my feet were taking me. The night was so dark, I couldn't figure out where I was. With the onset of dawn, I recognized the path that leads to our town. Dead tired, I dragged myself to the home of a relative and knocked on the door. Frightened, they opened the door and took me in. In response to their questions as to why I was out at this hour, I burst into tears and for a while was unable to utter a word.

That morning, it was told in town that Moishe Tchaplik and his little girl drowned in the river. When Moishe's son, Eliezer the CHEKIST, heard this he went to Yosef Wargon (the contrabandchiks said that he was the owner of the boat), dragged him out of the house as he was eating his breakfast, pulled out a revolver and shot him several times. Then he went to my parents and told them to find me, promising them that no harm would befall me.

As the wave of people trying to cross the border increased, the greater the vigilance of the CHEKA. In order to put the CHEKA off my track, I spread the rumor that I was already on the other side of the Dniester River in Bessarabia. Once again I tried my luck. This time, my brother-in-law accompanied me – a boy of twelve years. Through circuitous routes, we made our way to the village Goyani that borders the town of Yagorlik where I had relatives. We visited one uncle, then another uncle but nobody offered us a morsel of food. I did not request anything because I understood that if they did not invite us to the table, it was because there was nothing in the house. In the end, we went to Shmuel Pachis. He was the most well to do in our family. There I waited for a messenger who was supposed to bring me money from home. At two in the afternoon he arrived and told me that tonight the smuggler would be waiting for us in the town of Koshnitzy. Everything was ready. However – Koshnitzy was 30 kilometers from Yagorlik. How would we get there without horse and wagon? There wasn't too much time left to think. I took off my boots and heavy coat and in spite of the bitter frost, I started on my way in my thick socks. It was my luck that a strong wind was blowing and I was sure that in this weather the patrol guards would not be found on the roads.

I was already two and a half hours on my way and I had at least another hour to go. I pushed myself to get past the crossroads of Dubossar/Grigoriopol/Kishnitza before sundown as robbers had recently killed seven Jews in that area. At that time I saw the murdered victims and this terrible picture was very much on my mind. The closer I got to this tragic place, the more vivid was my recollection of this horror. As much as I tried to force it out of my mind, the scene remained before my eyes. I became very fearful. Soon I felt that someone was getting closer and closer and I was certain that it was one of the patrol guards. Avoiding him was already impossible. The man came right up to me and asked me my name. He took me by the hand and led me on. It turned out that he was one of the smugglers and had been on the lookout for me.

After an hour and a half, we arrived at the river. My guide told me to lie own between the shrubs and not to fall asleep in case one of the guards would discover me. he went off to find the other smugglers. I was so tired that I could not overcome my fatigue and did doze off. When I woke up with a start, someone closed my mouth. it was the same man from before. he told me that the smugglers hadn't arrived. I was to go home with him and spend the night there. In his home, he took me up to the attic and brought me a blanket to cover up with... but he gave me no food. The next day, he woke me up and informed me that I had to leave the house as he was under surveillance. I was to return at night. From afar, he pointed out a Jewish home. I went quickly to the house and sat down on the doorstep. The owner opened the door and asked me what I wanted. I told him that I had to wait there until nightfall. He ushered me into the house and directed me to the stove, saying:"please crawl up on top and lie there quietly". He then went off to town to take care of his affairs.

It was a Friday. His wife woke up and started to prepare Shabbes dishes. The delicious aroma of the cooking taunted me and my hunger pains tormented me. She did not offer me any food. When the man returned home, the first thing that he asked her was whether she had offered me any food. Before long, the wife brought me something to eat. As soon as I saw her, I recognized her and called her by name. She was the sister of my friend Zaitchek from Dubossar. When she recognized me, she turned red from embarrassment and apologized for not being able to offer better food. I thanked her with my whole heart. That small amount was enough to still my hunger.

When it became dark out, I parted warmly from them and went back to the appointed place. Soon the smugglers also arrived. This time everything went as planned. Crossing the river took no time at all. In one hour I was sitting in the house of a peasant in the Bessarabian village of Onitzkani.

The troubles of a refugee were not over once he reached the other side of the Dniester. In Kishinev, the capital city of Bessarabia, there were 80% of the Jewish refugees from Russia. Many of them decided to remain in Romania and with money were able to buy Romanian citizenship. For others though, Romania was only a transit station. They signed up with the Jewish Committee that had been organized by the Jewish community to assist the refugees. The Committee had lawyers that were connected to the Romanian authorities and they assisted the refugees with the legal procedures and documentation that was required. By law, each refugee was required to appear before a military court to stand trial for entering Romania illegally. Many were sentenced to various periods of time in jail while with others, entry was denied and the order was to return to Russia.

After a few months in Romania, I had my trial and was sentenced to three months in jail. Fate had it that the day before my trial, my family – my wife, may she rest in peace, my one year old son and my ten year old brother – arrived in Romania. They did not sign up with the committee but rather waited until I was released from jail. After my three months in jail, I was brought before the judicial inquiry where the verdict was that I must return to my place of origin. In the meantime, I had to return to jail. The Refugee Committee handed over my case to a well known Romanian lawyer and after energetic interventions on my behalf as well as guarantees from Rabbi Tzirelson, Dr. Bernstein-Cohen and Madam Babitch, I was set free on condition that I must leave within the month and emigrate to Eretz Yisrael.

Now we had to find a solution for my family who were not even listed with the Committee. The lawyer Dr. Landau was the liaison between the Refugee Committee and the authorities. I asked him what to do. He did not ponder it too long and said: "Come with me to the police station." We came to a room with many closets stacked high with files. There was one official in the room and Dr. Landau requested to see my file. There it stated clearly that I had been sentenced to three months in jail for illegal entry into Romania; that I had then served an additional period of time in jail and was obligated to leave Romania within one month to emigrate to Eretz Yisrael. In the meantime, the official left the room and Dr. Landau took the file and next to my name, added the names of my family. The official came back and Dr. landau handed him my file. We parted from the official and left the building.

Outside, Dr. Landau told me that the whole transaction had cost 20 Lai (a shilling according to money values at that time). I just could not believe my ears. A few days later when I received an appointment to pick up my travel documents, I was convinced that Romania was "A Golden Land" with unlimited opportunities.

* * *

The years 1920-1922 mark a tragic chapter in the history of Dubossar under the Soviet regime. The hopes for salvation that were in the very atmosphere during the years of 1917-20 were now gone. Persecution by the CHEKA, requisitions, contributions, hunger, need and the formidable efforts to escape from the "Soviet Paradise" created a chain of pain and suffering.

My escape from Russia, in spite of all the tribulations and failures that I had to overcome, finally had a good ending. Many refugees, however, did not even live to cross to the other shore. Many were killed in the boats; many drowned before reaching the other side; many were robbed and then murdered even when they reached the longed for shore and many were sent back by the border guards or the Romanian officials. Many found their deaths in the waters of the Dniester and no-one ever found out what had happened to them.

May these words serve as a monument and in memory of the thousands who perished – the men, the women and the children – those whose names are known to us and those who are anonymous - who in their struggle to free themselves from the "Soviet Paradise" died during this stormy, raging period – be it from hunger, epidemics, the sword or the depths of the River Dniester.

May their memory be honored.

Dubossarer Landsleit to Plant Forest of 10,000 Trees

The Dubossarer Committee presenting a check for 3,000 trees to Mordecai Rudensky, Assistant Secretary of the Jewish National Fund. Left to right (seated): Mrs. Louis P. Levine, Mrs. Louis Levine, Mrs. Harry Sheer, Phyllis Levine. Standing, Martin Choina, execut.ve secretary. JNF Landsmannschaften Dept.: Harry Sheer, Dubossarer Committee chairman; Louis P. Levine, treasurer; Louis Levine, member of Executive; Mordecai Rudensky; Moshe Feldman, co-chairman and organizer of the project.

The Dubossarer Landsleit Society, with branches in Israel, Argentina and Canada, as well as the United States, has already turned over to the JNF funds for the planting of 7,500 trees toward their goal of a forest of 10,000 trees to perpetuate the memory of their 18,500 martyred townsmen who perished at the hands of the Nazis in their home town Dubossari-Moldavia in the Ukraine in 1943.

The New York chapter of the Dubossarer Society provided the funds for 2,000 trees; the Philadelphia chapter, 1,000 trees; while 1,000 trees were planted by Dubossarer members in Israel, 2,000 by members in Canada and 1,500 by members in Argentina.

Realization of the project for Dubossarer participation in the JNF Martyrs Forest was brought about by the initiative of Morris Feldman,

co-chairman of the Dubossarer Emergency Relief Committee, with the active cooperation of the late chairman, Ben Zion Itzkowitz; the newly-elected chairman, Harry Sheer; treasurer, Louis P. Levine; secretary, William Nerenberg and the following members of the Executive Committee: Hyman Frost, Louis Levine, Harry Singer and Abraham Sobel.

Harry Singer is president of the Dubossarer Society of New York.

Officers of the Philadelphia Dubossarer Society are: Benjamin Finkelstein, President; Joseph Kipnis, Vice President; Harry Kuchuk, Treasurer; Morris Bender, Recording Secretary; Morris Blaufield, Financial Secretary.

On the Committee: Jack Babek, Max Lerner, Louis Dickman, Morris Gazer, Louis Gordon, Sam Mansky,

Dubossar Landsleit in the United States To Plant Forest of 10,000 Trees

Dubossar Landsleit Organization in Philadelphia

Dubossar Relief Committee in America (New York)

Sitting, right to left: Harry and Henya Scheer, Bentchik Benjamin Shuster, Benjamin Finkelshtein (Philadelphia), Fayge Teitelboim, Yose Kipnis.
Standing, right to left: Mendl Lerner, Nelly Teitelboim, Anshel Nirenberg, Moshe Bendersky, Moshe Feldman.
At the back: Parcels to be sent to Dubossar.

[Page177]

The Dubossar Association in America

by Harry Scheer (New York)
Translated by Sarah Faerman

In the years 1901-2, for the first time, immigrants from Dubossar who were living in New York got together and laid the foundation for our own Landsmanshaft (fellow townspeople organization). The loneliness and isolation that each immigrant feels in a strange land makes him cling to other immigrants, his fellow townspeople who share with him many memories, a similar childhood and similar customs. Thus, there sprang forth on American shores, dozens of Landsmanshaften of Jews from Eastern Europe and this was also the motivating factor in establishing our own association.

At the end of 1918, when Moshe Feldman returned from his military service with the Jewish Legion, the organization embarked on several endeavors in aid of the Jews remaining in Dubossar who, although impoverished during World War I, became totally destitute after the Bolshevik Revolution. Throughout all of the years, the spirit and strength behind these efforts of our Society was Moshe Feldman who poured his heart and soul into this work.

Moshe Feldman belongs to that class of people, who, from an inner sense of duty, take it upon themselves to be the shepherd of a community and to respond to its needs. Nor did he hesitate to call upon those who had been spared from the bitter fate of annihilation, to help in the name of those unfortunate ones who had been the victims of bestiality at the hands of the evil ones. He was molded of the very clay that providence itself assigned to him so that with his restless soul and fiery words, he would accomplish the feat of creating a memorial for the Martyrs, saying Kaddish (prayer for the dead) for them and providing a record for the coming generations. He was one of the few that is summoned by destiny – and in the long history of the Jewish diaspora there have been too many occasions – to be the mourner of the destroyed communities.

He traveled throughout America and with Diogenes' lantern searched out the names of the forgotten – the living and the dead – who were still in Dubossar as well as in the countries where fate brought them. Moshe Feldman never married. Who knows? Perhaps he left his dreams of a family behind in his hometown and brought only his bachelorhood, his solitude, to this strange new land, where, in spite of the dozens of years that he lived here, he was unable to lay down roots in America. He even preserved a certain Dubossar manner and style and did not seem capable of fitting into the day to day, grey, practical American way of life. He always lived in the world of the Dubossar past until he became the founder and inspiration behind the Dubossar Society's Emergency Relief Committee to provide for the Dubossar survivors. This campaign, into which he poured his very soul, assuaged, in part, his solitary, lonely life.

In our generation, Moshe Feldman was the most knowledgeable about Dubossar. He would recall the charm of the Dubossar landscape, the pristine surroundings not yet developed, the streets and alleys, the naive, simple small-town way of life, the quarrels and the peacemaking, the struggles to make a living, the Jews in the market place, the storekeepers and tradesmen, the rich merchants and the paupers. All these were his spiritual world, and like a veil, it obscured the American landscape and the human practical necessities. The American "Hoo Ha" was foreign to him; the notion "to make a living" or "time is money" didn't govern him. He lived outside of this time and place. Physically, he lived in America – spiritually, in Dubossar. Even when he fought in the Jewish legion for the kingdom of Israel, he did not cease to be a citizen of Dubossar and so until the very last day of his life.

And, because he always listened to the voice of Dubossar in him, he carried with him an alert conscience and a sorrow for the people of Dubossar. That is why he went from door to door for years on end, urging always that we "do something for our landleit from Dubossar"

* * *

The war ended. The Holocaust was revealed in its full extent of atrocities – seven ciphers: six million – buried alive, shot, gassed and burned. From the ashes of hundreds of towns and villages came the shrieks of the never ending Jewish catastrophe. The remnants, the survivors scattered in every direction, wandering and clamoring for help.

One fine day, Moshe came to this author and to the Levines. Distressed and sorrowful, he expressed his complaints: "Why are we silent?... We must immediately form a relief committee of the Dubossarers in America to address the needs of those that are still alive – our Dubossar brothers who are spread out in Russia and in other countries.

We did not have the addresses of all the Dubossarers, but trust Moshe Feldman's sixth sense to locate Dubossarers miles away. He gathered them like individual stalks and they began to gather around him, responding to this holy debt.

The Dubossar Landsleit in America responded warmly. Not only we, the old activists, but now new recruits added their strength and threw themselves into the work. I would like to give special honor to the young lawyer, Abraham Shimon Sobel who came as a child to America with his parents. Here he grew up and became a licensed lawyer. This Abe Sobel threw himself into the campaign with a youthful energy and expanded it to cover Philadelphia, Chicago and other cities as well as making the connection with Dubossarers in Argentina. Thanks to him and the other Landsleit, by 1949 the committee had sent 5,000 parcels of food and clothing to the Dubossar needy in Russia, Poland, Romania, Germany, France and Israel.

The New York Emergency Relief Committee was in contact with approximately 150 families of the 200 that had been evacuated to the Asian part of Russia.

From this contact, we slowly accumulated information about the tragic fate of our relatives and fellow townspeople of Dubossar.

As a result of the knowledge accumulated by the Dubossar Emergency Relief Committee, a souvenir journal was produced in 1950. This was mainly due to the efforts of Moshe Feldman, Abie and Rose Sobel as well as the author of these lines who served as chairman of this journal.

One of the most important projects of the American Dubossar Society was the planting of 18,500 trees in the Jewish National Fund's Martyr's Forest in the Jerusalem Hills to commemorate the 18,500 Jewish inhabitants of Dubossar who were mercilessly slaughtered. (I must mention here that the Philadelphia branch was very active in the planting of the first 10,000 trees). To our great sorrow, Abraham Sobel who had devoted himself totally to this undertaking, suddenly, at the young age of 48, had a heart attack and died. To this day, 8,500 souls wait for trees to be planted in their memory in Israel's earth.

* * *

On his way to my factory over a period of weeks and months, Moshe Feldman developed the idea of a "Yizkor Book" that would reflect the multi-faceted, colorful life of Jewish Dubossar over the generations; where the dreams of the youth as well as the wisdom of the old could be passed on to the coming generations who would learn about the life of this Jewish community in South Russia by the Dniester River. The book would portray the week days, the Sabbaths, the holidays, the unique and the general; the old and the young; prominent people and ordinary ones; the camaraderie and the hominess.

Night and day we dreamt the "Yizkor Dream" not noticing in the meantime how days, weeks and years sped by. The ranks of Dubossarers was thinning out. Just yesterday, the young became old and today they wish to live peacefully in their old age, in their own quiet corner....

And suddenly, in the year 1961, Moshe Feldman became seriously ill. He took to his bed and there he remained. From his sickbed he once again developed his dream of the "Yizkor Book". Unfortunately, he did not live to see it published.

I accompanied my dear friend, Moshe Feldman, to his burial and felt myself dreadfully orphaned. I did not become discouraged however. Right after his death, I realized that the great responsibility for the book now rested on my shoulders. Luckily, the Dubossar Landsleit in Israel took on the task of gathering material and organizing the book.

The "Yizkor Book" where these very lines appear along with the other writings from America, is a fact – a memorial for a Jewish community that lived, that created, that dreamed, that was joyous, that battled ... and tragically was decimated along with hundreds of other Jewish communities by the evil butcher who raised his murderous hand against them.

There was a Jewish community in Dubossar and it is no more. May this book be a memorial for Dubossar.

**Dubossar Landsleit in America. Active in organizing help for
survivors still in Russia. Harry Sher, Moishe Feldman,
Hene Sher and her sister Teitelbaum from Argentina.**

Dubossar Landsleit in Argentina. 1953. Credit Co-op "25 de Maja".

Seated R-L: Motl Shapiro (vice pres.), Simon Greenberg (pres), Leon Rubin (secretary).
Standing R-L: Joel Kuperman (treasurer), S. Salata (cherente?), G. Belinkin (acting secretary), B. Rashkovsky (syndica suplente ?), D.I. Vinishtok (director), N. Belinkin (active secretary), B. Rashkowsy (syndica suplenta), D.I. Vinishtok (director; yes…listed twice this way, see one line up), Malamud (director suplenta), P. Dubner (director suplenta), I. Gurevitch (secretary), A. Melman (director)

**Monument to the Dubossar Martyrs in the
cemetery in Mablada, suburb of Buenos Aires, Argentina.**

Israel and Fayge Jenin and grandchildren in Philadelphia

Dubossar Landsleit in Argentina

Argentine Dubossar Credit Union "25 of May"
Sitting, right to left: Moshe Shapiro, Simon Greenberg, Leon Rubin
Standing, right to left: Yoel Kuperman, S. Salata, N. Belinkin, B. Rashkovsky, D.I.Weinstock, Malamud, P. Dubner, I. Gurevitch, A. Melman

Executive Committee of the Argentine Dubossar
Organization and Women's Committee on the 25th Anniversary, 1953.
Sitting, right to left: Pauline Wexler, Mani Dubner, Paulina Meshbein, Dora Greenberg, Chuma Rubin, Chana Zeltzer, Rivka Samialof, Jenny Zeltzer, Rosa Itzkovitch, Miriam Brodsky.
Standing, right to left: Pesach Dubner, Zev Polinsky, Shimon Greenberg, Levi Yerusalimsky, Isaac Melman, Moshe Itzkovitch, Chaim Tzirulnik.

Dov (Bernardo) Gurevitch (Argentina)

[Page186]

Former Residents of Dubossary in Argentina

by L. Rubin (Buenos Aires)
Translated by Sarah Faerman

On the 25th of July, eleven Dubossar Landsleit (people from the same town) gathered together in the home of Bernardo Gurevitch, z"l, to meet with our guest from New York, Moshe Feldman, z"l, who just recently passed away. We heard his impassioned description of the destruction of the Jewish community in Dubossar and the terrible bloodbath carried out by the Nazi murderers against our brothers in our home town.

After hearing the tragic details, it was decided to establish an emergency committee that would immediately contact all the Dubossarites in Argentina and mobilize material aid to the survivors of what was once our community.

The elected committee consisting of Bernardo Gurevitch, Moshe Winokur, Hershl Yerusalimsky and the author of these lines, immediately got busy. Although we lacked the addresses of many, in a short time we were able to locate them and we overcame other difficulties as well. We launched the campaign and very soon were able to send funds to our friend Moshe Feldman in New York who was in contact with those Dubossar Jews who had miraculously managed to survive in Europe.

Women's Committee of the Dubossar Landsleit Society in Argentina.
Sitting R-L: Paula Meshbayn, Nechama Rubin, Rivka Samoyloff, Ana Melman, Jenny Zeltzer.
Standing: Paulina Wexler, Miriam Weinstein, Catalina Viler, Miriam Dubner, Clara Brailansky.

After the first spontaneous aid was sent out, it became clear that we needed a permanent and intensive organization that would address the following issues:

First: We needed to be in direct contact with the survivors in order to provide supplies according to their needs; Second: We wanted to let them know that we, their brothers in Argentina, would neither abandon nor forget them; Third: There was a need to create locally a permanent body to carry out in an organized fashion the above two objectives but also, in order not to neglect the local Dubossar Landsleit in Argentina, it was important to develop cultural activities and to create a family atmosphere that would reflect the spirit and traditions of our old home. This home-like environment would also help to stem the winds of assimilation that were blowing toward the Jewish homes.

As is typical, all beginnings are difficult. It was not easy to gather together all the Landsleit and to unite them after the passage of so many years, especially when each had his own struggles in adapting to the new land. We had to resort to all types of tactics. We appealed to the conscience, we played on sentiments, we recalled memories that over the years had dimmed and slowly, slowly, thanks to the diligent work from a couple of the activists, most of the Dubossar Landsleit responded and together we accomplished the creation of the Dubossar Landsleit Association as well as the Relief Committee.

We obtained the list of survivors from Moshe Feldman. They were spread out throughout Russia and to each address we sent packages of food, winter and summer clothing, various house-wares and also medicine for which we received heartrending, emotional letters of thanks that underlined the great importance of our work.

When the needs of the Dubossarites in Russia were alleviated, we decided to devote our efforts to helping needy Landsleit in Israel. We contacted our friend D. L. Granovsky in Tel Aviv and requested from him a list of those Landsleit of ours that needed some assistance. We then sent them dozens of parcels also.

With our actions, we realized the wisdom of the saying that the satisfaction is greater in the giving than in the receiving. You would have had to observe with what joy and enthusiasm the men and women threw themselves into the work for the Relief Campaign, with the buying of the goods, packing the parcels and sending them off with no regard for cold in winter or heat in summer, in order to demonstrate the strength of our brotherly solidarity and the happiness of one's soul to be able to help. In our case it also expiated some of the guilt we felt because we were the lucky ones who had managed to escape in time and had been spared the terrible catastrophe that our unfortunate brethren had lived through in our old home.

As usual, one good deed causes other good deeds. The Relief Committee revitalized our Association and fostered the desire to meet more often for cultural programs because of the convivial atmosphere we had created. We often gathered for lectures and concerts which were on a high level. We started to celebrate holidays together as well as remembrance events for both Jewish and gentile personalities. In general we used every opportunity possible to "Shevet Achim Yachad" (sit together with our brethren).

I must laud the exceptional and unstinting efforts of the Women's Committee that was formed within our Association. They made sure that our gatherings were always cozy with a family-like ambience and often with tables laden with refreshments prepared and served by the women. These gatherings were always a great success both from the point of view of our objective goals and also for the high morale generated.

Throughout its existence, our Association has had a dual purpose – the Relief component and the cultural programs which encompassed national (Jewish) and local concerns. Never was there a meeting without a collection for the Jewish National Fund. Our Dubossar Association was also registered in the Jewish National Fund's Golden Book.

Dubossar Landsleit Society in Argentina.
Nechama Rubin presents Bernard Gurevitch with a silver medal
for his dedicated work on behalf of the Dubossar Survivors.

The Jewish community of Argentina erected a monument in the cemetery in Tablada (a suburb of Buenos Aires) to memorialize the six million martyrs annihilated by the Nazis. The Dubossar Association placed a panel on this monument in the memory of our destroyed home town. Every year, the Dubossar Landsleit gather there with their families for the Yorzeit (anniversary of death) of our 18,000 martyrs that the Nazis murdered in Dubossar. We end the ceremony with a eulogy and a collective Kadish (prayer for the dead).

When the idea was initiated by the Dubossar Landsleit in Israel and Diaspora to create a memorial for our martyrs by planting a grove in the "Forest of the Martyrs" of the Jewish National Fund near Jerusalem, we undertook the mission to participate in this initiative. I hope it will not be considered boastful if I mention that when the world wide Dubossar Landsleit were discussing in what manner to commemorate our destroyed community, the idea of planting a forest of 10,000 trees in the "Martyrs' Forest" was the suggestion of the Argentina Relief Committee. And, at the end, when it was decided to publish this Yizkor Book, the Argentina Dubossar Society immediately supported the project and did its share in making it a reality.

With the passage of time, the Relief Committee's work lessened and the cultural programs of the Association required better facilities than those used in the early stages. At that point, the activists in the Association decided to establish a Credit Union which would provide the financial base for us to obtain a centre of our own that would have the necessary facilities for broader cultural activities and could also serve as a "home" for the Dubossar Landsleit and their families who could then enjoy its special close and traditional atmosphere.

In 1955, at a well attended meeting, the foundation of a Credit Union was established. An executive was elected consisting of Shimon Greenberg, Hershl Yerusalimsky, z"l and the writer of these lines, as president, treasurer and secretary respectively. The president, Shimon Greenberg, was not even from Dubossar but his wife Dvorah was. He feels, however, as close to us as if he had been born in Dubossar. Because of his experience and knowledge of co-operative ventures, he was invited to head our newly created institution. Thanks to his expertise and the co-operation of the board that worked tirelessly with him, in a comparatively short time we had our own "home" that was equipped with the facilities we needed to carry out our cultural activities. In time, we attracted new members, not necessarily people who had lived in Dubossar. Their relationship with the others in our Association has been a very positive one and the organization has continued to thrive both financially and spiritually.

I believe that this is perhaps the first time that a financial-economic institution (at least in Argentina) was not created for material considerations but rather because of our desire to help the survivors of the great catastrophe that befell our people during World War II. The result was an ongoing Association of a group of Landsleit bound together because of common memories, traditions and the desire for a rich cultural life. The Credit Union was not established to increase the number of Jewish financial institutions in Argentina but rather as a support for the Dubossar Landsleit Association which itself is an intensive cultural corner of Jewish life.

* * *

The following Argentinian institutions participated in creating the funds for the Dubossar Yizkor Book:

Credit Union "25th of May"	President – Simon Greenberg
Credit Union "Palermo"	President, Natalia Aidner
Credit Union "Cangallo"	President, Natalia Nigeles
Credit Union" Buenos Aires"	President, Israel Davidovitch
Credit Union "Bessarabia"	President, Davla Derky
"Flores Norte" Society	President, Israel Lyezhin

Our friend L. Rubin worked endlessly to raise funds for our Yizkor Book as did Israel Gurevitch, Vice President and Orlando Melman, Secretary of the Dubossar Association in Argentina.

[Page192]

A Plea to My Fellow Countrymen in Argentina

by Bernardo Gorevitch

Translated by Sarah Faerman

As we were preparing the materials for this book, I received a letter in the mail from Mr. Bernardo (Berl) Gurevitch, who has been living in Argentina since the early 1920's. The letter contained a newspaper clipping from "Di Yiddishe Tzeitung" (The Yiddish Newspaper) in Argentina, dated September 17, 1926 – between Rosh Hashana and Yom Kippur – relating to a request from the Jews of Dubossar to their Argentinian Landsleit (fellow townspeople) for help in erecting a new fence around the cemetery.

We had had very little information about the period of the Communist regime's stranglehold on Ukraine until the invasion of Hitler in 1941. This letter, undersigned by respected people in Dubossar – the Rabbi and the Shochtim (ritual slaughterers), in spite of its brevity, provided a glimpse of the life and hardships of the Jewish community under the Soviets in the 1920's.

The original letter had been written in Hebrew but as we do not have access to it, we are reproducing it here the way it appeared in the Buenas Aires Yiddish newspaper – in the Yiddish translation. The appeal was addressed to Messrs. B. Gurevitch, Bendersky and Yitzchak Dayan:

> "We the undersigned inhabitants of Dubossar beseech you to gather donations for a new fence for our cemetery. Since these days of hunger, our town has become impoverished and we do not have the possibility to provide everything that is necessary for our cemetery. Because of many deaths, the cemetery filled up and we had to enlarge it. God will enter your name for life for your generosity. We request that you send the money to the address of Rabbi Shmuel Rabinovitch, the Rabbi of Dubossar and in the names of Reb Dovid Tobin and Dovid Lifshin.
>
> Signed: Shmuel Pinchas Rabinovitch, son of Rabbi Chaim Shimon teacher and instructor; A. Kramer- Shv'B (Shochetand inspector); M. Z. Bronfman, Ben-Zion son of Efraim, z"l, Shv'B. Greenblat; M. son of Elkana, Shv'B; A. Plchikov, Z.Bendersky, D. Lifshin, D. Rabinovitch, A. Miyuches, S.Volovig, Y. Melamed, H. Sadetsky, V. Kurvitz, Y. Koifman, Z. Shdenkin,M. Rivilis

As a result of this plea, B. Gurevitch placed the following appeal in "Di Yiddishe Tzeitung" to all people from Dubossar in Argentina and in other countries:

> "We the undersigned beg you to permit us, via "Di Yiddishe Tzeitung" to appeal to our fellow townspeople of Dubossar as well as to all Jews who hold dear the Mitzva of "Chesed Shel Emes"

(commandment of true grace for burial). May all who read the following request from the citizens of our town Dubossar, remember in these High Holy days their own dear departed loved ones for whom they can no longer do anything other than a "Chesed Shel Emes. On Yom Kippur when we recall the departed souls, let every person vow to carry out the good deed by helping our poor friends on the other side of the ocean and by virtue of this, the blessings that they send us for the New Year will be realized.

Bernardo Gurevitch"

This campaign was carried out by B. Gurevitch and Nachum Feck and the sum of $180.00 was collected and sent to Dubossar for the erection of a fence around the cemetery.

[Page193]

Episodes from My Youth in Dubossar

by Louis (Eliezer) Tchernik
Translated by Sarah Faerman

As I recall, in the first ten years of the 1900's, a theater troupe was founded in Dubossar comprised of local talent. The 'father' of the troupe was Budeinsky – a Jew, a dreamer, an idealist with the soul of an artist. Actually, by trade he was a wall and sign painter at which he was very skilled. I don't know of any prior involvement he had with theater, I only know that one fine day, he gathered together the youth, mainly shop clerks and suggested that they form a theater troupe for the Dubossar Jewish community.

I remember with what great enthusiasm we embraced the idea and with all of our youthful energies we devoted our evenings to rehearsals. First of all he taught us what exactly 'Theater' was and gave us guidelines about acting. Then we applied ourselves to the work.

We performed various plays, even attempting Gordon's: "God, Man and Devil" as well as plays by other playwrights. Our performances were successful and we brought much joy and celebration to the Dubossar Jewish community.

The main actors were Hershl and Shmuel Postalov, Jacob Novimay, Neche Berkovitch and Averbach.

* * *

For my first contact with a political organization, I have to thank Zerach Flam, a shoemaker by trade. As it turned out, he was an activist in the Bund (Socialist organization) in our town and it was in his house that I attended for the first time in my life a clandestine meeting of the Jewish Dubossar Socialists. I came thanks to his younger brother who was a schoolmate of mine and he actually dragged me to this secret meeting. They made proposals that I partly understood and partly had no clue what they were talking about. Zerach also had a projector and showed pictures of various animals accompanied by explanations. As I understood it, this was a popular lecture about nature. This meeting made a powerful impression on me, perhaps because of the atmosphere of conspiracy, perhaps because of the projector. For whatever reason, that first meeting that I attended at a political organization was a great event for me.

* * *

In Dubossar, there was a Jewish doctor- Laybele Polinkovsky – a diamond of a man. He healed the poor without taking any payment and the people, particularly the poor, loved him. As a government doctor, one of his duties was to protect the town from epidemics. This Laybele Polinkovsky would often go out in the mornings to the market together with Nikita the policeman who carried with him a can of kerosene. They would go from stall to stall and wherever he would see rotten fruit or other spoiled products (i.e. baked goods) covered with flies and worms, he would immediately instruct Nikita to pour kerosene over the food. Then, even the destitute would not purchase these goods. Who knows how many people – children and adults - Polinkovsky protected from infectious diseases with his original campaign tactics.

* * *

There was a Jew, Chaim Finkelstein in our town. Actually, in Dubossar he was only a part-time inhabitant. He was a merchant of the "Fur Guild" (a prestigious guild which enabled Jews to live outside of the pale of settlement) and lived in Petersburg. He spent a lot of time in Dubossar, however, where he was the owner of the big Tobacco Factory "Loffers". Chaim Finkelstein was a Jew with a stately appearance and it was rumored that he had access to the Petersburg high society. Chaim Finkelstein employed many people, both Jews and gentiles. A special position in his factory was held by Yosef Visoky, his bookkeeper.

Yosef Visoky was a great idealist and the virtual Zionist leader in Dubossar. When the followers of the Haskala (Enlightenment) movement began to establish their classes in the Jewish towns and villages in Russia, Visoky convinced Finkelstein to help establish a modern school in Dubossar where, along with Yiddish studies and Hebrew as a spoken language, there would also be Russian and General studies. With Finkelstein's help, the first modern Hebrew/Russian school was founded in Dubossar. The school was located in the loveliest part of town, opposite the boulevard. It was housed in a sparkling clean building with spacious, airy rooms. There was a fine yard for gymnastics and games. I had the luck to be one of the first students.

The first director and teacher was Abraham Isaac Yogalnitzer (Golani), a God – sent pedagogue that was greatly loved by his students. He treated each one of us with such affection as if we were his own children. In no time at all, we achieved wonderful results. Particularly outstanding was our usage of Hebrew as a living language. When Yagolnitzer decided to leave Dubossar to make his home in Eretz Yisrael, we had very mixed feelings: We were happy for him as he would be realizing his dream but we were very sad to lose such a good and dear teacher.

Our second teacher was Israel Greenshpan. He was a gifted pedagogue and he thoroughly taught us Hebrew literature and Jewish history. He was also our guide in later years when the organization "Hatchiya" (Revival) was founded, attracting all of the best youth in town as members.

Under the leadership of Yosef Visoky, we the members of "Hatchiya" initiated many practical Zionist activities such as raising money for "Keren Kayemet" (organization for buying land and trees in Eretz Yisrael). The "Hatchiya" period was one of the nicest and most productive epoch in the lives and development of the Jewish youth in Dubossar.

Herzlia High School 1912. Children sent from Dubossar by parents to study in Eretz Yisrael. Shimon Ben Ami (sitting, second). Standing left – Chochomovitch

Herzlia High School 1907
Back row standing, right to left: Isaac Horwitz, Yaakov Mayerov, Nahum Resnik, Nahum Horwitz, Aharon Horwitz, Eliezer Gutterman.
Right to left, sitting: Shmuel Guzman, Bracha Mayrov, Liba Filler, Lev Shochat, Shlomo Vertheim, Yosef Ben Ami.
Below: Yosef Katsap

Dubossarers in Rishon L'Tzion 1923

A Group From Yagorlik (near Dubossar) in Ein Ganim

Right to left: Menki and Zalman Puchis, Neeman - son of Gedalia and Rachel Rechev, Avraham Gluzman , mother and father of Ben Zion Gluzman (among the first to Ein Ganim), Rabbi Puchis and wife Yenta, grandaughter of Miriam Bat Yakov, Gedalia and Rachel Rechev, David and Chaya Puchis with son Isaac who fell in the War of Independence.

Sorting Tobacco in Rishon L'Tzion, 1925

1.Avraham Fier, 2. Michael Tomshin, 3. Mordecai Tomshin,
4. Maier Rash, 5. Yishayahu Kan-Tor, 6. Avraham Moshkovitz

**A Big Reunion In Rishon L'Tzion, 1924, upon the
Aliya to Israel of Michael and Masya Shteinberg**

Dubossarers In Israel

Israel and Chana Tabachnik, their son Yehoshua (Aliya to Israel 1905), his wife Chaya Sarah, daughter Malka and her husband Yehoshua Levin with sons Moshe, Benjamin and Aryeh.

Moshe Bick of Dubossar conducting a choir in Haifa

[Page204]

Way of Life – Folklore and Legends

In the Place Where the Penitents Stand
by Yechiel Resnick z"l
Translated by Lancy Spalter

Rabbi Yechiel Resnick, a great scholar and respectable man in our town of Dubossary, wrote the following pages based on a legend known in our community about the famous "Baal Teshuvah" (Penitent) who is buried in the Old Cemetery of Dubossary. Rabbi Yechiel was born in Kalarash and he married the daughter of Rabbi Shimale Dayan, a pious man, a Torah scholar and a Kabbalist. After his marriage, he settled in our town, until he immigrated to Israel more than 50 years ago. He was among the first denizens of Tel Aviv, in which he lived and reached old age. Until the very last moments on the day of his death at the age of 93, on the 6th of Heshvan 5723 (November 3, 1962) he was lucid and kept his wits. He wrote these pages in 5714, when he was very old, getting close to 90. He engaged in writing and research and among others wrote a work titled "David beveit Shaul" (David in the House of Saul) and "Hachayim Bitkufat Hashoftim" (Life in the Age of the Judges).

He wrote the legend about the Penitent especially for this Yizkor Book.

Baruch She-hecheyanu Ve-higgiyanu (Blessed be the One who has kept us alive and brought us to reach this moment)... My soul is full of gratitude to the Compassionate God, Blessed be His Name for His benevolence to me, bringing me to this moment, to the time of the Messiah, the Beginning of Salvation, as we bless... And yet, my soul is torn and my heart is in pain for the terrible tragedy that was brought upon us, on the loss of 6 million, brothers and sisters, holy martyrs, pious and righteous, working people and scholars, dear and shining stars whose light was forever extinguished. For all of them, my soul cries.

The Jewish people mourn heavily, even in their most joyous times. They moan and cry on their holidays for the tragic death of their martyrs and pray for the rising of their souls. We shall now weep for generations to come , in public with the Congregation of Israel and in solitude, each one for his own kinsmen and for the people of his community that were removed from the Book of the Living. At this time, I would like to deliver "a blessing of gratitude" and to thank the Compassionate God, Blessed be His Name, for giving me the strength to participate, even minimally, in the eternal memorial being built by the people of our town to the community of Dubossary, in compiling this book.

I hope that these pages will satisfy the readers and will serve as one brick in the memorial being built here.

Tel Aviv, 5714, the Sixth Year since our Independence.

* * *

We were a bunch of silk youths in our town of Dubossary, engaged in Torah studies. The Beth Midrash served as a place of learning as much as a place to meet for Hassidic discussions and for a friendly chat. Twice a week for years we had the benefit of a special spiritual joy. Once: on Thursday evenings when we gathered for our lesson of Parashat Hashavua (the weekly Torah reading) with Rashi commentaries from Rabbi Aharon "Der Bobbes" (to this day I do not know whence this name originated). It was a special delight to learn the Pentateuch with Rashi from Reb Aharel; it was a joyous tutoring. His fascinating lessons will be justly remembered and his soul will illuminate with the light of eternal life. And once: on the evenings when we sat for several hours in the company of Rabbi Israel Leib Shochet z"l, the father of Rabbi Kalman Feinshel, Shochet Uvodek z"l. He used to come to our Beth Midrash and immediately after the evening prayers we would crowd around him to hear Hassidic stories from his mouth. Rabbi Israel Leib was a gifted storyteller. His audience was captivated by his words. He was a man of truth. Out of caution and fear lest he fail, God forbid, in an unchecked word or in transmitting an inaccurate fact, he would always remark in humbleness: "Children, be careful; I am not accountable for the precision of these events. I think I can remember so far the things I tell you."

On one of the evenings dedicated to the memory of the Baal Shem Tov, Rabbi Israel Leib opened his story as follows: As you know, the Baal Shem Tov z-tz"l (may his sacred memory be blessed) departed three times to Eretz Israel, thus risking his own life and the life of his daughter Hudel, and each time he had to renounce. The purpose that moved the sacred Baal Shem Tov to risk his life three times to reach Eretz Israel by the tortuous ways of those times was to meet with the Great Tzadik, Rabbi Chaim Attar, who compiled "Or Ha-Chaim". All the Tzadikim of that time believed that a meeting of the two would bring redemption. After the Baal Shem Tov had been miraculously saved three times from fatal dangers, the Tzadikim concluded that the postponement was dictated from Heaven and decided to send someone else in the Baal Shem Tov's stead. They sent his brother-in law, Rabbi Gershon from Kitov, and Rabbi Joel, author of "Maggid Meisharim" from Nemirov, an ancestor of my father-in-law, the righteous Rabbi Shimele Nachum Levi's; my father-in-law is fifth generation to Rabbi Joel. After this mission also failed, they resolved to take other measures, one of which was to place great Tzadikim in certain places. One of them was the pious Rabbi, author of "Tzafnat Pa'neach", and the other was the pious, enlighted Rabbi Mendele, who rests in the Old Cemetery of Dubossary.

Reb Israel Leib mentioned the name of Reb Mendele by the way, as an introduction to his story. But I was especially interested in him and wanted to hear more details about the life and work of this Tzadik, and sought an opportunity to talk with my father-in-law, Reb Shimele z"l. I succeeded and one day my father-in-law, may his soul rest in Paradise, told me this story:

The question of who was Reb Mendele, his ancestry and whence he came remains a mystery till this day. Many years later it became known that the Baal Shem Tov and his group, the Tzadikim of the Kloiz of Brody, headed by the preacher from Polonne, assigned him to settle in Dubossary. Nothing else is known. There must have been a reason.

In time, there was a mysterious event which was later elucidated thanks to Reb Mendele. And this is the story.

On the eve of Yom Kippur, during the Kol Nidrei prayer, when the crowd that filled the synagogue was entranced by Reb Mendele's prayer, a stranger sneaked into the synagogue. He was tall and ruddy, a typical "Muscovite". With furtive steps, so as not to be heard, he sidled into a corner and he broke out in bitter crying. Bewildered, the praying Jews asked each other: "What is a powerful Gentile doing in the synagogue on Yom Kippur eve?" During the first recess, someone approached Reb Mendele and told him about the peculiar occurrence. The Tzadik gestured with his hand so as to say "there is nothing to it".

After Kol Nidrei the crowd started to disperse. Only a few stayed behind for the Psalms, as is the custom, and by midnight they, too, retired , each to his home for the night's rest. Nobody approached the stranger and the last to go left him where he stood. The next morning they found him standing in the same corner and he remained there all day. From time to time, heartbreaking sobs came out of his mouth and his eyes were filled with tears.

The closing prayer was over and the sound of the Shofar echoed in the air. People wished each other a good year, a year of forgiveness and acquittal. The crowd and the Rabbi went out to the synagogue's yard to bless the moon. The stranger joined them and pushed his way to come close to the Rabbi. His sobs did not cease during the moon blessing, as if the source of his tears were endless. At the end of the ritual, Reb Mendele turned around to look for the stranger and gestured to him to approach. There was a spark of joy in the eyes of the stranger. Reb Mendele invited him over to his home.

When the meal was over, many Hassidim came to the Rabbi's home, as usual, to listen to his teachings. They were all eager to hear from Reb Mendele the explanation of the mystery of the stranger in the synagogue on Yom Kippur. After a few moments of silence, the Rabbi lifted his eyes and told the stranger: "Well, tell us the story of your life". And the man began his narrative.

"My father was a "Sibiriak" (a prisoner sentenced to exile in Siberia). I never learned what was his crime and why he was exiled. After he ran his sentence, he never returned to European Russia and he settled in Siberia. He married a woman and for many years did not beget children. I was born when he was almost an old man. He always reminded me that I am a Jew and when I was born he brought a Mohel surgeon from far away to introduce me to the Pact of our Father Abraham, which had cost him a large amount of money. One day he took out a book, pointed at it and said: "Look son, this book is called a Siddur". It is a book of prayer. He taught me the alphabet. At first it impressed me, but in the course of time it vanished from me.

My father had a fabrics store and once a year he traveled to Moscow to buy merchandise directly from the manufacturers. When I turned thirteen, I joined my father at the store and, before long, I showed a talent for trade. I learned about the quality of the fabrics, became acquainted with the customers and very involved in the business. My mother died a few years later and my father, who loved her very much, turned suddenly old, lost his vitality, and did not have the strength to travel to Moscow, a long and tiring journey that lasted several weeks. For lack of alternative, it was decided that I should travel in his stead. My first journey was a success. I bought good and nice fabrics at a reasonable price and the manufacturers and tradesmen of the capital treated me with warmth and appreciation. One large manufacturer named Timoshenko became especially fond of me. On my next journey, Timoshenko invited me to be his guest for the length of my stay.

Timoshenko had a single daughter, a good-looking young girl of about my age, and we became friendly, much to her father's joy. He urged us to go out and seek entertainment every time I was in Moscow. Thus, a few years elapsed. Frequently, when I arrived in Moscow, I went directly to the Timoshenko residence, where I was received with happiness and affection. One day Timoshenko summoned me to his study, made me sit in front of him and told me: I am sick and getting old. As you know, I have many assets and only one daughter. My anxiety for the fate of my daughter after my death grows with each passing day. My friends and relatives are waiting for me to close my eyes, to give Natasha's hand to one of her many hollow suitors. They are superficial and gamblers and I shiver at the thought of my only daughter falling in the hands of one of them, whereas I liked you since the first time I set eyes on you, and I wish you would take Natasha for a wife. All that is mine will become yours while I am still alive, because I am convinced that Natasha will find happiness only with you.

Timoshenko's words made me feel good; indeed he had many assets, and I also liked Natasha. Nevertheless, I evaded giving him a positive answer. "The future will tell" was my reply.

I returned home and told my father nothing about Timoshenko's offer. However, in the solitude of my bed, I spent many a sleepless night pondering...Soon after, my father became incurably ill; I felt his end was close. I nursed him day and night but his condition worsened from day to day. For days he lay unconscious. One day, when I was standing by his bed, he suddenly opened his eyes and there was a flash of recognition in them. He glanced imploringly and it tore my heart. For a long time he stared at me and two big, burning tears rolled down his sunken cheeks. In a barely audible voice, he whispered: "My one and only son, be a Jew". Those were his last words. He closed his eyes, never to open them again.

For many days I mourned my father's death. I was left alone and forlorn in the world, without a friend or a relative. My soul cried in solitude and I could not find consolation. The days passed and time, that cures all ailments, eased my sorrow. I departed for Moscow to buy merchandise. My stay at the Timoshenkos in the company of Natasha, who did her utmost to comfort me and to make me forget my father's death, alleviated my grief and I recovered completely. On my next visit to Moscow, I married Natasha.

I closed the shop in Siberia. Before I left the town where I was born forever, I went to the cemetery to part from the graves of my parents. Standing by my father's grave, I was seized by guilt feelings and regret for not having fulfilled his last wish and for having married a Gentile. And yet, when I reached Moscow, the crowded and boisterous city, and took over the management of my father-in-law's business, I soon forgot my father and my past. Business prospered and my assets grew year by year. My wife bore me two sons and shortly after the birth of my second son, my father-in-law passed away.

To expand my business further, I decided not to wait for the merchants to come to Moscow for the fabrics but rather to take large quantities of merchandise to the large rural towns. I organized a convoy of tens of carts loaded with merchandise and set out with them for Odessa. The venture succeeded, the merchandise was practically snatched from my hands, and several months later I arranged for a second convoy".

On reaching this point of his story, the stranger's voice trembled, his throat choked and tears came out of his eyes. After he calmed down, he continued: "and yesterday. When I was passing by the synagogue with the convoy, my ears detected the sounds of the Kol Nidrei prayer coming from the Rabbi's mouth... I felt as if a string of my heart snapped... I got off the dray, ordered the convoy to continue and came into the synagogue..."He choked once again, burning tears rolled down his cheeks and he sobbed for a long time. The Rabbi put a hand on his shoulder and the man calmed down.

"And now, what do you intend to do?" the Rabbi asked softly.

"I want to be a Jew. All day I have been seeing my father's eyes begging me to go back to my sources. Today, on this holy day for the Jewish people, I have separated myself from the Gentile world in which I lived for so many years. Holy Rabbi, please help me return to the bosom of Judaism!" And my father-in-law z-t z"l ended his story: "He became a Penitent, and who can measure up to a Penitent? And his end, indeed, attests to his greatness."

One icy winter morning, the sun appeared to warm the Mikve and found the Penitent sitting on the step stones, inert. In the cold of the night, he had breathed his saintly last.

The following day, the funeral was performed and the entire town participated. Reb Mendele himself, the Tzadik, chose the burial spot and ordered: "When my day comes, please bury me next to the Penitent's grave".

In the Old Cemetery of Dubossary you can still see the two Tzadikim's graves side by side, Rabbi Mendele's and the Penitent's. May their merits in Heaven protect us and the People of Israel. Amen.

Glossary:

Beth Midrash	Place of Judaic learning
Hassidic	Belonging to the Jewish current of Hassidism
Kol Nidrei	Prayer sang on the eve of Yom Kippur
Mikve	Ritual bath
Mohel	Ritual surgeon who performs circumcisions
Pact of our Father Abraham	The circumcision
Rashi	Abbreviated name for Rabbi Shlomo ben Itzhak, commentator of the holy books
Shochet Uvodek	Ritual slaughterer and overseer of compliance with precepts, who served as religious leader in small communities, in the absence of a Rabbi
Shofar	Ritual horn blown on High Holidays
Tzadik (plural Tzadikim)	Pious and devout Jew
z"l (Zichrono Livrachah)	Blessed be his memory

[Page220]

The Beginnings of Theater in Dubossary

by Isaac Horvitz

Translated by Sarah Faerman

A

The year was 1901. Yiddish (Jewish language) stage performances in those days were basically readings from books. Yiddish theater was associated with the name "Goldfadden" who would come from time to time to Dubossar. They say that his acts were usually selections about comic and ludicrous characters like: "The Two Kuni Leml" – two pathetic characters – or "Babba Yachna" who performs magic, cooks kettles of pitch and tar, crawls on rooftops searching for days gone by, and so on. Upstanding, respectable Jews did not deign to attend these silly comedy spoofs and Goldfadden was practically chased out of town after a few weeks barely scraping together a few coins to buy food for the "actors" and toward their traveling expenses.

That was the extent of Jewish theater in those days when there was no library in town and no thought yet of a cultural center. Even a Yiddish or Hebrew newspaper would come to the very few. Preachers and lecturers would appear from time to time to expound on ethics or on "Love of Zion". Then notices would go up in the synagogues and schools announcing that this one or that one would be lecturing Saturday night in the old synagogue and everyone was invited to attend. However, staged performances aimed at the broader public were not yet heard of or even desired.

The Jewish folk was devout and God fearing, totally opposed to the modern, progressive speakers. Whatever was associated with the theater would be greeted with the complaint: "What do these "actors" want? Painted faces! with the Talis Kotn (tasseled undergarment worn by Orthodox Jewish men) on the left side! Brazen women showing naked legs with... with...!!! May God watch over them and protect them... Who are they? Trayfinyakes (not kosher)! Licentious men and women; depraved clowns that besmirch our Jewish name and blacken our reputation! who lead our Jewish little children to strange ideas and to blasphemy; May God save us!"

To this backward, small-town atmosphere, chance brought the young man, Kalman Baylis who came to Dubossar to visit his brother, Israel Mayer Melamed. Kalman had already had a great deal of experience in theater in his city Horodek where he had been both actor and director. We immediately recognized in him someone who was capable of pushing forward our stagnant, provincial, staid young boys and girls. After a few meetings with Kalman Baylis it was clear to us that we had to initiate something in Dubossar.

With Kalman's initiative and help we assembled a theatrical troupe of approximately ten people to perform the play: "The Song Of Bread" by M. M Varshavsky. Kalman, together with Velvl Kazatzker – a singer with a fine baritone voice and very talented in music – began to rehearse us for the performance. Dressed in white shirts and with pitch forks in our hands, we sang with elevated spirits and in great ecstasy this lusty song of celebration:

> Mighty God, We are singing songs
> You alone are our help.
> Brothers gather the sheaves
> Until the sun has set.

On the stage, lit with special lighting, we were like silhouettes against a magical horizon; twilight shadows moving like spirits from a far off strange world. We rhythmically swayed and whispered:

> May the sun bake and burn us
> It lightens our way to happiness.
> See – the bread is plentiful
> Youth, never retreat.

The scene electrified the audience; the singing enchanted them; the mysterious light seemed to fog their minds and from hundreds who sat with warmed hearts, wide open-eyes and mouths agape, came the murmuring: " May the sun bake and burn us, children. Never retreat!!"

Hershl Chaikl's hall suddenly was transformed into a temple of art and paeans of praise along with tears of joy fell on the heads of the "dear Jewish children that have brought such joy to our heavy hearts."

This first sprout of Yiddish theater, like a planted kernel in a ploughed field, flowered and heralded the beginning of theater in Dubossar. With that first performance, the foundation was laid.

B

After the overwhelmingly positive reception of our first offering, our courage soared and so as not to lose momentum in our aspirations, we decided to immediately plan for our next show. This time we named our troupe "Lyubiteles" (Theater Lovers).

Kalman proposed that our next theatrical undertaking should be the musical melodrama "Zerubavel" – a play by L. L. Lilienblum – based on the exile in Babylon and the return to Zion. Kalman had played the role of "Zerubavel" in his town of Horodok and it had been very well received. After giving us a reading of the eight act play, we decided that we wanted to present this as our next production. Three troupe members were chosen to assign the roles and to take responsibility for the preparations. The three members were: Velvl Kazatzker, Kalman Baylis and the author of these lines.

I only remember the names of several of the participants of this endeavour: Kalman, Velvl and his brother Nachman Kazatzker, Joseph Faynshil, Jacob Imas, Berele Molyer, Yankl Nissenboim, and Yankl (or maybe a different name) Shayke Glazer's. Kalman gave me three roles to play, and like the obedient horse that pulls a heavy load, I acted in roles that were distributed throughout the first, second, fourth and fifth acts. Aside from these three roles, I was also the cashier, the ticket printer (by hand with a rubber stamp as there was no printing shop in Dubossar), announcement writer and distributor of fliers in the synagogues. I also, together with Velve and Kalman created the costumes, beards, makeup and all the other incidentals that are associated with mounting a play.

I must mention another two people who, although not directly part of our theater troupe, were of great help to us: Moishe Tzelnik who donated all of the necessary makeup from his apothecary shop and Shmuel Guzman who simply loved the atmosphere of the theater and would help us whenever we needed something.

This same Shmulik Guzman did actually solve a difficult problem for us. We had to put a sacrifice on the stage and fire from "above" was supposed to descend and burn it. This was a difficult situation for us as we could not figure out how to execute this. Shmuel filled his mouth with kerosene and got up on a table behind the set. In one hand he held a burning candle and through a big crack in the scenery, he spit out the kerosene in a big 'swhooosh' . It passed through the candle and onto the stage. The 'sacrifice' burst into flames and dense smoke covered the whole stage. The audience, in great fright, began to run to the doors. And that is how in Dubossar theater, we burnt sacrifices. And now back to the main story.

We applied ourselves diligently to our theater although there were some lazy ones that had to be dragged to rehearsals. We were unable to entice any women to take two female roles in our play so we had no alternative but to use Berele Molyer in the role of Shulamis and Shayke Glazer's boy in the role of the mother.

The week after Sukkot we began to rehearse two or three evenings a week in the cheder (small Hebrew school) of Israel Mayer Melamed. As everything that we were attempting was new and strange to us, we had great difficulties in equipping ourselves with the necessary costumes, props, etc. We wanted to create the best of effects and this cost us a lot both in time and in money. We bought material and conscripted our closest girl friends to sew the costumes in the style and fashion of the historical period we were depicting as written by the playwright and as instructed by Kalman. We also had to make our own wigs and beards and these were painstakingly created by Paike, Nachman's daughter and her sister who were by profession wig makers. In our courtyard, In Kayle Chaim Mordecai's little shul (synagogue) we stored all of our costumes in the women's section and each time a new item was completed, it was brought right over and stored there.

Around the end of November, we decided to rent the "Gorodskay Theater" for a day in December when it was not being used. On December 11th we obtained the theater for five ruble per night. Now we encountered another difficult problem. We had to have a permit to perform in the theater otherwise we could not get the hall.

We started to run here and there, hunting for a way or a person who could help us to obtain the permit. I was given this heavy assignment. To my great luck, a very good friend of mine, Shmelke Melamed, came to my assistance. It turned out that he was close to the authorities, an acquaintance of the Police Commissioner. Shmelke agreed to approach the Commissioner but only if I would accompany him.

We both set out one morning taking with us, at Shmelke's suggestion, the book "Zerubavel" and three rubles that Shmelke placed between the cover and the first page. To put us at ease, he joked that that was a lucky place to put the money as there was a stamp on the page indicating that the book was "Permitted by the Censor". When we arrived at the office, Shmelke asked to see the Commissioner and we were told to go into the reception area where he quickly explained to the chief our request. At the same time, he handed over the book saying:"Here is the book with the permit from the censor." The Commissioner opened the book, skillfully rolled the money into his hand and with an officious expression said: "Yes, yes, the necessary permit is here." He also advised us to send a telegram to the chief of police in Tyraspol stating:"I request permission for the Jewish-German play to commence without a fee" and to sign his name to it. He said that when he received a reply, he would inform us.

I did as he commanded and on the third day, a policeman came to summon me to the Commissioner's office. I went to get Shmelke and we repeated the same steps as before – the book, the three rubles – and off we went to see the gentleman. And he, the gentleman, seeing the book in hand, became very cheerful and told us that the permission had been granted. Shmelke handed over the book and Commissioner, while swiftly extracting the money, read aloud the reply: "Notify Isaac Gurevitch that I authorize the production of the Jewish-German play – to be performed free" (meaning without tickets).

December 11, 1901. Evening. A rush; shoving and pushing at the entrance to the theater. Most of the tickets had already been sold. Many were waiting to be let in but there were no more seats available. We had worried about just such an eventuality and were prepared with a plan. We had gathered together a pile of rocks and quickly assembled a "gallery" behind the benches, near the entrance. "Come people, and if you like, you can watch Yiddish theater standing on the rocks". Needless to say, there were many willing takers for our "gallery".

The hall was so packed that not even a pin could be squeezed in. The ushers were perspiring, yelling and working hard to maintain order. Eight o'clock. The kerosene lamp was extinguished. Everyone held their breath with great anticipation. The curtain slowly rose and Dubossar was privileged to see, for the first time in its history, her own children acting in the theater, acting in the Yiddish theater. (The gentiles had already been involved in theater for a long time).

Around midnight, when the production came to an end, a thunderous applause poured forth from the enchanted audience. "Bravo!" they shouted and stayed as if glued to their seats. They applauded loudly and even wildly, drawing out their great appreciation of the actors. Much later, outside on the street, groups of exhilarated people were still exclaiming: "How they acted!!!" "They were so talented!!" "How did they learn to do this? Where did they learn to act like this?" "I would forfeit a great meal and the best glasses of wine to be able once again to view such wonderful theater!!!" These and similar words of praise were heaped upon us and we, the "actors" behind the scenes, who had struggled and grappled with all the myriad details involved in mounting the production both before and during the play, finally, finally also had some "naches" in listening to the compliments of our enraptured audience.

Our theater group, acting for the first time and being neither trained nor disciplined, had made many mistakes. In one case, we threw away one actor's total costume; in another case, a beard wouldn't stay on; In yet another instance, everything was in order but one half of a mustache refused to stay in place and hung down like a second beard. It wiggled, it moved and made everyone around the actor nervous. What to do? He was due to step out immediately onto the stage. His partner was pacing impatiently; the unruly mustache was waving to and fro until with more clay patted onto his cheek, he finally was able to go onto the stage.

Others, perhaps twenty individuals – among them children – were positively underfoot and getting in our way. This along with the clamor and commotion back stage was disturbing, disappointing and painful and we were worried sick. In spite of all this, the play was a great success. Each scene and then the finale were executed with great finesse. Our collaboration and efforts paid off. We all stepped down from the stage after the last act deeply satisfied with ourselves in the knowledge that we had inaugurated a good beginning. We had laid the foundation for the Yiddish theater in Dubossar.

After the performance, the entire ensemble as well as several backers and helpers were invited to a banquet in our honor at the home of my sister and brother-in-law Reuben and Pearl Bartniker. We celebrated all night until dawn. It was here, around the table laden with tasty dishes and glasses of wine that we decided that all of the proceeds from the sale of tickets for the play would be used to create a library and a reading room. The Bartnikers immediately offered the use of their house for the library and reading room. Reuben Bartniker volunteered to be the first librarian. This was the origin of the Yiddish Theater and the Culture Center in Dubossar.

[Page228]

Reb Isaac Shargaradsky
The Dubossar Klezmer

by Harry Scheer

Translated by Sarah Faerman

As with most Klezmer (musicians) in the Jewish towns and cities of long ago Russian and Poland, my father, Isaac Shargaradsky did not have a formal musical education. Although self taught, he was not merely one more of the many who played instruments; he was an artist, a virtuoso. Had he the opportunity of a musical education and had he lived in different circumstances, who knows the heights he might have achieved.

Itzhak Shargaradsky and family. 1897. The boy on the right is Harry Sher.

I have no doubt that my father was not even aware that a couple of hundred years previously, there lived a master craftsman – Stradivarius – who crafted such superb violins that they far outlived him and to this day they enchant and enthrall whosoever hears their magnificent resonance and tone. I also don't know if my father was aware of the prestige of his own fiddle. Of course, the exquisite sounds that he would coax out of his violin were an authentic reflection of his own unique individuality. When he would take the violin in hand, the music would flow like a river on a calm summer day. Suddenly there would be a winter storm howling through the forest with a soaring to the highest octaves; a wailing would be heard, of one, forlorn and homeless in the frozen, snowbound winter. From the violin would emanate the haunting lament of sorrow and longing; then again there was the rapture and joy of celebration. His virtuosity and artistry elevated him above all the other musicians and he was the focal point of his Klezmer Kapeleye (band). His playing was like the blessing while the rest of the band were like those who say "amen"; he was the bright light and they, the butterflies that warmed themselves in its glow.

There is a folk saying "A Klezmer has a happy profession, but makes a very poor living". The Jewish calendar is full with days of sorrow and weeks of sorrow; with days of misfortunes and difficult times when one is forbidden to celebrate weddings and other festivities. On these days, Klezmer have nothing to do. Even in the permitted days, the earnings were small, insignificant unless it was a wealthy wedding (and how many wealthy people were there in a small town?) There were weddings where the musicians would receive money in the hand for the dance and the amounts given were not uniform. The rich gave more; the poor gave less. When it comes right down to it, the Klezmer's income was that of a pauper and meager was the Klezmer's table. And – when the Klezmer Kapelye ventured forth to the surrounding towns seeking "engagements" – then their families were indeed left with very little.

Therefore, when my father's two brothers-in-law, my uncles from my mother's side – Mordecai and Hershl – wrote to him from America, telling him that Klezmer there have opportunities to perform, not only at weddings but in the Yiddish theater, my father acted upon their suggestion and left for America at the turn of the century. He went alone with the hope of soon bringing over the family and he was soon successfully performing in the Yiddish theater. He was unable to remain long as my mother became ill with consumption, an illness that was a frequent guest among the Jewish poor. When grandmother Menya wrote to him that in God's name he must return to save his wife, the mother of his children, he wasted no time and returned.

He did leave America, but he could not save mother. The illness advanced mercilessly and in the year 1903, my mother – Fayge, "The Klezmerke" (Klezmer's wife) – passed away. Isaac Shargaradsky once again became Dubossar's 'star' Kapelye musician – a live legend on both sides of the River Dniester wherever there were to be found Jewish folk.

* * *

I have no doubt that my father was also gifted as a composer. In spite of the primitive resources at hand, he composed melodies and songs, particularly of the "folklore" genre. One who personally witnessed this is our friend Moishe Bick, himself a composer and also born in Dubossar. Just recently, in 1964, the Museum of Music in Haifa presented a musical folklore concert featuring one of his compositions: "A Jewish Wedding". Among the various dances and wedding songs were also several melodies that were composed by my father.

How or from whom did my father learn to read musical notes? I do not have a clue. I doubt if there were special sheets of paper for musical notations in those days in Dubossar or even regular sheets of paper. And if yes, surely that would have been too expensive for him to purchase. I do remember seeing him take regular white paper and with a ruler, pencil in the lines and the notes. Then he would teach his newly composed dance melodies to his Kapelye. These melodies were soon absorbed within the repertoire of folk music that was sung at family gatherings around the table, at celebrations and at parties in the homes where the young men and women would gather at the end of the Sabbath, after Havdala, to socialize and to dance. These melodies were picked up by other Kapelyes and soon spread out to the surrounding towns and cities.

It would be a pity not to take this opportunity to mention the names of the musicians in my father's Kapelye in the order of their position in the ensemble:

First violin:	He himself
Second violin	Yossl Shual's
Third violin	Vassily Plinzhi (in Moldavian, plinzhi means "The one who cries".
	He was called that because his eyes were always running.
Flute and Clarinet	Matye-Mordecai
Clarinet	Timashke
Trumpets	Shaya and his son Abraham
Bass	Shual
Trombones	Arke from Krivilan and Godl the Blind
Tuba	Israel "Everything Holy" (nickname)
Drums	big Israel and small Yossl

Among the students that learned to play violin from my father, I remember: Moishe Fagis, son of the Shoichet; Solomon Fishgold's two children – Marusya and Grisha; Vishnivetsky's youngest son; the two sons of Mordechai the Zhelyeznik (metal worker) and Lipa Siratzky's little daughter.

[Page231]

The Insight of a Torah Scholar

by Yechiel Reznik, of Blessed Memory
Translated by Shula and Morton Laby

I, Yechiel Reznick, have been asked by my friends and fellow people of Dubossar to participate in writing a memorial book for our sacred community in which I grew up, married my wife and had my sons and daughters. Hence, I feel an obligation to bring from the depths of my memory an episode of which the hero was a brilliant rabbi who worshipped G-d with fasting and prayer. He was my father-in-law, Rabbi Shimon ben Rav Nachum Levi Yitzchak of blessed memory, known as Reb Shimele Nachum Levi, whom I was honored to serve and to pour water over his hands. I basked in the light of his Torah knowledge and hope I have inherited a little of his teaching ability and scrupulousness in every aspect of religion and law.

It was one day in 1894 or 1895, while I was studying with Reb Shimele that a young man of some 22 years of age entered and introduced himself to the Rabbi as a "de-veiner" of the hind parts of cattle (Ed. note: This was necessary in order to make certain cuts of meat kosher.) The conversation between the Rabbi and the young man went as follows:

Rabbi:	Do you have a diploma as a de-veiner?
Young Man:	Yes I have a hechsher (permit).
Rabbi:	Where is the diploma?
Young Man:	It is with the dayan (judge of rabbinic law) Rabbi Yerucham.
Rabbi:	Did you get permission from Rabbi Yerucham?
Young Man:	Yes.
Rabbi:	(sighing). If so then why did you come to me?
Young Man:	I was told that the majority of the townspeople would not buy meat unless you also gave me your approval.
Rabbi:	If so, then why did you not bring me the diploma? Did you think that I would write my approval on your forehead?

The young man mumbled something, said his goodbyes and left empty-handed. This happened on Wednesday. He returned the following day at noon and without saying a word handed my teacher a note signed by the rabbi of a neighboring town, beneath which was the signature of Reb Yerucham. After a few minutes he said: "I thought that it would be enough if Reb Yerucham approved and that you would accept his approval."

My master took the paper, turned it from side to side, read it over several times, looked at it again and again, and finally handed the paper back to the young man saying in an unmistakable tone: "I absolutely forbid you to make kosher any meat which needs de-veining – and not only this – I also forbid you to rely on the permit of Reb Yerucham, not because he is suspect in his own kashrut , but because he has made a very sad mistake in this matter. Do you understand what I am saying? If it were up to me, I would not have given you back this certificate but I do not have the right to keep it. I suggest that you leave our town immediately. Go in peace."

The next day – it was early Friday morning – my father-in-law was still in his bed when there came a knock on the door. My mother-in-law opened it and the shamas (sexton) burst into the house in great excitement. "Rabbi", he addressed my father-in-law, "A great scandal is in town!. The de-veiner is working and several women have already bought the treife (not kosher) meat!"

From the day when I first met my father-in-law, I had never seen him as swift and agile as on that morning. Like a boy, he jumped from his bed, washed, dressed in whatever was handy, and hurriedly left the house with myself and the shamas following behind.

Actually running, he reached the butcher shop shaking with excitement, and in a commanding voice proclaimed: "You are feeding Jews treife! In the name of our Holy Torah and in the name of the Halachah (Jewish law), I forbid you to continue selling this meat because it is treife." He turned to the shamas and said to him: "Go and proclaim in the streets of the town that everyone who has bought de-veined meat here should throw it to the dogs because it is treife. And if they have a question about the state of kashrut of their utensils, they should address the rabbis." He added that he had requested Reb Yerucham to come to the Beit Midrash (prayer house) to clarify the matter.

In an instant the town became a whirlwind. Reb Yerucham's entourage met to discuss the problem. The story is that Reb Yerucham at first did not intend to come to the Beit Midrash. He was deeply insulted by the verdict of Rabbi Shimele but his advisors pressed him to go in order to prove his innocence.

Meanwhile, many Jews were gathering in the Beit Midrash. Such a thing had never happened in our town. The great Beit Midrash was too small to hold the crowd and people were even crowded into doorways and windows in expectation of seeing a public confrontation between the two Torah giants.

Rabbi Shimele ascended the bimah (pulpit) and addressed the public: "I ask the crowd to choose from amongst themselves persons expert in handwriting, who will examine the note which this fellow has brought to us."

Dudl Lifschin and Yechilikl Tselnik were chosen and ascended the bimah. The Rabbi handed them the paper and said: "Look well at the date when this paper was issued." They looked and after a while replied: "The date has been altered; a forgery has been committed."

It is difficult to describe the tumult which erupted in the Beit Midrash. Cries and screams rang out. Suddenly a voice was heard: "Hush, hush; Rabbi Shimele wishes to speak."

Instantly a complete quiet prevailed. The Rabbi took the certificate, held it up to the crowd and said: "My friends, according to the date on this permit, it was given nineteen months ago. But look at the crumpled yellowed paper and you will come to the realization that it was actually issued at least fifteen years ago and has since been altered and passed from hand to hand." The appearance of the paper was as compelling as a hundred witnesses in illustrating the justice of Rabbi Shimele's case. The crowd quieted down and began to disperse. That Sabbath, everyone in town was speaking about Rabbi Shimele who had prevented the Jews of Dubossar from eating treife. Then, Sunday at noon there arrived a telegram addressed to the Rabbi:

"Be it hereby known, that should anyone arrive in town with a certificate in hand permitting him to de-vein the hind parts of cattle to make them kosher, I hereby proclaim that the certificate was stolen, and that any meat such a fellow de-veins is treife." The signature on the telegram was that of the rabbi of the town where the certificate had been issued.

Quickly the news spread around town; the telegram was passed from hand to hand and for many days the townspeople spoke about the imposter and the Rabbi.

In Reb Yerucham's favor, it should be said that he admitted his mistake and apologized for having let the culprit mislead him, for Reb Yerucham was a trusting and G-d fearing soul.

[Page233]

The *Gabbai* [Sexton] of the Makarover rabbi

by Nachum Peck
Translated by Sarah Faerman

"Yossi, the Makaraver Rabbi's Gabbai" (trustee). That is how they called my Zaide (grandfather) who was the head Gabbai of the Makaraver Rabbi and also the Cantor of the Rabbi's little synagogue. He was from Makarov and his wife was from Dubossar.

He was a tall man, my Zaide, with a gaunt, pale face, a sparse, white beard and a pair of big, penetrating eyes. His side locks were curly and round like two bottles and would rhythmically sway when he prayed, studied or even walked.

Almost 20 hours a day he was occupied with God's work. His "work" day started just before dawn when it was still dark outside. He performed the ritual of hand washing upon rising and immediately started to study Gemara (holy book) with a sweet melody that would suffuse his whole being. His melody for learning was additionally engraved in my memory because I could barely fall asleep unless I heard it.

As a child I was easily frightened. At night I would become startled at every little rustle. However, when my Zaide would sit down to study Gemara after his supper, his sweet haunting melody would quickly lull me to sleep.

He would study for half the night. Then to mark midnight, he would recite Tehilim (psalms) and at dawn he would go to the mikva (ritual bath). From there he would proceed directly to the synagogue to pray. He would then return home, wash before eating, say the blessings and once again devote himself to study.

Throughout the whole week, I did not hear my Zaide utter ordinary , everyday language. With a few words of the holy language and with a bit of a wink, my Bobbe (grandmother) Nechama understood him. When did I hear my Zaide speak Yiddish? At the end of Sabbath, after the Havdala (end of Sabbath ceremony). Then there would be a gathering in our house of devout Jews – all Chasidim (religious movement), all sons of the Torah such as: Reb yerucham Dayan, Hershl Yosl Zelig's, Avreml the Cantor and so on. They would discuss and learn Chasidic issues. One of their favourite topics during these Saturday evening gatherings was Cantors and Cantorial music. Zaide would tell stories about Nissi Belzer, the famous cantor and composer of liturgical music who was also his close friend. Nissi Belzer was also a Makarov Chasid and My Zaide's only son, my Uncle Nachum Matenko, practically grew up with him before he himself became a famous Cantor. He was Cantor in the Moscow Polyakov Synagogue as well as performing in concerts all the way to the Czar's court.

At the end of the Sabbath, Saturday night, they would sit and talk until late at night. The Samover was always hot and Bobbe was busy serving tea with preserves that she had prepared herself from all kinds of fruit as well as her home baked cookies. My Bobbe was proud of her husband, the scholar and Chasid. She took care that he would lack for nothing and by virtue of his good deeds, she was sure that she would also have a share in the world to come and would be as his foot stool.

My Zaide did not concern himself about income. For that, he had confidence in the Almighty , blessed be He, and the Rabbi. Being as it is, however, neither the Almighty nor the Rabbi will make the effort without an emissary. Bobbe took it upon herself to fulfill this role. My Bobbe Nechama, was an Eyshes Chayil (woman of valor). She ran a wool dying enterprise which provided a good income. This made it possible for her to run a respectable household, to marry off her children and to have the ability to entertain generously on Sabbaths and holidays. I remember also her feasts of Mitzva that she would prepare for the elite of the town when my Zaide would complete one of the tractates of the Talmud, a quite frequent occurrence during his lifetime. Until this day we can remember the wonderful taste of her varenikes filled with potato and chicken or goose gribn (cracklings). And what about the thick, red Borscht beaten with yolks that were cooked in fat marrow bones! My Bobbe's borscht with varenikes were famous in Dubossar.

My Zaide and I did not exactly live in great harmony. At the age of eight , I would forget to say a blessing or forget to wash before a meal or rush through my prayers. My Zaide would roar: " A total goy!" That was his greatest insult. If Bobbe was nearby, she would say "Leave the poor orphan alone already." She would take me aside and with mild words of reproof, encourage me to be an honest Jew so that my mother in the other world would not be ashamed and suffer because of her one and only son.

My Zaide was not always displeased with me. Friday evenings, for example, at the table, when we Sang Sabbath melodies or at the three Sabbath meals, he would have much pleasure from me. I had a nice little voice and I knew my Zaide's entire repertoire by heart. When we would sing our melodies together, people would stand outside under our windows to listen. Then my Zaide would give my cheek a pinch. That was his greatest compliment and expression of love and acknowledgment. In those moments, my Bobbe would look with triumph at my Zaide as if to say: "Ha, what do you say now about Nochem'ke. He's definitely not a total goy!"

My Bobbe loved me more than all of the other grandchildren. She would say that of the three children that God took away from her, I was the only one close by. The oldest daughter, Malka, had one daughter who married and moved with her husband to Argentina. The son, Nachum Matenko, had been poisoned by enemies jealous of him and he had two boys who lived with their mother in Odessa. My mother, the youngest daughter, Tzirl, was very young when she departed this world while I was still a small child. My Bobbe took me to her home and was the one that raised me.

My Zaide lived a long life and never went to see a doctor. He didn't believe in doctors. First of all, he had faith in God and then in the Rabbi. When his time came at the age of eighty-six and when his suffering was great, my Bobbe did not ask him but sent for Dr. Krasnovyetz. When the doctor came in and asked him:"Reb Yossi, how are you feeling?" my Zaide answered: "They are summoning me there but I go without fear." With a motion of his hand he requested that my Bobbe come close to the bed and he asked her to summon three of his friends. He confessed his sins to them, turned over with his face to the wall where all of his books were and without even a sigh, released his pure soul. He died in the year 1904, my Zaide, of righteous and blessed memory.

My Bobbe Nechama, the saintly woman, was a true Jewish matriarch. She passed away at the beginning of the Jewish month of Av, 1914, a few days before the outbreak of World War I. May her memory be honored.

[Page236]

My Town Dubossar

by Anna Scheer (nee Teitelboim)

Translated by Florence Steinberg Schumacher and Jennie Steinberg Brown

Where is the street, where is the house?

No longer the street, no longer the house.

... Perhaps you can explain how they took two low rows of houses with roofs decorated with red brick and placed them, one row opposite the other, at the very edge of the shore? Who knows how many generations, perhaps even as far back as the six days of creation, these houses hugged the banks of the river with its sloping hill... and maybe even found their reflection in the puddles that spread out in such a princely fashion in the days of endless rain, when ice and snow began to melt. Who knows for how many generations these houses have witnessed the water-carrier struggling pitifully with all his strength up the hill bringing up clay barrels of water on his horse who likewise, strained helplessly, begging the water- carrier in its own way to pitch in and help. Otherwise, the wealthy houses would be like empty pockets – without water.

In one of these very houses with gardens in the back yard, one could discern between the branches of the trees, a church, as if to spite the Jewish poverty that had spread out its tents not far from the River Dniester where the gardens blossomed on the riverbanks of red clay. Here, in one of these very houses, I was born to a family who, generations before, started out in the nearby vicinity of Grigoriopol (Charna) that is part of the overall Dubossar geography.

I was born to Nachum Teitelboim who was called "Nachum The Baker" because every morning he would favor the Dubossar early morning tea and coffee drinkers with fresh egg bagels and onion rolls "just taken from the oven", slightly browned like the forehead of a gypsy and with the tantalizing scent of poppy seed and delicious baked goods.

Our family grew larger than the "Number Eight" in the Yiddish folksong and "Sleeping in Twos" was necessary as our little house was very small. When the oldest sister, Pesia, married and moved to the small town of Rokalesht on the other side of the River Dniester with her husband Yangel Bronzilberg, the tobacconist (he was in involved in tobacco plantations), and the house became roomier. Afterwards, my second sister Sheindl decided to go to an uncle in Argentina and when I also left for America to re-unite with my fiancée Hershl Shargaradsky (Yitzchak the Klezmer's son) – for sure the house became even roomier and spacious for my sisters and brother who remained. There were my sister Dvora , my brother Moishe Yitzchak Klezmer's daughter Toibe, Rivka and Arel (all unfortunately died in Hitler's hell with their families) Faigele who lives in Argentina; and mother, Chaya Sorah, who in contrast to father's red beard was dark skinned,- a Jewish beauty with black hair under her kerchief (which started to get gray when she was young because she had so much trouble selling the bagels and from being afraid of the evil eye befalling the house with children.)

This doesn't mean that we children did not know the taste of working hard, we kept pace with our tasks: pouring flour into the troughs, carrying wood for the stove, fetching water from the well and in the morning carrying the strings of bagels, baskets of onion rolls and seltzer water to our stall in the market as well as to the other "merchants", small stores and bars. To do all this work – lest the evil eye befall us – our mother's hands were not enough, so we children eased the burden by helping with respect and pride.

Our grandmother, Baila Rochel, was an asset to the family. She also did not sit with idle hands. The whole market knew her because she used to help our mother. Besides that, her Shabbes and holiday food were famous; her gefilte fish and her horseradish – so strong that when the Messiah comes, it will help to wake up the dead. At the time of the Kishinev pogrom, she just happened to be visiting her son, Itzl (who later joined the Baron Hirsch Colony in Argentina). The hooligans broke her foot and so she limped until her death at an advanced age. She died in Arihev while with her son Yosef Velvl, the bath keeper, and her daughter-in-law, Rochele, the beauty. She had prepared their Purim party with her traditional delicious food. Then she lay down and after three to four days of sleeping, ended her account with life. Her father, our great grandfather, Yisreol-Leib, a distinguished scholar, died in Bogadelnia, in the Jewish hospital at the age of 115 years.

In this way, the little houses did not have anything to be ashamed of with their inhabitants, our neighbors: Zaydl the carpenter, his wife Miriam and their four children who lived right near the market; on the other side, Chaim – Moishe-Hersh the tailor and his wife Alte and their six children; on our side, Elia-Laybeche with four children and across the street was a school where I also went to learn a little Yiddish and Russian. The school had a name, which if you didn't pronounce it quickly, your tongue would stumble over it, neither here nor there. The school was called: "Tchitchilnitzkyes Otshilishte".

I have mentioned only a few of our neighbors but there were many. A gang of us children would descend like locusts and invade the weddings in Benyomin Rashkovan's hall near the police station. We called him "Benyomin the Blind" because one eye was useless. There was another hall called Hershl Chaykl's hall toward the old market down by the Jewish hospital across the street from our beloved rabbi, Rabbi Abel. We, however, were satisfied with "our hall" – Benyomin the Blind's hall – because first of all the other hall was quite far and second, we would have to fight with the children from the other neighborhood...and not always were we ready for war.

You couldn't make a living in Dubossaar alone for so many mouths to feed, as my father used to say. Indeed he would hitch up the horse and wagon several times a week and travel to nearby villages to sell bagels to the tenant farmers. My aunt Ennis, father's sister, tells the following story about one such trip. Her son – Moishe Bik (a composer who lives in Israel) in his childhood, would come during his summer vacations to our: crowded but comfortable house:

> Coming with Uncle Nathan to a village, I usually helped him carry the bagels into the tenants' guest rooms. The wagon with the rest of the bagels was left outside and the horse leisurely caught its breath and chewed from his pouch as if he was praying from a sidur with near sighted eyes... Suddenly, uncle saw a village boy stealthily swipe a string of bagels from the wagon. Swiftly, uncle chased after the boy and a fight broke out. From the screams of the defeated village boy, tens of goyim (gentiles) ran up and uncle suddenly had to show his courage against the whole village. Quickly with his tall frame and broad shoulders, he ran to a nearby fence and tore out a board, swinging it like a sword from left to right and driving away the goyim who were crossing their hearts in fear: "A demon has appeared in our village! A demon!" My uncle put me deep into the wagon and victoriously cracked his whip so that the horse would go quickly from this village to another tenant lodging in another village.

My father's legacy, "A Chad Gadya Nigun" (Passover melody) was recorded by the Israeli composer, Yehoicham Stotchevsky, in his folklore notebooks and was also published.

It is over fifty years since I left Dubossar and although my memories do not contain the aura of a carefree childhood or a worry-free youth, I carry in my heart a longing for those years, for that very hard working community and the warm-hearted, decent, homey, positive, confident Jews where I grew up in this world to carry out and nurture the continuity of a new beginning, a new fate...

[Page239]

Laybe's Cross

by Chaim Greenberg

Translated by Sarah Faerman

… It happened that I had to travel from Argayev to Dubossar with a Moldavian coachman. After a few hours into our journey, I asked him if we were far from our destination. "It is exactly half way", he answered. "We are now very close to Laybe's Cross." Laybe's Cross? Laybe's Crucifix? I expressed my bewilderment.

I saw before me, by the light of the moon, a well – a typical Bessarabian well – with a wooden sculpture of Jesus on a ladder and with a wooden cross at the very top of the ladder. A very common sight and a typical part of the scenery. But then, how does a Jew happen to have this named after him? The coachman related an ancient story.

Not far from here – he gestured at the village on the right side – there lived two neighbors – a Jew and a Moldavian. The Moldavian man was accused of a murder he did not commit. His Jewish neighbor, Reb Layb, took all the money he had and traveled all the way to Petersburg to hire lawyers to defend and exonerate his Moldavian friend. Eventually, the Moldavian was set free from prison but soon after, the Jew died. The Moldavian then dug out a well by the side of the road (a traditional gravestone in that district) and erected everything that accompanied a well - a carved figure of "The Saviour", a ladder and a crucifix – in order to memorialize Reb Layb's name. This happened, he said, long, long ago when the present landowner's grandfather was still alive. From then on, all of the peasants in the vicinity refer to this place as "Laybe's Cross."

The coachman was engrossed in his thoughts for a few minutes and then he said:

"Now we live like wolves. Before we lived like human beings." He took the reins in one hand and with the other hand he first made the sign of the cross over himself and then over me. He quickly became frightened at his own impertinence – making a cross over a Jew! However, he soon arrived at a solution and begged me to make the cross over him in "Jewish". I didn't know what he meant but he reminded me of the "Jewish Cross" that hangs over the door at the entrance to the Synagogue. I felt that I could not refuse him and (I'm ashamed to admit it) I made the sign of the Magen David over him.

From "Bessarabish", published in the book "Pages From A Diary"

[Pages243-251]

"May His Great Name be Magnified and Sanctified..."

by Moshe ben Yaakov Feldman, of blessed memory

Translated from the Yiddish by Harvey Spitzer

[Unrhymed translation]

On that sad day of weeping and
moaning,
Of terror which took place,
The hill was as red as burning ashes.
With a blood-soaked chain
The wicked one kept up his endless
slaughter.
And, as if out of shame,
The sun hid in her butter-barrel
corner.
The blue sky grew dimmer and then
became dark
From the bloody vapor drawn up
onto the red clouds.
The curses of the dead
Overtook the storm.
Trees, ears of corn and flowers
Were overthrown, broken and bent.
Everything, everything around
moaned.

Brother! You order me to write to you
What happened to us.
What happened to the Jews in
Dubossar?
Who can describe the terrible grief?
Who can paint the pictures of horror,
Of ruin and martyrs
Numbering in the thousands?
They frighten me and drive me out
of my mind.

They make me drunk
And my head is of no more use to me.
It is empty and bare.
My brain is confused.
I'm weak and have no more strength.
I'm swollen from weeping
And my eyes are feeble.
The sources of tears have dried up.
I'm bent over; I've aged prematurely
And can no longer hear.

Do you remember the lovely hill
Where the young people leisurely
spent their time?
They dreamed and meditated
In the magic of the moonlit nights.
The mountain... and now
It's drenched in blood.
Neither would you recognize
Our lovely town
Dubossar and its streets.
The Nazis tortured and shot them...
The houses are demolished,
Burned and scorched.
Nothing has remained of them.
Jews from near and far
Were driven and herded together
And were led to the slaughter
Like slaves in chains.
A hundred in each group,
Jewish men and women
Caught hiding in holes.
They were tied by their necks to
horses.
They were chased and dragged
Over streets and stones.
Blood flowed from their wounds.
They went out of their minds. From
the *Lunke* to the *Maholes*
From Synagogue Street to the *Fantoles*
From the length and breadth of the
town
They fenced us in with a chain.
They drove groups of Jews together,
Men, women and children
Like sheep and cattle.

They chased and drove them
Through the old and new market
places
Upwards, upwards to the hill.
Ukrainians, Romanians and Germans,
Riding on horses.
And with clubs and whips
They beat and flogged their bodies.
Jews in great numbers
Fell along the way.
Suddenly, the beatings and driving
on stopped.
A shout was heard:
"Remain standing! ...
And get into rows!"
They counted everyone.
They gave everyone a shovel
To dig a grave.
With just their own hands.
Every limb was paralyzed.
We remained glued to the place.
The marrow in our bones solidified.
Every word was silenced.
Not a rustle was heard.

Suddenly, one person
Just one and no more –
Hershel Fostolov
Like a hero
Risked his life courageously –
He wants to recite the final *El Maleh
Rachamim* ("O Merciful God...") for
every Jew.
And at the end, let them shoot him
And let his blood be first to flow.
By the Nazis, the murderers,
By the head of the bandits
Hershel's courageous words
Were heard sarcastically
And recited ironically.
Thus his request was granted...
Zvi Simcha ben Yerachmiel
Ben Simcha Fostolov
As though suspended in the
heavens,
Intoned the *El Maleh Rachamim*

In a moving and holy way.
Word by word
The confession was repeated
And the end came right on that spot.
Hershel Fostolov
Gave up his soul with perfect faith.

The "master" race rejoiced gleefully.
With planning and order
The Nazi chief gave another command:
His demon-soldiers are waiting to
kill all those standing there in
desperation –
The Jewish community
Which they drove to the Sacrifice.
Machine guns thunder and crash
With lead bullets and fire,
Flashing and piercing the bodies
Of everyone who was dear to us.
With sadistic pleasure,
The bandits threw themselves on
the Jews
Torquemada Jesuits
Anti-Semitic cliques
With bayonets and axes
And finished off those dying in agony.
They murdered them,
Silenced them forever...
For days Jewish blood poured forth,
Streamed and did not rest.
It flowed into the brother graves;
It foamed and was saturated
Even after the long, wide pit was
covered over.
Their eternal, eternal home...

Eighteen thousand five hundred
slain, martyrs
Together, not separated
In peace
Without a wall, not fenced off.
And in the town, among the ruins,
The little of life that remained
Is a shadow, skin and bone;
Naked, barefoot, driven in hunger,
Searching for something to sustain

them, a morsel of bread.
They wait in despair,
Looking around and hoping
That their countrymen in America
will not delay
In sending them help, clothes, bread
To alleviate their grief and need.

Brother, I have no more strength.
I've already written about everything
That happened to us,
The misfortune that befell us,
All the Jews in Dubossar.
Near Bessarabia, on the Dniester.
Will you understand, feel the grief
Of your misfortunate sister?
Now you know, it's no longer a
surprise.
You must remember, not forget
Yorzeit, Yizkor, saying *Kaddish,*
Awaken the world and its conscience.

[Page248]

Under Soviet Rule, and the Holocaust
I shall forever remember
by D. L. Granovsky
Translated by Eti Horovitz

These we shall remember:

... The fertile land in the devastated countries fertilized with the blood and marrow of the folk who believe in one God. The chain of torture, suffering, the blood and tears of the chosen people, the nation of prophets.

The vast fields strewn with graves of fathers, mothers, sisters and brothers, thirsty for life and wishing for redemption.

The ashes. Ashes created by the incineration of one third of a nation; Living ashes of six million holy Children of Israel who once lived and existed among wild beasts; who were educated upon holy commandments, on values, and followed them carefully and correctly.

Among the waves of these ashes, I will dig, look for the shred of an organ or a remnant of a bone. With thirst, I shall mend and mend with my tears. The thousands of dear ones who were buried alive while the defiled soil trembled above them for days and days without rest; our chopped down Cedars, abounding with the freshness and vitality of youth; our tender flowers at the end of their childhood and their wondering eyes.

The best of our sons who died deaths of heroes whilst on their lips the song of life, creation and redemption. What other nation has suffered so?

And heaven was not shaken, and the revenge is yet to come, and their world has not been darkened, and their arm has not been cut off, and their pride has not been shattered, and their home has not been destroyed like our home, and their children were not torn to shreds like our infants, and they didn't lose their minds, and they are not crying for their families like us – a nation of survivors.

And what if we shall shout?

Along the altars we have built in our long path, we will be silent! And we will stand alone with the memory of our fallen in the forest of the Martyrs and we will become one in the passion of our pain and grief, and our tears will join with the tears of generations. A forest of Martyrs on the way to the eternal Jerusalem. A monument we have built for the memory of the Holy Ones of Dubossar and surrounding areas. Its trees will blossom and grow, and will become a thick forest in which the souls of our precious ones will be tied to them and they will be like the continuation of their lives. Their names and memories will exist and be illuminated forever. And when we will come to this sacred place – we will pour out our bitter words and we will pray that their souls will join with the souls of the holy ones of our people.

Yisgadal v'yiskadash shemaei raba (prayer for the departed)

(These words were taken from a speech given at the Martyrs' Forest in memory of the martyrs of Dubossar and surrounding vicinity.)

[Page250]

**Mordecai Volman, Lieutenant-Colonel in the Red Army.
Died after the war.**

Under The Soviet Regime And During The Holocaust

by Arkady Timor

Translated by Eti Horovitz

The October Revolution and the following years fundamentally changed the lives of everyone in Russia, in Dubossar and especially the lives of the Jews in it. The nationalization of private property and the means of manufacturing created problems in work arrangements and work relationships.

The Jews were not able to solve these problems themselves but had to co-ordinate with the general policies initiated by the Soviet Union. Even though these policies were extreme, the Jews of Dubossar carried them out in the best way under the circumstances. In this case, I do not refer to the agricultural sector, which I will discuss later. The primary units of industries and manufacture in Dubossar were "Artels" – co-operatives of professionals. Even though the local authorities supervised them, there was also some "freedom of creation". In Dubossar there were the following Artels:

The Craftsmen Artel whose members were tailors, hatters, leather industrialists, furriers and seamstresses who were called underwear-makers. This Artel was organized by Idel Tzveighaft, Itzik Barenboim and Isaac Schrier (the three of them were murdered by the Germans).

252 Jewish school before World War II

The Artel of the needle workers (cutters of the upper part of shoes), the shoemakers and the piercers. Its organizers were Abraham Livnet (died 1961) and Idel Plum (died in the Siberia deportation because of Zionist activity). Most of the production of this Artel was aimed at the foreign market.

The Artel of the barrel makers, blacksmiths, carpenters, locksmiths, tinsmiths and other professionals of this field. Even in 1936 this Artel was the foundation of machine repairing factories, a workshop of carpentry products and a factory of military vehicles. The other departments served only Dubossar and its surrounding areas. This Artel and the factories that followed it were organized by the Lindenboim brothers (murdered by the Germans) and the Zemel brothers (the older one murdered by the Germans) and by Yitzchak Belfer (killed in the front against the Germans).

The General Service Artel, whose members were the barbers, the watchmakers, the painters, the washers, etc. Its organizers were Idel Ladzinsky (died 1958) and Samuel Tzolsky Vaktzker (died 1941).

The chain of commerce was in the hands of the government. The government also held the tobacco factory, the dairy, two factories for fruit preparation, two wineries, brick factories, the flour mill, the butter factory and other factories that were not only managed by Jews but most of the employees were Jewish as well.

The construction workers (more than 60% were Jews) and the miners (in the "Big Fountain" district) were organized in one organization close to the town's council.

I can safely say that from 1922 to 1941, the industry of Dubossar took a big step forward. The extensive electricity mains and water pipes system significantly changed the appearance of the town. Until the Second World War about 2,000 Jews worked in the factories in Dubossar, with approximately 1,800 of them laborers.

The situation in the agricultural field was different, in fact, it was a total failure. At first, there were attempts to forcibly create agricultural communes. Moshe Weiner arranged the first commune in Okna. Twenty-six families from Dubossar were sent there. The second commune was arranged in Yagorlik. Those two communes failed during their first year and their residents went back to Dubossar worn out, thin and starving. Some of them were deported to Siberia due to "Failure in Agricultural Operations." One of the victims of these communes was Chaim Kiner, who died in Siberia. From 1930-1931, the first sample Kolkhozes were established in Dubossar, Lung, Cochiery and other places. These settlements specialized in growing tobacco, grapes, fruit and vegetables. Jews took part in each of these fields. Until the beginning of the war, there were about 200 Jewish families from Dubossar indirectly associated with agricultural labour in the kolkhozes and sobkhozes. Among them were the following families: Greenberg, Imas, Barenboim, Shulkleper, Feitel, Wolf and others who lost their lives in the ghetto of Dubossar.

This review does not intend to analyze the outcomes of the kolkhozes and sobkhozes, but factually, I must mention that despite the great efforts of their members, they never could accomplish the level of agriculture production of 1914. In 1930 and 1935 there was great hunger in Dubossar. There was no bread, no meat and no vegetables. Thousands of hungry people could only dream about mamaliga (a popular dish made of corn). People walked around swollen with hunger and many starved to death. In our town, 100 people died of hunger. Keep in mind that those were times of peace.

During the years 1922-1941, the Jews of Dubossar were known for their passion for education, especially the children and youngsters. In addition to a Russian school, a Ukrainian school and a Moldavian school, there were four Jewish schools in Dubossar where the studies were conducted in Yiddish. The level of education in the Jewish schools was high and most of the graduates continued their studies in technical high schools and in higher educational institutes. It is interesting that even though there were enough open spaces in the Russian, Ukrainian and Moldavian schools, many non-Jewish children studied in the Jewish schools because of their high level. Of those, 11 of the graduates of the Jewish schools in Dubossar were 6 Russians, 3 Moldavians and 2 Ukrainians who then graduated successfully in their studies at the Jewish Technical University in Odessa (on 71 Kantana Street). Three of them became engineers.

Up until the outbreak of the war, 1,610 Jewish children graduated from the Jewish schools in Dubossar. 912 of them continued their studies and graduated from professional high schools and higher educational institutions in Odessa, Kiev, Krakov, Moscow, Leningrad and other cities. 38 students of the Jewish schools graduated from military academies and achieved the rank of officer. There were 23 doctors, 41 teachers, 54 engineers, 18 agronomists, 4 archeologists, 361 technicians of all kinds and many other professional experts that contributed to the Soviet society.

The most mentionable Dubossarers are my colleagues: the excellent scientist – the scholar Pavlov, the professor Yosifovich Bernboim, the famous mathematician Boris Leibovich Shternberg, one of the engineers who built the Moscow Metro (subway), -David Abramovich Zemel (died close to Moscow in 1941), the steam turbine expert - Abraham Yosifovich Shulkleper, the ship engineer – Jacob Davidovich Goryevsky, the surgical doctor – Dora Yefimovna Saditsky and more. Private schools for religious education existed in Dubossar until 1929. From 1930, religious education was officially forbidden.

At that time, they also started to close down synagogues and turned them into warehouses (the Main Synagogue, the Attendants Synagogue, the Synagogue on the Gypsies' street) or into workshops (the Craftsmen Synagogue and the Old Synagogue).

In the synagogue that was next to the new market, a club was built. After closing the synagogues, the Jews gathered for prayers in private houses. Until 1941, there was a shochet (ritual slaughterer) and most of the Jews consumed kosher meat. Although the education seemed Jewish (it was taught in Yiddish) and continued until 1941, it no longer reflected any Jewish national value. Even in the twenties any Jewish "deviation" was persecuted and during the thirties all Jewish content had disappeared. Still, no draconian rules could silence the Jewish hearts. The Jews celebrated the Jewish holidays, kept the Mitzva of circumcision and other Jewish rituals. The national Jewish identity had left its mark upon the lives of the Jews in Dubossar after all.

A rich collection of Yiddish books was found in the public library, which was managed by the comrade G. Grodzinsky (who was hung by the Nazis for Partisan activities). Literary gatherings were held in that library, with participation of various Jewish writers. In Dubossar, there was extensive artistic activity that appealed also the non-Jewish public. The best Russian theatres – from Moscow, Kiev and Odessa – played in Dubossar. The writers – David Bergelson, Peretz Markish, Otkin, Leib Kwitko and others were frequent visitors to Dubossar. In one of the meetings with the Jewish youth of Dubossar where we participated as students who came especially from Odessa, the great actor, Shlomo Mikhoels said: "You, the people of Dubossar, are strong and we are proud of you." I will never forget those words of our great actor who was murdered by Stalin's people.

An important part in nurturing the Jewish consciousness of the Dubossar Jews was the model Jewish hospital and the good maintenance of the old and new cemeteries. Dr. Kalman, who died in the Dubossar Ghetto, managed the Jewish hospital for many years. It served also the non-Jews of the area and gained the status of one of the high authority medical institutes of the area. While speaking on the subject of medical assistance, I must mention the paramedic Frucofance, the devoted and loyal Israel sympathizer, who assisted Jewish families for many years. Day or night, rain and storm, he was always there to help the sick and suffering. When he died in 1938, thousands of Jews, young and old, accompanied him in his funeral. Everybody felt obligated to pay their last respects to this kind and noble man – Frucofanco.

I will allow myself to mention also the dentist, David Yefumovich Weintroib – a warm-hearted Jew who took upon himself the task of guarding the Jewish spark in our town. Jewish ceremonial weddings were held in Dubossar all those years. I remember how the Moldavian violinist, Diorda, played with his musicians "The Seating of the Bride" dance and how they accompanied the departing guests until dawn with hearty Jewish tunes filled with joy and melancholy. Diorda died in 1948. This talented Gypsy musician was known as a faithful friend to the Jews during the dark days of the German occupation. Heroically, while risking his own life, he helped the Jews. Up to these days, I can hear his Yiddish speech, fine speech, spiced with Jewish humour with traces of melancholy.

Besides hunger, the Dubossar Jews suffered other calamities before the outbreak of the war. Twice, in 1937 and 1941, many know public activists and Zionists were detained as part of massive arrests. In 1937, the following captured and then shot: The Malkis family, Idel Plum, Veloil Zemel, Jacob Tolmatsky, Berl Steinberg, the brothers Chaim and Aaron Belfer, The Goryevsky family, Chaim Dunievsky and others. All together 48 people were arrested and only two remained alive.

In 1940, right after the annexation of Bessarabia to the Moldavian Republic, more than 60 people were arrested. No official charges were filed and no public trials were held. Among the victims of these arrests were Velvl Katzker and his son Gregory, Yankel Gurevich, the Lipshein brothers, Moshe Kishiniovsky, Lea Shragorodskaya, Aaron Trachenberg and others.

A great loss to the Jews of Dubossar was the killing of two of its famous sons – General David Urman and his brother, Colonel Abraham Urman. The brothers Motel, David and Abraham Urman were raised as orphans. During the First World War, while serving in the Czarist Army, David Urman performed as a highly brave, gifted military man. He won three Geiorgy Awards. Right after the Revolution, he received his officer rank following his graduation from the Military Academy of high-ranking Headquarters. He achieved one of the highest possible ranks. He was appointed Deputy Commander of the Soviet armies in the Far East, second in command to Marshal Blucher. His younger brother, Abraham managed, as a military engineer, the fortification works at the Russian-Chinese border. In 1937, David Urman was unjustly accused of spying. He was captured and shot to death. His brother, Abraham, could not consent to his arrest and when they came for him, he shot himself in the chest. David's widow and son are living now in one of the Russian towns.

Special trading centers named 'Turgasin' were established in Russia during the thirties. These trade centers held the best quality of merchandise that was sold in exchange for dollars or gold. The Soviet Union needed dollars and gold at that time. Trade centers of this kind were also opened in Odessa and Tiraspol. Many Jews of Dubossar, who received dollars from their relatives in the USA, Canada and other countries, enjoyed the services of these official and state trade centers.

In 1938, for approximately six months, Russia conducted punishment campaigns called 'Gold Fever', where innocent buyers as well as people who did not buy anything were arrested and were held until they were bailed out with dollars (whether or not they had any). Only with dollars would the authorities pardon the 'sins' of those who did not have dollars and who had to sell their last belongings to buy the dollars that would free their dear ones.

And the Dniester kept on flowing; the river didn't hear and didn't see; the vineyards spread out to the horizon along with the green apple and walnut trees. Lives were full of fear and danger, sometimes unbearable. The people, our people, the Jews of Dubossar, lived their lives bravely, unable to know the horrible destiny they would face.

In the beginning of 1941, among the 20,000 residents of Dubossar, about 8,000 were Jews. The majority of the employed Dubossar Jews were occupied in local industry` and some of them in the Kolkhozes, Sobkhozes and in the Tractor Stations. 80% of the local educated professionals (doctors, teachers, accountants, etc.) were Jews. There were over 4,000 Jewish children and teenagers below the age of 18, and 1,500 over 60 years. In Dubossar, there were people who also lived to be over 100 years old. Among them were: Chaike Kishinevska who was 105 years old, Velvil Belfer who was 102 years old, and Chaim Kalinovsky who was 102 years old. All of them were killed in the Ghetto that the Nazis built in Dubossar.

On June 22 1941, Germany started the war against the Soviet Union. Dubossar was air bombed on the first day of the war, and our first war victims died that day. The Jews of our town were realistic enough to anticipate what would happen despite the fact that the Jews, like the rest of the USSR citizens, did not know the truth about the horrible actions of the Nazis since the Molotov-Riventrup agreement on 1939. Even though for many years the Dubossar Jews had good work relations with the German citizens of nearby regions, most of them decided to leave behind their homes and everything they had achieved over many years and move east.

The members of the special committee that handled the evacuation were: Isaac Orbuch, Baruch Bendarsky, Lea Barzovskya, Mordechai Mechinovsky, Ida Schuster and Shlomo Yusim. The major problem in organizing the evacuation was transportation. The local authorities and the head military commandment recruited almost every means of transportation for the clearing of the archives, the industrial equipment and the gasoline stocks (Benzene and Diesel oil). For the migration of the Jewish residents they appointed two old cars, one tractor with a cart and six carts with horses. These vehicles were not enough even for transferring the sick. So the thousands of Jews from Dubossar, our fathers and mothers, our sisters and brothers, women carrying their babies, went ahead marching east.

During the first days of the war, the military drafted more than 1,300 boys and girls from the Dubossar Community. The Germans aimed their attacks north of Dubossar using the following forces: the third Armenian corps of the fourth camp, the fifth Armenian corps and the 26th Romanian corps. The northern division moved ahead towards Leveznensk, and the southern division turned towards Odessa. Heavy forces of tanks and aircraft supported the attack. The Russian forces that acted heroically, tried every possible defense, but had to retreat. While crossing the Dniester in several places, the Germans proceeded east and southeast. At the end of July 1941, they reached the southern Bog border and severed all the roads leading east.

Thousands of Jews from Dubossar and the surrounding areas, exhausted from the long walk and the persistent hunger, were chased back west to the

Dubossar Ghetto. Even while they were walking back, on their way towards their total destruction, the German Commandant already started applying the monstrous plan of exterminating the Jews, with the active assistance of the majority of Ukrainians and the local Germans. The Selection was performed during this walk. They separated children from their parents, the sick from the healthy, and the elderly from the young. Those who could not walk were immediately shot.

Quarantine camps were built at the entrance of Dubossar, beyond the roads leading to Balta and Tiraspol. Pregnant women and old people were forced to dig their own graves and were immediately shot at the site. By the middle of August, 400 people were murdered that way. Esther Imol was murdered during the last month of her pregnancy, and into the pit that was her grave, they threw alive her 3 year old son and her old mother. The Moldavian, Sekortol from the village Longi, who was one of the eye witnesses to the murders of the Jews, told me that they forced a group of old people to tighten with their feet the fresh grave of the murdered Jews. The elderly lay at the edge of the grave and did not move. The Germans ran over their bodies with tractors. They brought another group of people, and again, over the bodies of the old Jews, went a heavy tractor.

Thus, the brave Jewish Community of Dubossar was sentenced to brutal death. At the end of August 1941, the Dubossar Ghetto was built and over 600 of the Jews from our town were imprisoned in it and the road for their salvation was blocked and sealed. The ghetto in Dubossar was concentrated in the heart of the town, in the streets leading to the Dniester and the area called 'The Gypsy Triangle'. Each zone of the ghetto was divided into three camps and they were all fenced with electrical wire. The guards were Ukrainian police officers from the region and different divisions of the S.S. Two of the camps were intended for those Jews who were able to perform physical work, and the third one was for those who were destined to be killed first.

The people in the Ghetto were deprived of everything. They were deprived of the elementary living conditions. There were hardly any food and water and there was no medical aid at all. Upon organizing the Ghetto, the Germans decided to establish a Jewish self-administration and to hand over the internal guarding to Jewish Kapos. We can say, to the credit of the Dubossar Jews, that the Germans were not able to tempt any of them to co-operate. No traitors were found among them. Furthermore, no one bowed his head to the German murderers!

We shall honor and glorify you, our brothers, the brave people of Dubossar.

Due to the lack of cooperation with the Germans, they hung, in the public park, Yankil Leibovich, Doctor Fine, Ruben Levin and the Isaac Brothers, Idel and Moshe Bernboim. I will mention one more thing: From the first day of the occupation, the famous group of Partisans started to operate. Its leader was the Dubossarer Yankil Guzinsky. Their attacks were very painful for the Germans. Among other actions carried out by this group, I will mention:

bombing of the Dniester bridge, bombing the local power station, and other locations. The members of this underground group also organized the transporting of food and medical supplies into the ghetto.

One night, not so far from the "Valley of Death", where those brave ones who would not cooperate were killed, they hung the council's chairman, Metbienko.

The suppression in the Ghetto got worse every day. The local police were placed in the house of the Malkises, where the well-known sadist, Demanchuk, worked. (After the war, he was sentenced to 15 years in prison, and now he is walking around, free, in Moldavia). Once, after one of his frequent intoxications, he took three Jewish girls to one of the rooms on the second floor – 16 year old Raia Tzelnik, 15 year old Mania Rabinovich and 18 year old Velia Reisman. He tore their dresses from their bodies, tossed them through the window and shot them as they were falling down.

Human beings, Remember this forever!

Shlomo Tumashin had beehives. The Germans locked him in a room and put in several swarms of bees. Without any food or water, stung by the bees, he died with dreadful torments a few days later.

At the beginning of 1941, the Germans seized about 600 Jewish elderly, brought them to the former synagogue, blocked the doors and windows, and burned them alive with everything that was inside. An eyewitness of this horrible death, the violinist Diorda, told me many years later: "I only heard sounds of praying and the noise of the breaking fire. Then, the ceiling collapsed. I could not bear it anymore and I ran as fast as I could."

Doctor Worobiov's wife, who passed near the Craftsman's synagogue at the time, saw how the officers tried several times to light the building and the fire went out a few times. Finally, they poured gasoline on top of the entire building, and the flames flared up completely. She also heard the praying voices rising from the burning building.

On the following nights, Jacob Guzinsky and one of his men killed the German chief and the anti-Semitic woman Sonia Kogotanco, who was one those who co-operated with the Nazis. A second group, commanded by Aaron Dorfman, blew up a big military equipment warehouse located close to the old Jewish cemetery. After these acts of retaliation and some others, the Germans began to grasp the nature of the Dubossar Jews. Often I wondered about General Kobpek's Partisans, who were located nearby. I could not understand why they did not try to save the Jews from the Ghetto. They did not help them at all.

At the beginning of September 1941, the Germans finished all their preparations for the mass destruction of the Ghetto in Dubossar. They chose a field outside of town, on the way leading from the Russian-Parboslavian cemetery to the 'Great Fountain' as the place of murder. In normal times, this was a favorite traveling road for the Jews. The shooting lasted day and night. They dug holes of 50 meters length and 4 to 5 meters width. They intended each hole for 1,500 people. People were brought to the holes and shot at the edges. Killed and wounded, dead people and living people were buried together in one enormous mass grave. One man, living today in the town of Tiraspol, Cheven, told me "They shot day and night, non-stop. According to the shooting, one could think there was a great battle going on over there".

On September 10, the 'Women's Rebellion' broke out. Jewish women, mothers and wives, demanded to be taken to die with their families. They dropped themselves down on the ground and refused to get up. The Germans shot the children – and the women didn't get up. The Germans gave up. They starting taking complete families to be killed together. At the end of September 1941, the day after Yom Kippur, the extermination of the Dubossar Jews was completed. Only one woman, Hanna Paskar, survived miraculously. She went mad and died near the time of the liberation of the city by the Red Army.

According to the Government Committee investigating the horrific actions of the Germans, the numbers of people buried in the first four graves (there were totally 12), is estimated to be 6,000. So there are 6,000 Dubossar Jews buried there. The committee also confirmed that the Germans abused the bodies of the murdered after they died. They pulled out gold teeth, took away their clothes and more.

Until the end of 1943, the Germans brought many Jews to the ghetto in Dubossar and there killed them. From Odessa and Kishinev, from Tiraspol, from Balta and Ribnitze, and even from Czechoslovakia, they brought Jews to Dubossar to be murdered. That way, Dubossar become a huge cemetery for 18,500 Jews.

As was mentioned before, over 1,300 young Jewish boys and girls from Dubossar joined the military. In addition, over 600 of the Jewish students from our town, who studied in Odessa, in Kiev and in other towns, and many of those who managed to escape from Dubossar also joined the armed forces. By the outbreak of the war, over 2,000 of the Dubossar Jews, about 25%, were part of the military. Approximately 900 of them lost their lives in battle. I must mention, that every one of the Jewish Dubossar soldiers, up until the very last of them, received honor awards or medals for their bravery.

More than 200 of them were officers. Elia (Eliahu) Leibovich Pesis was a Major General in the artillery corps; David Grigorovich Glozberg was a Colonel. He lost his life while commanding a tank brigade attacking Posnan; Lieutenant Colonel Gregory Leibovich Litmanovich who served in the Air Force, downed 11 German aircraft during battles. In one of the battles, his plane was shot down and he was critically injured. After a long struggle for his life that lasted more than a year, he died at the end of the war and was buried in Moscow. The commander of the Partisan group, Jacob Guzinsky, died with the people in the Ghetto in the arms of his family after being mortally wounded.

Heroism is probably innate in the Urman Family. At the beginning of the war, 50 years old Motel Urman joined the frontier. His daughter, Riva, also volunteered and served as a Medical Corps instructor in the Tank Squad. She saved many wounded and was injured herself three times; Motel Urman's son – Vladimir – was the commander of a transportable Artillery Battalion. Several days before the end of the war, he died in the battle at Berlin. They granted him six awards and medals. The brothers Liova and Yitzhak Livnet were exceptionally courageous. Liova was an electrician in a submarine in the Baltic Navy. On one of the voyages to the coast of Germany, the submarine was sunk and Liova died. Yitzhak Livnet, Captain in the Soviet Army, was a commander of a brigade and was killed on October 1942 in Stalingrad.

Monia Bondiriov, a Major in the Soviet Army, was a commander of a Bomber Squad at the front in Leningrad. He performed over 100 flights. On January 1943, during the battle to break the siege of Leningrad, his plane was downed and he was killed.

Misha Shkolnik, an Officer of the Soviet Army, was wounded during one of the battles in the Minsk District on June 1944. It was the fourth time he was injured. However, Misha did not leave the battlefield until the enemy retreated. I saw Misha Shkolnik after the war. He was unrecognizable. His face was mutilated and changed completely. Only Mishka's good and brave eyes remained. And so was his spirit. Well Done, Misha!

Lieutenant Colonel Jacob Rashkovan, the commander of a brigade, had maintained a high level of performance in the military. He was granted many awards and medals. I would like to dwell on the role of the Dubossar Jews in the defense of Odessa. The special Soviet Coast Guard had retreated down the Dniester towards Odessa due to extensive pressure by the fourth Romanian Corps. On August 19, Odessa was surrounded. It was very difficult to protect the city, because the supply of ammunition and food could only arrive through the Black Sea and then, only in limited quantities. During that time, there were 182 Jewish students from Dubossar in Odessa, and all of them willingly joined the forces. The battle for Odessa lasted 68 days. 54 of the Dubossarian students lost their lives defending the city. Yefim Dunayevsky, a 3rd year student in the Odessa University, was the commander of one of the major defense units in Fersip Area. In one of the battles, he was mortally wounded and died within an hour.

On December 1944, when I was at the front, I received a letter from one of the Dubossar girls, Lena Tulmatsky (I have kept the letter until these very days). Below are some paragraphs of her letter:

> "Very few of us remain. 99% were shot and buried alive. Our friends are no longer with us; our dearest ones are gone. Avenge us Arkady! Revenge for all the torments we are going though! On January 29 1942, my husband was killed during the battles of Krakow, and I became a widow at the age of 22. Do not spare the enemy! This is not only I who ask. I am asking on behalf of all the widows, all the orphans, on behalf of the thousands of our tortured. Revenge!"

Later in this letter, Lena referred to our warrior friends:

> "Dear friends! Avenge the death of Arkady's wonderful mother,
> avenge the death of his little brother, his two younger sisters.
> Vengeance for me too. You see, I also desire happiness. Vengeance
> for thousands of women like me." Well, the Jewish soldiers from
> Dubossar did take revenge, courageously, at every frontier.

Finia Glozberg and Esther Bandersky started a committee to search for
Dubossarers in Bozulok during the war. These noble people had a very
important task. After an exhausting 12-hour day of labour, they made the effort
of sending hundreds of letters throughout all of the country, searching for the
people of Dubossar. Whenever they found someone, they informed everyone else
about him. In addition, they assisted each son of Dubossar that came across
their area, close to Bozulok, to settle down. This committee also collected
information about the soldiers, and sent them modest but precious gifts.

Holocaust survivors of Dubossar meet in their hometown after the war.

At the end of March 1944, the Second Ukrainian Frontier Corps reached the
border of Dubossar and heavy battles took place. On August 30, 1944 the
52nd Corp battalion, under the commandment of General Lieutenant Korotiev,
coordinating with the Sixth Tank Brigade, started the decisive campaign to
release the town from the Nazi Occupiers. The town was indeed released, but

its 8,000 Jews did not live to see the liberation. The Jewish Section was burned down, destroyed. The chimneys protruded from the destruction like pillars. It was almost impossible to recognize the town. Some of the tombstones in the graveyard were shattered and the fences were broken. The factories and workshops were completely destroyed. The town was a ruined place. From every corner, from each pile, the voices of the tortured screamed silently. An Acacia grew in the yard of my home (that was also the yard of the Litmanoviches), and around it, I saw piles of stones... Only stones.

The monument by "The Brothers Grave"

The remaining Jews started returning to Dubossar on October 1944. Among them were the war invalids: Aaron Belfer, David Ladginsky, the Greenbergs, Abraham Sokolnik and Abraham Tukman. Thirty-six families – 80 people – returned. Some of the Dubossar survivors did not return at the end of the war, but settled in Eastern Europe and in Siberia, (about 40 families), in Kishinev, Riga, Moscow, Leningrad and in other places. Today, there are 200 families of Jews from Dubossar, living throughout Russia. The very few Jews returning from the war felt it was their obligation to humanity and to history to commemorate the thousands of martyrs, and to renew the community life in our town.

On July 1945, the old soldier, Motel Urman, came back to Dubossar. Motel was an extremely gracious and vigorous person. Soon he also became known for his excellent organizational skills and his brave struggle for the honor of the Jewish people. I said "brave struggle" because it took great effort to fulfill the tasks he took upon himself. The economic situation of the people who were returning was very poor. There were no apartments. There were not any jobs and no food. Under these conditions, Motel Urman started the activity of the Jewish Committee on August 1945. One of their assignments was reconditioning the apartments for the returning people and arranging for heaters for the winter. (This was not an easy task).

When winter came, they somehow managed to find housing for everyone and then in December of 1945, the Dubossarers living in the USA, Canada and Argentina started sending their support. This assistance literally saved many from hunger. When they had managed to provide appropriate living conditions, they decided it was time to renovate both of the cemeteries – the old one and the new one. They also wanted to give a dignified appearance to the "Valley of Death" of the Dubossar Jews. This was one of the most difficult missions they faced because the local authorities had explicitly disapproved of the committee's plan. While the Prevoslavic cemetery had already been renovated, the military cemetery repaired, and the monument for the "Anonymous Soldiers" had been built in the park, the burial place of the Jews was still wild with weeds.

After a long correspondence and many travels to Kishinev and to Moscow, Motel Urman got the approval for renewing the Jewish Cemeteries – the old and the new, and to build a fence around the location of the mass murder of the Jews. In 1956 the people of Dubossar who served as officers in the Soviet army, requested from the Soviet Union Marshal, G. K. Zukov, to assist them to commemorate the 18,500 Jews that were murdered in Dubossar. After several days, the local authorities granted their authorization to build a monument to the memory of the eighteen thousand "Soviet citizens" from Dubossar, that lost their lives during the war. "Soviet citizens", without mentioning the word Jewish.

The funds were raised among the Jews from Dubossar who were spread across Russia, as well as from those who lived in USA and Canada. In 1957, I flew to Dubossar specifically in regards to the building of the momentum. When I asked if it would not be more appropriate to add to the words "Soviet Citizens" the word "Jewish", and also add to the inscriptions that were there in Russian and in Moldavian, an inscription in the Jewish-language, I was accused of being a "Bourgeois-Nationalist"! My high military rank, my 14 pledges, my 5 times being injured in battle – none of those helped. I must admit this was one the hardest blows I suffered and it hastened my return to Judaism.

The fence around the area where the mass killing took place, 800 meters long, was built twice, and twice was ruined by those who were foraging for housing material. Nevertheless, the committee and its chairman Urman did not give up. Instead of stone substructures, they laid out concrete and dug around it a deep canal. This is how the fence appears today: Eighteen pits protected by 60 cm high concrete walls. A low fence with a deep canal around it surrounds the entire area. At the entrance, in the middle of the pits there is a statue of a soldier holding a machine-gun, kneeling down with his face lowered toward the graves. Next to him stands a little grieving girl.

The committee and its chairman, Motel Urman, maintain a connection with all of the Dubossarers in Russia. They also keep in touch with all of those who were hospitable to the Jews of Dubossar during the war, in Siberia, the Urals and Middle Asia. They are often sending those letters and gifts of produce from Moldavia. We must forever remember the compassion and self-sacrifice of those people, to whom we shall be grateful for all time. Thank you, Kind Russians from Siberia, the Urals, and Middle Asia for sheltering and feeding our brothers and sisters during the difficult years of the war!

Our old Dubossar no longer exists. Its ruins are covered with weeds; its chimneys, that seem like tombstones have disappeared. In its place, we have built the new Dubossar. A hydro-electrical power station was built 1.5 kilometers north of Dubossar. Between "the Small Fountain" and the Cocheers is the living zone. The Jewish cemetery is at the heart of the living zone. Most of the families who came back are living in reconstructed houses from the old Dubossar. They are not re-building Dubossar as it was.

In an empty field near the house of the Mulokshers a bus station was built. Four times daily there is a bus to Kishinev, and three times to Tiraspol. Once a day, a bus travels towards Kotobesk (Birzula) and Balta. A new bridge was built over the Dniester River at Lunga. A port was built in the river (near Kiner Gardens), and light boats sail from there to Grigoriopol and to Bender. From the port near the hydro-electrical station, it is possible to sail to Rivnitze. In the old mill's location, there are car repair shops. There are three cinemas and a few clubs in Dubossar. The tobacco factory was enlarged significantly, and so were the fruit drying and other agricultural industries.

These days, there are 150 Jews among the 25,000 residents of Dubossar. One hundred and fifty Jews out of a population of 25,000 people, as opposed to 8,000 Jews among 20,000 residents before the war. There are no Jewish schools in Dubossar, no Jewish library or Jewish hospital. There are hardly any Jews, and there is no Jewish atmosphere. The typical atmosphere of old Dubossar, the known and beloved Jewish Dubossar - is lost for good. Some of the old people gather for prayers in private houses and life goes on. A new generation is growing up that will know about our beautiful heroic lives only from the stories of the seniors.

The Jews in Dubossar are working in different jobs. Some of them are working in the hydro-electrical station, which supplies electricity also to Kishinev, Tiraspol and Odessa. There is an eternal sadness in the eyes of every Jew. Each stone in Dubossar is screaming. Each stone is brushed with the blood of the Jews.

Every year, on Yom Kippur, the Jews from all over Russia gather for the Memorial Prayer for the Dead. I came to say goodbye to Dubossar on Yom Kippur Eve, before I left Russia. We walked in silence from one ruined place to another and we thought of scenes from the past. We walked holding each other's hands, dreading the moment of departure, although we knew, in our hearts, that we would be together again. Present were the soldier Yefim Zemel, and Fima Granovsky the son, an excellent engineer in the flour industry. There was Misha Finezilberg, the metal expert- his gray head bent and his wide shoulders secretly shaking. There were Doctor Rashkovan and Riva Litmanovich, the daughter of Leiba Limanovich, and Rosa Livnet and Jacob Shulklepfer. We walked silently but full of pride! People stopped, uncovered their heads and bowed to us.

We saw the dry land. Very soon, we saw the place that had become the destiny -- the bitter destiny of our most precious ones. Motel Urman led the group. Suddenly we started singing a sacred song from the Day of Atonement. Mournfully, the tune went on, entered our hearts and re-opened the wounds that had yet to heal: "Remember, human being. You are mortal and the Judgment day awaits you! Dear God, please undo our vows. Release us from them, our dear God, God of our ancestors". Tears washed our faces, and everyone whispered:

"Great lord, accept out oath: We shall never, ever forget them, for as long as we shall live."

November 1964, January 1965.

Pilot, Lieutenant-Colonel Litmonovitch

A Group of Dubossar Jews Days Before the Outbreak of War.
(Numbers go from left to right, bottom row to top.)

Murdered: Yidl Zweighoft (4) Faygeh Vasserman (5), Esther Brilian (7), Shimon Kinor (8), Toba Rashkevan (10), Sarah Shkolnik (11), Shenkar (12),Rachel Poskar (13), Yitzchak Barenboim (15), Boris Katzavman (16), Menia Zemtzer (20), Chaike Tefler (22), Chaim Rashkevan (23), Layb Barenboim (24), Yakov Chayat (27), Isaac Shreier (29), Israel Koifman (30), Yakov Schinder (31), Layb Mordkovitch (34), Yakov Laybovitch (35), Sherl Kiner (37), Bentchik Shlit (39), Idl Sandler (40), David Shneiderman (41), Shifra Maydanik (43), Reva Barenboim (44), Menya Soibelman (45).

Suvivors: Riva Urman (1), Motl Urman (2), Zweighoft (28), Lena Berelechis (6), Velvl Festuyicher (9), Sarah Bashkansky (14), Avraham Livocht (17), Shmuel Tshoylsky (18), Hershl (22), Yosef Finkelstein (25), Yosef Volovick (32), Hershl Bander (33), Berl Bakman (36), Pessy Glimberg (38)

[Page286]

Upon the Ruins of Dubossary

by D. L. Granovsky

No elegy, no weeping – the disaster is too great;
Only mute silence and abysmal grief and pain.
In mourning over one third of the nation destroyed by foe
We remember the Holy Community of Dubossary –
A cherished town – went up in flames and blood
And living heaps of human ashes.
Vision and deed, innocence of heart,
Splendor of childhood, charm of youth,
All that was loved and treasured –
Hopes for the future – all was buried,
Buried alive by defiled hands.
Eighteen Thousand and Five Hundred.
Forever the remnants shall weep
For the calamity of our town Dubossary.

[Page287]

The poem on page 286 is set to music by Moshe Pik.

It is to be sung as a *Recitativo* "in mourning and sorrow"

**1953. Planting the first trees in the forest in honour
of the martyrs from Dubossar and surrounding area.**

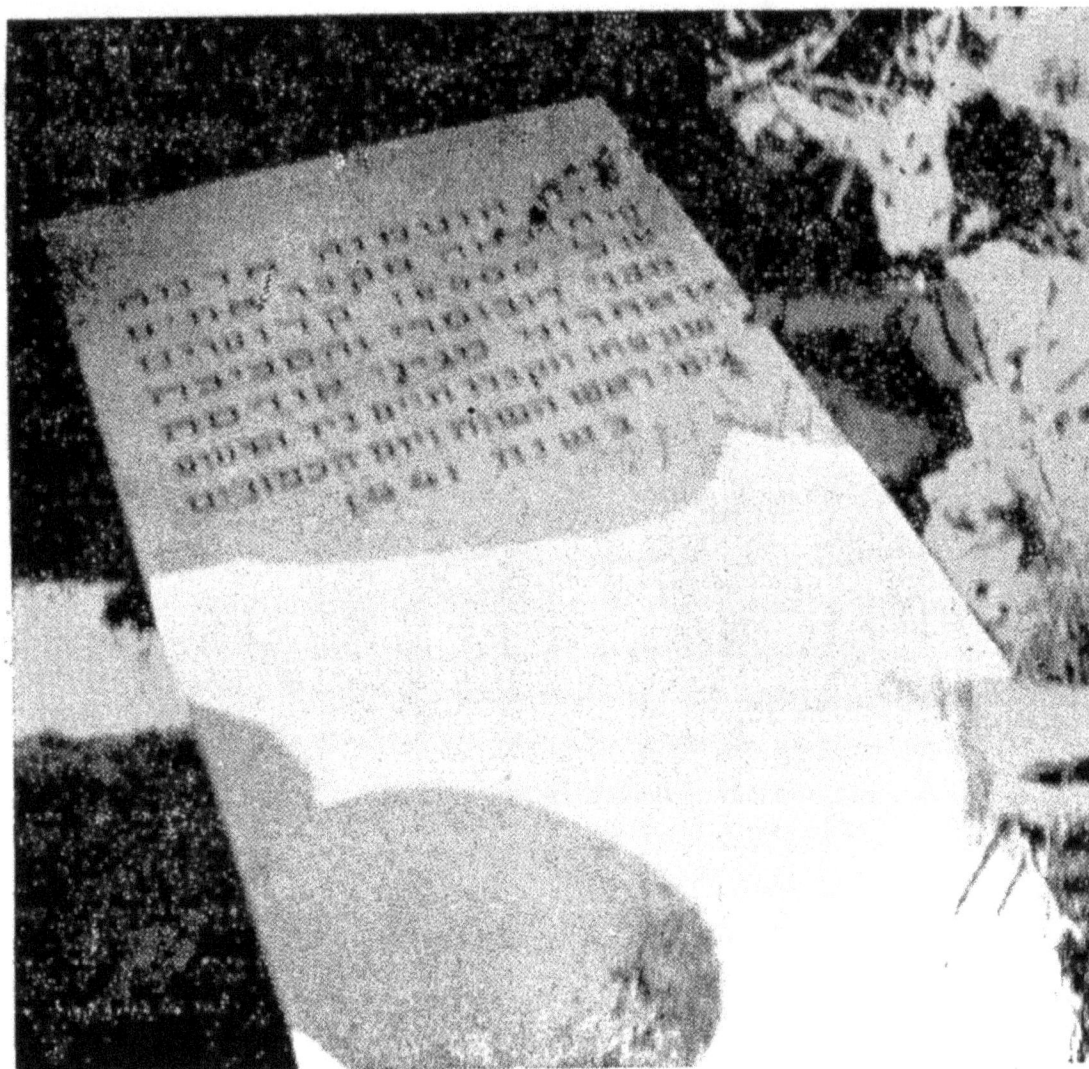

**Commemoration gravestone in the Martyrs' Forest. Beneath the
gravestone lies a sack with earth from the "Brothers' Grave" in Dubossar.**

[Page292]

Planting trees in the Martyrs Forest in Israel

A Memorial – Forest of the Martyrs
by D. L. Granovsky
Translated by Sam Blatt

At the end of World War II our Landsleit (fellow town-dwellers) in America, at the head of which was Moshe Feldman, of blessed memory, and his friends Harry Sheer, Leibish Levine, and others, may they live to a ripe age, – organized the first "help-action" for the Jewish survivors of Dubossar in the Soviet Union. In the course of a short time they sent over thousands of packages of food and clothing, as well as medicine to our Landsleit in Russia, an "action" also joined by former Dubossar Jews living in Argentina, at the head of which was Bernardo Gurevitch, of blessed memory, and L. Rubin, may he be well. We should stress – thanks to this material help, the majority of our surviving brothers and sisters in Russia were spared hunger and cold.

A good deed brings on a good deed.

In addition to the "help-action", for us Dubossarer Jews, whom fate spared the terrible catastrophe that happened to our brothers in Europe, it became clear to us that with material help alone for the survivors we were far from fulfilling our debt owed our martyrs and heroes who perished "Al Kiddush Hashem" and in the battles at the fronts against the most deadly foe of Jews of all times. We saw it as a holy duty to create a memorial work to eternalize our community, and the nearby communities, which, in the course of its four hundred year existence, had a rich lore in the history of Ukrainian and Russian Jewry.

Remembrance day. Baruch Bassin lights a memorial candle in the "Martyrs' Cellar".

After the liberation, our brothers in the Soviet Union undertook an initiative to erect a concrete fence around the looming "mass-grave" in Dubossar, where are buried 6000 of our Lansdleit, and another 12,500 Jews from the near and farther communities, from towns and villages: Akneh, Zacharivkeh, Yagarlik, Tyrospol, Grigoriopol, Kryulyaneh, Argeyev, Rizineh, Rivnitzeh, Balteh, Kishinev, and Odessa, as well as Jews from Czechoslovakia, who were brought to the Dubossar ghetto and murdered by the Germans and their helpers from the local non-Jewish population. This initiative was enabled thanks to donations of the Dubossar Jews in Russia, the U.S., Canada, and Argentina.

With the creation of the State of Israel the idea of eternalizing the memory of the martyrs of Dubossar and surrounding areas began to mature through a special undertaking in Israel. It is to be noted that this time also our Landsleit in America – Moshe Feldman of blessed memory, and Harry Sheer, may he be well, L. Rubin of Argentina, and Moshe Faerman of Blessed memory, of Canada, were those who raised the thought to plant in the Martyr's Forest a treed area in the name of the martyrs of Dubossar and surrounding areas.

Families Sher and Levin of America at the Martyrs Forest

This idea was accepted with much support by the Dubossar circle in Israel, and in the month of Sivan, (May) 1951, the first meeting of a group of Dubassar "members" took place, with the goal to found an administrative committee to undertake the practical implementation of the memorial work. A temporary committee was elected at that meeting, which immediately started on the actual work.

In the month of Tamuz, 1951 the founding assembly of the Dubossar Landsleit Organization in Israel took place, at which participated sixty-five persons. At this meeting we declared that we would plant a forest in memory of the Dubossar and area Martyrs, in the Forest of the Martyrs. We also elected an Actions Committee, which consisted of the following members: A.Y. Golani, of Blessed memory –Chairman, Ram-Visoky, of Blessed memory, and may they be well, the following members: B. Basin, Y. Kantor, D. L. Granovsky (Secretary), Moshe Bick, Ze'ev Brodsky and Zvi Sukai. At the same meeting we started a campaign to collect funds for the memorial.

Working closely with the Dubossar Landsleit Organization in America and Argentina, we collected the funds necessary to plant the memorial forest in the Jerusalem hills, on the grounds of the Keren Kayemeth. After three years we planted the forest comprising 10,000 trees.

Three years ago a Dubossar family emigrated to Israel, who related to us many details of the massacre in our city, and about the amazing heroic actions of many Dubossar Jews in the ghetto, and the many fighters from the front as well as partisans – sons and daughters of our city (as described in detail by A. Timor in this book.) This family also brought along a little sack of earth form the mass-grave. We immediately contacted the Keren Kayemeth office and advised them of our wish to bury the sack of earth in the forest, in the name of the Dubossar Martyrs, and also our wish to erect a monument in memory of those killed. The office of the Keren Kayemeth immediately concurred with our requests, and also undertook the planning of this initiative.

As the eleventh of Tishrei (a day after Yom Kippur) 1941 was the day that the Nazis completed their extermination of the Dubossar ghetto, the Dubossar survivors in Russia decided to make the eleventh of Tishrei the memorial day for the murdered. On that day the Dubossar Jews come together from all corners of Russia to the mass-grave, to be united in the memory of the Martyrs. The Dubassarer in Israel, Argentina and the U.S. also accepted this day as a memorial, and the day after Yom Kippur we stand together with the memory of our Martyrs.

Also, on the day after Yom Kippur, September 29, 1963, the Dubossarer living in Jerusalem gathered in the Forest of the Martyrs to uncover the monument (the office of the Keren Kayemeth had taken on the responsibility to have it ready for that day), on which was inscribed the following:

> *Here lies buried earth which was brought from the mass-grave, wherein lie 18,500 Jews from Dubossar and environs, and the last defenders of the city of Odessa, who were murdered and buried alive at the hands of the wicked, in the days between Rosh Hashana and Yom Kippur 1941.*

In the sack of earth was also buried a history about the destruction, written on parchment, signed by all the participants in the memorial.

The monument stands near the sign: "Forest planted in the name of the martyrs of Dubassar and surrounding area".

With a shiver those assembled listened to the details of the mass grave, told by the man who brought the sack of earth. The grave is made up of 12 pits; in each pit are buried 1500 Jews. The man who told these details was a high officer in the Soviet army, and together with other officers, Dubossarer, succeeded in obtaining permission from the government to erect a concrete fence around the mass grave. At the entrance, in the center of the pits, the government erected a monument, which portrays a soldier with a machine gun, kneeling, with bowed head at the graves of the murdered.

The man also related that the cement wall around the mass grave in Dubassar is the only one in the whole area, and perhaps even in all of Ukraine. Unfortunately there are disquieting signs that the local regime is not interested in maintaining the grave site. However, those few Jews who still live in Dubassar undertook to care for this holy site their whole lives.

The monument that we erected in Israel in memory of the 18,500 buried in the Dubassar mass grave is located in the "Forest of the Martyrs of Dubassar and Region", near the Sheuva highway, at kilometer 17 on the road to Jerusalem.

Thanks to the contribution of Harry Sheer of America, we hung a plaque in memory of our Martyrs in the Cellar of the Martyrs in Jerusalem.

This particular memorial book is in its third publication. Here-in is told the history and the life of the Jewish community in Dubassar from the first days of its founding until today. And if tomorrow your children will ask you what is the purpose of this book? You should answer them: This book serves to note and to memorialize the wonderful Jewish community in Dubassar, where a creative, exuberant and heroic Jewish life was cruelly cut-off together with hundreds of other Jewish communities in that horrible time, when the most terrible enemy of the Jews lowered his murderous axe over Jacob's tent in the *galut* (diaspora) of Europe. With their deaths they sanctified our lives, instructing us to continue to build a Jewish life in the State of Israel and wherever Jews live.

[Page298]

Personalities

Rabbi Gaon Reb Yerucham, son of Reb Shabtai Hacohen, z'l, z'tzl

Yerucham, son of Rabbi Shabtai Hacohen, z'tz"l

by his grandson, Shabtai Kardonsky

Translated by Eti Horovitz

Reb Yerucham was an erudite person, great in the Torah, in his devotion to God, exquisite and proficient. He studied the Torah and the Jewish laws all his life, and even passed away while studying the Talmud. He was not only a great scholar, but also had a pleasant voice for singing. He was very talented in music and the reputation of his public prayers was spread throughout Dobossar and the surrounding areas. Whenever he and his sons came up to the podium for the Benediction of the Cohens, their prayers sounded like a musical group and the praying public enjoyed very much listening to it. There was a reason for that: the sons of Reb Yerucham were all gifted with pleasant voices and musical talent. They all served as cantors in big communities – one in Kishinev, one in Odessa, and the young Shlomo in the USA. The three of them are no longer alive.

I was a boy and I grew old, but until today I remember the chanting of grandfather in the Benediction of the Cohens and in Halel.

The rabbi Reb Yerucham wrote a book named "Cohen Zedek" – interpretations about the six books of the Mishna, to settle the questions of the Gaon Reb Akiva Eiger of blessed memory. He also wrote Questions & Answers "Hatishbi", which is a big book about the four parts of the "Shulhan Aruch". This book elucidates the laws and clarifies the abstruseness when one is corresponding and the other is contradicting. And indeed, "Hatishbi" answered the questions, clarified everything in good taste and wisdom. For this book, grandfather received approvals from many Rabbis, and he worked many years preparing for it to be published. In my youth I had seen the thick book in my grandfather's handwriting. It took a great deal of money to publish it, and unfortunately he didn't get to see it printed in his lifetime. My uncle, Reb Shlomo Hacohen of blessed memory, will be well remembered for contributing to the publishing of the book in USA.

As well, Reb Yerucham wrote other books that are not familiar to me. But I do possess his essay "Be Reish Galei" – an interpretation for the Hagadah of Passover. This small book excels in its beautiful explanations and magnificent simplicity. It also has collections of other interpretations about Torah verses and stories of Hazal (our Sages of Blessed Memory). At the end of the Hagadah there is a discourse for Shabbat, an answer with a moral. Grandfather named the book "Be Reish Galei" after the latest redemption awakening movement, and the verse "and the children of Israel are leaving fearlessness" is translated by Uncalos As "Be Reish Galei". These letters imply the initials of the writer, Yerucham son of Rabbi Shabtai.

According to what they told my mother, of blessed memory, Fige, daughter of Reb Yerucham, it was the 10th of Adar 1908, while grandfather was studying the Talmud. His daughter Rachel suddenly heard the sound of his velvet hat falling to the floor. She went into the room to see what this noise was and she found Reb Yerucham bent over the Talmud, not breathing. He died painlessly while studying the Torah.

His wife, grandma Adila, offspring of the Baal Shem Tov, and like her husband, the offspring of the "Shach", was a righteous woman and his right hand her entire life. May her memory be blessed as well.

[Page302]

Rabbi Yehoshua Yissachar Abel z'l

Rabbi Yehoshua Issachar Abel, z"l

by D. L. Granovsky

Translated by Sarah Faerman

Rabbi Abel occupied a very special and honored place in our community. He was a Talmud scholar, a sage and a man of good deeds. In short, he was the leader of our community in every sense of the word.

He came to us from Odessa, brought to Dubossar by Reb Yechiel Tzelnik, himself a learned man and one of the most respected Jews in our town. Rabbi Abel came to us in 1907 to occupy two Rabbinic positions – that of Rabbi and head judge of Jewish law, as well as being the crown appointed Rabbi – both positions that he held until the day of his passing on Shavuot (holiday) 1925.

The period that Rabbi Abel was the spiritual leader of Dubossar was the most productive period of our communal life and his influence was felt by young and old throughout his tenure.

As mentioned, he combined scholarship with general education and a deep knowledge of the wisdom of Israel. His greatness and influence, however stemmed from his warm Jewish heart, his love of Yisroel and his love of people. Thanks to his lectures and teaching of the Talmud, Bible and the wisdom of Israel that he gave to so many study groups, Dubossar became a center for Torah learning. He also involved himself in broader Jewish topics which were of benefit to the community.

His influence was also beneficial to the youth for whom he opened new horizons in his knowledge of Man and Society. Uppermost was his knowledge of the Jewish nation, its past and its aspirations for the future. Like a good father, he was always ready to devote himself to his community and he invested much effort into influencing it toward peace and understanding.

His activities became even more time consuming and diverse after the outbreak of the Russian Revolution as he pinned his full hopes on it. He believed that the Revolution would herald in a glorious new chapter for the Jews and bitter was his disappointment when all his hopes were dashed one by one with the realities of the new regime.

In 1917, right after the outbreak of the February Revolution, he was elected as delegate to the 7th Zionist Conference that was held in Petrograd and together with Chaim Nachman Bialik, Moishe Kleinman and others, he was appointed to the Cultural Commission. When he returned home from the conference he gave a wonderful report to an audience of hundreds about the new era that was ushering in expanded, widespread possibilities for Jewish national and cultural work in Russia and of the many projects that the Zionist Conference had planned.

Unfortunately, instead of pouring his energies and talents into the cultural work that he loved so much, a short time later he was forced to involve himself in activity of a totally different character. After the October Revolution plunged Russia into a bloody Civil War, Pogroms and the slaughter of Jews proliferated, particularly in Ukraine.

Before my eyes I see the image of Rabbi Abel, flushed and disheveled, with stones in his hand, running throughout the Dubossar streets yelling at the top of his lungs: "Who is for God, Come with Me!" This was the Dubossar combat cry to summon the Dubossar Jews against the mobs heading our way to start a Pogrom. At that time, many of the Russian Army soldiers deserted the front, crossed over the Dniester River and would attack our town. The alarm that Rabbi Abel raised, saved our town from a great misfortune. In a matter of minutes hundreds of Jews gathered around him, armed with sticks and pitchforks. Some managed to lay their hands on revolvers and rifles and with great gusto and enthusiasm managed to chase off the attackers.

Sometime later, Rabbi Abel once again was actively involved in rescuing the town from the Petlyurists. His fiery words gave us courage and faith and with this fortified strength we stood up against Petlyura's men and vanquished them. When the Pogromists advanced toward our town, the bells from all the churches were rung, sounding the alarm of an attack. The farmers who were in town (it was coincidentally a Market day) quickly disappeared. The Jewish Self-Defense was ready for battle.

I would like to mention here that a certain number of Christians helped in our attack against the hooligans. The Petlyurists assembled in the suburb of Lunke and from there marched into town. From their machine gun and rifle shots we knew exactly where they were. The distance between the Haydemaks (Ukrainians) and town became shorter and shorter. Suddenly the shots sounded further and further away until there was complete silence. What could have happened? Yosef Barbarash, a short, swift Jew who had once served in the Russian army, had crept quietly up to the machine gunner and with the pitchfork that he had in his hand, knocked the machine gun out of his hands, quickly grabbed it and started to shoot at the Haydemaks. Panic spread among the big "heroes" and in great fright they fled wherever their feet took them, leaving behind many dead. With great joy the Dubossar Jews celebrated their victory over the Pogromists. The joy, however, was spoiled because of the death of one of our own Self Defense heroes – Avraham – who was killed by a flying bullet.

As mentioned, our victory was due to Rabbi Abel for he had planted the seeds of courage in the Self Defense organiztion.

During the First World War, when day-by-day, the numbers of Jewish refugees increased because of the Russian Government's Anti-Semitic politics, Rabbi Abel organized Refugee Committees and worked intensively to ease the burdens of the dispossessed and forlorn souls. He would extend full aid to the most needy but himself he could not help. His own sorrow, he carried silently locked away in his heart.

I will never forget his visit to our house on Simchat Torah (holiday) 1921. As was typical of him, his conversation was sprinkled with wisdom and Torah. Suddenly he stopped talking and began to sing with a sweet voice Bialik"s "Hachnisini Tachat Knafayich" (Take Me under your wings). He sang with great emotion while hot tears fell from his eyes. We were startled by the depth of his soul. We sat like stone and could not move a muscle. We felt that this time the man had revealed the sense of suffering and tragedy that he felt so deeply but had kept hidden from everyone. Such a "Hachnisini" we never heard before nor in the days to come until this present time.

All his life, Rabbi Abel had an unlimited love of Zion. He deeply longed for the opportunity to settle in Eretz Yisrael. His luck did not give him his fondest desire. In the year 1925, his soul departed when he was only 48 years old.

[Page305]

Rabbi Yehoshua Issachar Abel, z"l

by Yosef Visoky (Ram)
Translated by Sarah Faerman

Rabbi Abel was a refined, aristocratic person and greatly respected. He embodied love for people, for his folk and had great enthusiasm for our national resurgence.

With his honesty, gentle nature and interesting manner of conversation, Rabbi Abel was much loved and won over everyone's heart.

His extraordinary depth of knowledge in both the old and the new Hebrew literature, as well as in the world's general literature and his exceptional ability to include in his lectures the appropriate expression of our nationalist strivings, placed him in the same league as the great orators and activists of the Zionist movement.

Rabbi Abel came from Odessa to occupy the double positions of Rabbi and Crown appointed clergy. From his first day in Dubossar, he did not restrict himself exclusively to the Halacha (Jewish law) but also devoted himself energetically to instill in the youth and the community a nationalist, Zionist consciousness. His lectures and talks that he gave always drew massive audiences.

He was a proud and courageous Jew. As a member of the city council he would fight energetically against any expression of Anti-Semitism and discrimination against the Jewish community. With his powers of persuasion and the strength of his arguments, he usually was able to squelch projects and actions that ran counter to the interests of the Jewish community.

As a member of the city council, he always defended the interests of the poor and the working class.

Rabbi Abel was a true spiritual leader of his people. Until the very last day of his life, he did not lower the flag that he unfurled on the first day of arrival in matters of holiness to serve in the Jewish community of Dubossar.

[Page307]

A. Y. Golani (Yogalnitzer, z"l)

by Yishayahu Kantor

Translated by Sarah Faerman

In memory of our teacher and leader whose last post in the diaspora was in Dubossar before he made Aliya to Eretz Yisrael.

1906. One year after the defeat of Czarist Russia at the hands of Japan and after the oppression of the 1905 Revolution. At that time, we and six other Jewish families lived in a Moldavian village four kilometers from Dubossar. I was a little boy then and I remember how every evening we would leave our house and go to sleep at one of our Christian friends' homes while my father and a few other gentiles would stand guard over our house.

One sunny morning we found out that the night before, Pogromists had attacked one of the Jewish houses in the village and brutally beaten the head of the household. At noontime we noticed a commotion in the town. The gentiles were running, frightened – a sign that something had happened. Soon the source of their panic became clear. A special emissary of the mayor of our town came to my father and told him that Mendele Patron of Dubossar had arrived at the mayor's house demanding the extradition of the hooligans that had attacked his uncle.

Within minutes this news spread throughout the village and a special delegation was sent to beg pardon of Mendele. He, however, did not want to hear of it: "Give me the criminals and I will teach them something." Finally, finally, he was convinced that it would benefit all sides if this was handled in a milder fashion. Wine poured that day like a river and in the evening he was escorted home to Dubossar to the accompaniment of drum -beats. Soon after that episode, we moved to Dubossar.

Great was my joy at the prospect of living in Dubossar and having the opportunity to become acquainted with the famous Jewish heroes of Dubossar, including Mendele, who were feared by the gentiles of all the surrounding villages. I, however, was in for a great disappointment. Instead of showing me these great heroes, my father directed me to the "best" Talmud Torah (Hebrew school). We arrived at recess time. All of the children were playing or engaged in games and activities in various groups. In the midst of one group, an adult stood out. He had a mustache and was dressed in black pants and a white shirt. The children chased him and he ran away. They "shot" a ball at him, which he caught and he "shot" it back at them. I asked father why a grown man was playing with the children and he explained that this man was no less than the teacher and director of the school... and not only that, he was also the head of all those heroes that I had been so eager to see.

Great was my chagrin at seeing this leader of the heroes. In my fantasy, I had imagined the heroes to be giants and their leader at least a head taller than all of them and here suddenly, was this very ordinary person, playing with children my own age – not particularly tall, not especially broad shouldered. Here he was – dressed in a white shirt with a tie... not even with a special hat... and they didn't call him 'Idl Katarzhan' and not 'Laybl Dishovke' but by a strange name that was hard to pronounce – 'Yagolnitzer'.

Slowly I became accustomed to this "strange" teacher and along with all of the other students I started to love him. During our lessons, he was the most beloved teacher; during recess he was the most devoted friend and during the vacations and holidays he was a conscientious guide.

I heard my father say that in the evenings, Yagolnitzer taught the youth how to use weapons. One day, I plucked up my courage and asked our teacher if he could tell us about some of those activities. He indulged us and told us about the Jewish heroes of our time and of our town. He particularly emphasized the heroic exploits of Idl Katarzhan, Nachum Chaim Isser's, Mendele Patron, Laybele Dishovke and others. True they were simple men and not literate in Hebrew but they were proud Jews with straight backs; upright individuals prepared to risk their lives for Jewish honour. He would also tell us a great deal about Eretz Yisrael and he planted in our childish hearts the seeds of a warm love for our land. During one summer vacation, word went around that in the coming school year we would have a new teacher because Yagolnitzer was leaving for Eretz Yisrael.

1937. At this time I was already a Vatik (long timer) in the land (since 1923). On a certain day, riding in a bus to Ramat Gan, I glanced at an elderly passenger who appeared very familiar to me. I wasn't shy and approached him, saying: "aren't you Yagolnitzer?" In the Jewish manner, he answered with a question: "Aren't you from Dubossar" If I am not mistaken, your father was a tall, blond man. First your family lived in a village and if I am not mistaken, your name is Kantor." He immediately began to describe to the friends who were with him in the bus, all about Dubossar and the town heroes of whom he had been so fond.

When the dreadful revelations became known, of the great destruction of European Jewry and the Jewish community of Dubossar at the hands of the Romanian and German murderers, the seventy-five year old Golani was the first to urge the landsmen (fellow townspeople) from Dubossar in Israel to honor the memory of the Dubossar martyrs by planting a forest in their name in the "Martyr's Forest" of the Keren Kayemet (Jewish National Fund).

Ten years after the destruction of our community, during the high holidays of 1953, the Dubossar landsmen in Israel held a special evening to mourn their annihilated brethren and to proclaim the plans to commemorate Dubossar. Golani was the chairman and after the Cantor chanted the "El Mole Rachamim" (prayer for the dead), he rose, with a voice choked with tears and said the 'Kaddish' (mourner's prayer). When we parted we did not know that this was to be our last meeting with our beloved teacher and devoted friend, A.Y.Golani.

[Page312]

Moshe Feldman in the Jewish Legion 1920

Moshe Feldman, z"l

by D. L. Granovsky

Translated by Sarah Faerman

A sorrow engulfs us whenever one of our circle of friends is no more. Greater yet is the pain and much deeper the grief when the one torn away from us was the lion of the group... whose life was dedicated to the well-being of our community... who devoted himself totally, with love, to those in need.

Like thunder on a bright day, we received the bitter news. We never imagined that so soon would the light of our dear friend, Moshe Feldman, be extinguished. He was full of life, energy and thirsty for action. Throughout all of his years he always found time for communal involvement. Apparently, his father Reb Yakov Feldman the sage – an enlightened and upright individual who faithfully served his people – passed this admirable trait on to his son.

In spite of the fact that Moshe emigrated to America in his youth, his heart always yearned for Eretz Yisrael and during World War I, he joined up with the Jewish Legion. Although he tried his best to settle in Eretz Yisrael, there were extenuating circumstances that forced him to return to America. In spite of this, he kept up a life-long close connection to Israel and participated in many projects for the land.

His crowning accomplishment was the establishment of the Dubossar Landsleit (Association of the people from the same town) in the United States and throughout all of his years he was the main force behind it. Thanks to his initiative, a similar group was established in Argentina and he did much to organize the Dubossar Landsleit chapter in Israel.

Between the two World Wars, Moshe was active in organizing parcels of food and clothing to our impoverished brethren in Dubossar and also for many in Eretz Yisrael who found themselves in dire straits. After World War II, he was also involved with organizing help and support for those of our town that had survived the Holocaust. Moshe also invested great efforts into the creation of the forest in the Jerusalem Hills that would be our Memorial to the Dubossar Martyrs. In the beginning, he was the only one who battled against those who opposed this plan. He carried on his campaign with energy and courage until he succeeded in winning over all who were hesitant. The forest was planted, largely through the contributions of our Landsleit in America but also because of the immense efforts that Moshe Feldman invested in this holy project.

When we began to prepare the materials and content for this Yizkor (memorial) book, Moshe Feldman was very caught up with the idea and together with his friends in America – our Landsleit – tirelessly helped to raise the funds for the book. While we eagerly awaited his article with his recollections of our town for the Yizkor book, we received the sad news of his illness which would confine him to his bed until his last day. Moshe Feldman was not destined to live in the land he loved, nor to see this Yizkor book, his last labor of love where he poured out his very last efforts.

Moshe Feldman was a faithful leader of his Landsleit. His whole life was devoted to others and least of all for himself. He did not build a house for himself, nor did he establish a family. He died alone because his whole life was dedicated to the community.

The last letter we received from Moshe was written on his death bed and was full of longing for Israel. He knew that his end was near and that the Yizkor book of the Jewish community of Dubossar would be like his will to all of his friends.

With great sorrow and pain, we remember the dear friend Moshe Feldman who was too soon torn away from our midst.

[Page313]

Moshe Feldman, z"l

by Baruch Bassin

Translated by Sarah Faerman

Moshe Feldman was born in Dubossar, the son of Reb Yakov Feldman – a known Talmud scholar, a follower of the Enlightenment movement and a community activist. When still a youth, he made his way to America. During the first World War, he voluntarily joined the Jewish Legion. I did not personally know him in Dubossar and met him for the first time in Tel Aviv after World War I. After the war, when he was discharged from the military, he wanted to settle in Eretz Yisrael in the village that was to be established by his friends from the Jewish Legion but for various reasons he was forced to give up these plans and he returned to New York. Sometime later, when the Moshav (co-operative village) Avichail was founded by his comrades, Feldman remained one of their greatest friends in America.

During his whole life he strove to settle in Eretz Yisrael. He was however a proud man, intent on being independent but his material resources were not sufficient to allow him to establish an independent life in the land. Thus he postponed the move until such time as he would be able to afford the move. Another factor that held up his Aliya (emigration), was his self-imposed mission to care for the Jews still in Dubossar between the two world wars. He organized the Dubossar Landsleit (fellow townspeople) in America, founded a "relief" organization and made certain that the neediest would receive assistance from their American brethren.

With the outbreak of World War II and the destruction it wrought upon European Jewry, Feldman threw himself heart and soul into this relief work. He neglected his own affairs and devoted himself to the needs of the Dubossar Survivors of the Holocaust. He and his friends, Harry Scheer and Leibish Levine – long may they live – took up the initiative to provide a fence around the new cemetery in Dubossar (where the thousands of Martyrs, murdered by the Nazis, lay buried). They also provided for additional needs of the Survivors as well as others of our community.

Feldman was the instigator and driving force in this undertaking, urging others to involve themselves as well. He worked tirelessly not only in New York, but in the other cities as well where Dubossar landsleit lived – in Chicago and other American cities and he also travelled to Argentina to motivate others to throw themselves into the rescue work.

Twelve years ago in Israel, the idea was born to memorialize the Martyrs of Dubossar and the Surrounding Areas by planting a forest on Keren Kayemet land (Jewish National Fund). I wrote to my friend, Moshe Feldman about this plan. He immediately jumped in with all of his enthusiasm and zeal, expending every last drop of his energy into the actualization of this proposal. He interested his friends in this and together they undertook the raising of funds to establish a forest of 10,000 trees in the name of Dubossar and Surrounding Areas which would be part of the Keren Kayemet Forest Of Martyrs'.

In 1961, Moshe Feldman because seriously ill and, confined to his bed for almost half a year, fought his battle against death. Even then, he did not cease to interest himself in everything associated with commemorating the name of our Dubossar community. Two weeks before his death, he wrote to us asking for details about the Yizkor book we were compiling. He wanted so much to take part in preparing the book and in distributing it.

Moshe Feldman was an esteemed and valuable man – a symbol of self-sacrifice. May his shining memory be a solace to all who knew and loved him.

Harry Sher by Moishe Feldman's grave

[Page317]

Yosef Ram (Visoky), z'l

Yosef Ram (Visoky), z"l

by D. L. Granovsky

Translated by Sarah Faerman

Among the influential people in our town, Yosef Ram (Visoky) held a special place as businessman and Zionist leader. He was one of the founders of the organization "Hatchiya" (The Revival) and together with Chaim Greenberg and A.Y.Golani developed the first "Tzeirei Tzion" (Young Zion movement) ideological platform known widely as "The Dubossar Program". There was no Zionist education in Dubossar that Visoky did not have a hand in shaping and executing. As an articulate and compelling orator, he spoke at both small Zionist gatherings and mass meetings. If a noted lecturer or businessman arrived in Dubossar, the first address he would visit would be that of Yosef Visoky. At his initiative, Rabbi Abel was sent as a delegate of the Dubossar Zionists to the Seventh Zionist Conference in Petrograd, summer of 1917.

While Dubossar was flooded with waves of refugees during World War I, Visoky threw himself heart and soul into the necessary relief work to provide for their most elemental requirements - such as food and roofs over their heads. Later when Besarabia was occupied by Romania, he worked tirelessly to help them cross over to the other side of the Dniester. True, in these important humanitarian activities, Visoky had many helpers but he was the leader and instigator.

During the "honeymoon period" of the Russian Revolution, when all the various Russian populations, particularly the Jews, viewed the revolution as the "coming of the Messiah", Visoky, as the main speaker at a huge rally of thousands boldly stated that in spite of his belief in the new winds of change in this giant land, the Jewish salvation lay in only one direction – Zionism.

In that turbulent period, he was also elected to the Dubossar city council where together with Rabbi Abel, he represented the Jewish community. Yosef Visoky was by nature good hearted and always willing to lend a helping hand to those in need.

When the Communist regime reigned over Russia and the Yevsektzye (Jewish Communist Ministry) that ruled over the Jewish street began to persecute Zionists and Zionism, Visoky realized increasingly, day by day, that he had no reason to remain in this land under this regime. To deprive Visoky of his Zionist work was to deprive of him of his purpose in life. He began to seek a way to escape from the Soviet Union. He fled to Besarabia and after a lengthy struggle managed to make Aliya (emigrate) to Eretz Yisrael, settling in Jerusalem where he immediately obtained employment as head of one of the important Zionist offices.

When the Dubossarites in Israel organized for the purpose of memorializing the Dubossar Martyrs of the Holocaust by planting a forest in their name in the Martyrs' Cemetery in the Jerusalem Hills, Yosef Visoky took an active part in carrying out this project. He was also one of the initiators in preparing this Yizkor book. Unfortunately, he died a few years before the book was published.

Yosef Ram (Visoky) died the tenth of Tamuz, 1960.

May his memory be honored.

[Page320]

Our Great Teacher Gad Layb Rechev

Our Esteemed Teacher – Gad Layb Rakov, z"l

by Fruma Granovsky

Translated by Sarah Faerman

Gad Layb Rakov, a gentle, pure man, lived in our little shtetl Yagorlik (near Dubossar). Throughout his life he studied with fervor and a thirst for knowledge and this he imparted to others as a teacher. His lessons of the Bible and Jewish History not only enriched our treasury of knowledge but also planted a great love in our hearts for the Hebrew language, our folk and our land.

A town where the entire youth spoke Hebrew and even thought in Hebrew was by no means a typical occurrence some fifty years ago. That awesome achievement can be attributed to one person – our honoured teacher, Gad Layb Rakov who taught us Torah for its own sake and not for any prize or reward. Not only was he a wonderful speaker, but he was also a doer. The

Zionist 'Torah' that he taught us was carried out first of all by him. At the beginning of the Second Aliya (immigration to Eretz Yisrael) in 1906, he left everything behind and settled in Eretz Yisrael. With that move, he became a role model for many of his students.

Today, remembering him, I feel as if he lives once again amongst us, his students and his books that he so dearly loved. With deep feelings of gratitude and respect, we, his students, honor his dear memory.

[Page321]

Nachum Matenko, z"l

by Moshe Bick

Translated by Sarah Faerman

Nachum Matenko was a legend and in a legendary manner he disappeared – not even making an appearance in biographies or novels. With other folk, personalities of his caliber are retrieved from their obscurity so that they will not be forgotten. With us, however, they vanish like extinguished stars.

Nachum Matenko did not discover a new planet in any of the numerous skies; he did not produce any "never before spoken words"; he did not introduce any new methods to our way of thinking or in the existing art. He did however raise himself from the Dubossar surroundings and traveled far off into the world – all the way to Moscow where he enthralled all who heard his magnificent voice, his own homegrown talent.

The small town environment where he was born and raised lacked the resources to nurture his unusual talent which was apparent while he was still a child. He was taken on as a choirboy by the Dubossar Cantor, Reb Motel and he awed the worshipers with the sweetness of his voice and the warmth of his singing. He was the blessing that young mothers prayed for... His father was Reb Shmuel Yosef, or, as we called him – "Yossi the Gabai" (trustee) because he was one of the intimate circle of Rabbi Dovid'l Talner, of righteous and blessed memory, and also for a period of time, one of his trustees. He was very active in Chasidic circles and his mother, as the old folks in town told us, was busy with charitable work. Both she and Reb Yossi were well known for their melodious singing of Chasidic melodies, folksongs and lullabies. Nachum's singing talent had its roots in his family. It was a known fact that in the evening, people walking in the street would stand by the house of his sister Tzirl in order to hear her sing lullabies to her child Nachum Peck, who now lives in Argentina.

How did Nachum Matenko manage to leave his close knit family and small town and secure one of the most coveted positions of that time in the choir of the famous Cantor and composer-director, Reb Nisi Belzer in Berdichev? Did that happen with the approval of his parents, relatives and fans or did he have to fight to be able to pursue the development of his talent? The cantorial literature, memoirs and biographies shed no light on this. There is a paragraph in "My Life Story" by the famous artist, Boris Tomashevsky that describes how, when he joined Nisi Belzer's choir as a young child, Nachum was already there:

"Within the choir there were certain gifted individuals. One of them was Nachum Matenko. He had a very rare bass-baritone voice. He was a very handsome man and he wore modern clothes with a top hat. His long hair, artistic brow and graceful deportment elicited great respect and admiration. Looking at Nachum, one could assume that he was an artist of the Kaiser's Opera rather than a chorister in Reb Nisi Belzer's choir. When Nachum left Reb Nisi, he was appointed Cantor of the Great Odessa Synagogue in the place of the renowned Cantor Bochman. The Moscow millionaire, Poliakov, heard Nachman's voice in the Odessa Shul and was so impressed by his talent and personality that he built a synagogue in his courtyard and installed Nachum as Cantor, giving him a life-long contract."

This particular vignette perhaps misses the most important aspect of his struggles as he perfected and honed his abilities in cantorial music. From his clothes alone, one could surmise that he made an effort to elevate himself from his surroundings, saw himself as one who "would become" and apparently dreamt of becoming an opera singer. In order to conceive of wearing a top hat, modern clothing, long hair and to present oneself with a graceful carriage reflected his inner feelings of self worth and dedication.

Yechiel Tzelnik

The fact that he succeeded Bachman indicates that his confidence in himself was not a form of arrogance but rather the sign of a true artistic talent. This was also the impression he made on those who "The Great Odessa Shul" because after Bachman, the search for a replacement was not only for a talented cantor but also one who was an intellectual and a personality as was Bachman. As well, the millionaire Poliakov could afford the best and most gifted cantor for his shul in Moscow. Apparently Nachum satisfied all the above criteria, not only for Poliakov but also for the Muscovites – for the Jewish community and also the gentile intellectual circles.

This growth of Nachum and his outgrowing of his roots would make an interesting psychological study as well as a cultural illumination of our people.

I would like to believe that somewhere in the archives of the Poliakov family or in the dusty cellars of other prominent people of those times; somewhere lie the undiscovered memoirs of singers, artists, community activists, who were in close contact with Nachum Mateno and contain details and insights into the various facets of his personality – the singer, the cantor, the intellectual.

It is interesting that even Eliyahu Zolodkovsky, the writer of the worthy book:

"Culture Carriers of the Jewish Liturgy", (America 1930), was not aware of the above paragraph of Boris Tomashevsky and was satisfied with the following three sentences about Nachum Matenko: "Nisi's famous bass, Nachum Matenko, who later was the cantor of the Poliakov Shul in Moscow, had a phenomenal bass, was a great hero and an exceptionally fine personality. He died in 1894". (page 209). In 1924, "The History of Cantorial Music" was published in conjunction with the 30th anniversary of "The Association of Cantors of America and Canada". There was a picture with the following caption – "Nachum Matenko, the celebrated bass-baritone of Nisi Belzer's choir. Later Moscow Cantor. Died under tragic Circumstances" – and that was all!

From those very brief words, however, one can ferret out two details that are very consistent with the Nachum Matenko legend: "He was a great hero" and "died under tragic circumstances". These two revelations add to our understanding of this individual. Matenko's surviving relatives (Nachum Peck – Argentina and David Layb Granovsky – Israel) relate that a princess of the Russian royal family became enamored, not only with his voice but with his manly good looks. Wherever he went, she would follow him. With a wink from the ' ruling authorities' he was banished from Moscow and he returned to Odessa. It is a mystery to the family however, as to who the person was that slipped poison into Matenko's food. As a result of the poisoning, he became paralyzed. Hero that he was, he slowly overcame his illness and once again sang with all the octaves of his talent... Once again a stealthy hand poisoned his body.

His old mother took him from one doctor to another until finally, in Italy, the soul of Nachum Matenko, kissed by all the muses, departed his body.

[Page326]

Yechiel and Gittl Tzelnik (centre) and family

Yechiel Tselnik, z"l

by Baruch Bassin

Translated by Sarah Faerman

People approach holidays and week-days in their own unique way. Some people embrace the holidays, not only by changing their clothes but by putting on a festive face as well. On the other hand, there are those that even on a holiday do not have the strength to set aside their bitterness and to shrug off the everyday burdens of life. Finally, there is a third type of person, blessed with a very special quality, who on Sabbath and holidays – but also during the week – radiates a tranquil soul – not only in moments of joy but also, God forbid, in times of sorrow. These are the dreamers who observe the world through rose colored glasses and their natural optimism lightens their suffering and gives them strength to overcome with a smile the most difficult adversities.

Our fellow townsman, Yechiel Tselfnik, z"l, belonged to this third category of optimists. In Dubossar he was a wealthy merchant, the father of a large family (he had ten sons and daughters) and was a fervent Zionist. Even before the first World War, he sent one of his sons to study at the Herzlia Gymnasia who also was one of the founders of Kibbutz Kiryat Anavim. In his later years, he realized his goal of settling in Eretz Yisrael where he worked and lived the life of a pioneer. Arriving in the land with his wife, he first lived in a dwelling put together with rags that he himself sewed up. Later, with his own hands, he built himself a small house in the Montefiore district of Tel Aviv. He earned a living first of all by going into partnership in a grocery store and later by building wooden huts.

Before my eyes, I can see Yechiel Tselnik running with two baskets from Tel Nordau to the Shuk Hacarmel (market) and returning with them full and heavy. His face is red and perspiring from the great effort but his eyes are shining and on his face is a blissful smile. Yechiel Tselnik was a good man and in his modest house in the Montefiore district, he took in as a tenant, someone who had arrived on the boat with him, and charged him one groschen rent.

Yechiel Tselnik loved cantorial music. I will never forget how he sat by my father's bed, when he was near the end, and sang many cantorial melodies for my father in order to distract him from his pain. Yechiel was a dear man.

May his memory be honored.

[Page327]

Yechiel Tselnik z"l

by Y. Dunayevsky, z"l

Translated by Sarah Faerman

In our town, I had a bosom buddy, Yechiel Tselnik. He was the owner of the biggest business in Dubossar. His family was large – God blessed him with many sons and daughters. He was a traditional Jew and a devoted Zionist. He loved song and was always humming cantorial music. He particularly worshiped the famous Cantor, Pinchas Minkovsky and every time he returned from a business trip in Odessa, he would bring back a new Cantorial melody.

One bright morning, he confided in me that he was sending one of his sons to Eretz Yisrael: "This will be a good beginning", he said. "After him, the others will follow." That son was one of the founders of Kibbutz Kiryat Anavim and he lives there to this day. Tselnik's hopes were realized. In time, he and his other sons settled in Eretz Yisrael.

On his arrival to the land, he bought a small house in the Montefiore district of Tel Aviv. My friend hoped to live out his years in serenity in our own land. Unfortunately he did not live long in his country. Before his death he requested that he be buried in Kiryat Anavim. His request was granted and there he came for his eternal rest together with his wife. May the earth of Eretz Yisrael be sweet for them both.

[Page328]

Pinchas and Leah Bassin

Pinchas And Leah Bassin, z"l

by Yosef Ram (Visoky) z"l

Translated by Sarah Faerman

They were both refined and spiritual aristocrats, faithful Zionists and enlightened people. Leah and Pinchas Bassin established a wonderful Jewish and Zionistic home in Dubossar. In this spirit they raised their children (one son and two daughters) from early childhood. They transformed their home into a meeting place for Zionists and intellectuals. Often the local Zionist leaders would gather there to discuss Zionist issues or to celebrate National (Jewish) events. Rarely did a guest speaker or celebrity visit Dubossar without being welcomed with full honor into the Bassin home.

We, the young Zionist activists, were additionally grateful to Leah and Pinchas Bassin for permitting us to spend a few hours with our national poet, Chaim Nachman Bialik. He was traveling to Kishinev in connection with the Pogrom that broke out there against the Jews in 1903 and he stopped in at the Bassin's home for a few hours on the way. It was a joyous and inspiring experience for us to sit together with our great poet and to thirstily drink in his wise words that flowed from him as from a fountain.

Leah Bassin was also active in various Zionist and community programs and campaigns for the local institutions.

They settled in Eretz Yisrael in 1926.

May these lines serve as a crown of flowers on their grave.

[Page329]

Yosef Ben Ami (Nahalal)

Yosef Ben Ami of blessed memory

by Hanna Ben Ami

Translated by Eti Horovitz

Yosef was one of the people of the Second Immigration. He came to Israel shortly before the First World War, and as most of the pioneer immigrants of these days he fought the battle of the Hebrew worker for employment, and had many experiences.

Yosef was a man of deed with creative intelligence. He was qualified for many tasks and had a good reputation of being proficient of all branches of farming.

When the First World War began we lived in Beer Yaacov. The engine of the water well was broken and because of the war it was impossible to find a professional to fix it. And even if a professional was found, there was nothing to pay him with. Also the stone coals could not have been found. What did Yosef do? He cut the trees of our small Eucalyptus grove and with his own hands made coals out of the trees.

In 1921 we went with the first settlers to Nahalal. Yosef, who was skilled in construction, became the right hand of the chief engineer, helping building the cowsheds that were built even before the houses. Years later he built the school and the community center in Nahalal. He also made the synagogue of Nahala, planning it from top to bottom. He served there as Gabai until he died.

As mentioned, Yosef was very resourceful. He invented a method of building hen houses on a limited area, and guided the village members how to build their hen houses according to his method that was efficient and inexpensive. He also invented a new model of incubator that was accepted by almost every collective agricultural labor settlements.

At his initiation and under his guidance, the creeks and channels that caused the rain flooding the fields were straightened. This action contributed significantly to the quality of the fields and their readiness for agricultural processing. He also initiated the idea that the waste of the cities will not be burned, but will be made into fertilizer for the agricultural fields.

This was his way all his life in this country: Laborious, diligent, resourceful, and with a lot of understanding of labor and agriculture. Contributed significantly to the establishment of his village and to the collective agriculture labor of the entire country.

May his memory be blessed.

[Page330]

מיכאל ומסיה שטיינברג

מיכאל און מאסיא שטיינבערג

Michael and Masia Steinberg

Michael Steinberg

by Y. Kan-Tor

Translated by Eti Horovitz

Michael Steinberg was an innocent, righteous and honest man. He was born in Dubossar in 1876. He was drawn to the trade of Blacksmith from early childhood. In those days the young trainees were not so fortunate. The craftsmen were exploiting them for house chores that were irrelevant to the profession they had come to learn. It is no wonder then that only a few of the boys lasted long enough to learn the profession properly. But not Michael Steinberg. Thanks to his diligence, his patience and his talent, he became highly professional and was famous all around the area as an artist-blacksmith.

In that period, smithery was not considered a highly valued profession, and blacksmiths were ranked at a low stage on the social scale. However, Michael the Blacksmith was different. His innocence, his integrity and his kindness acquired him good and loyal friends among all layers of society, among Jews and among those who were not Jewish allies. Furthermore, his profession was not an obstacle when he came of age. Masia, daughter of a respectable family in Dubossar fell in love with him and married him. Together they built an excellent home.

When my family had to leave our village and moved to Dubossar, we came to live in the home of Michael the Blacksmith. My parents were delighted living together with the pleasant couple Michael and Masia.

Michael was twenty-five years old when he left Dubossar and moved to Ribnitze, about fifty kilometers from our town. Long after they moved, friends and acquaintances were speaking about them affectionately and respectfully. I remember that even the peasants from the surrounding area used to ask about Michael and were sorry to hear that he left. Michael acquired many friends in Ribnitze also, and was valued in the Jewish Community as well as in the non-Jewish one.

In 1925, Michael and Masia emigrated to Israel following their four sons. Our home in Rishon L'Zion was their first stop. By the next morning after his arrival, Michael made plans for arranging a workshop in the yard where we lived. He said and he did. On his first Shabbat in Israel, all the immigrants from Dubossar and Ribnitze gathered to welcome Michael and Masia. It was an encounter full of events. The people of Rishon L'Zion, our neighbors, could not understand this great honor for the new immigrant, knowing he intended to be just a blacksmith. However, his ability to capture people's hearts solved this riddle rapidly. Not many days passed until Michael became well known as a great craftsman as well as a good, honest man and he acquired quite a reputation. Michael was a gracious man. He honored his wife and cherished her. He educated his sons to love labor and was extremely happy to live in Israel with his entire family.

Since the age of thirteen the hammer and anvil were his loyal companions. "Working is our Life" was not only a slogan for him but the essence of his life. When his wife passed away his hold on the hammer was loosened, meaning the fountain of his existence dried out. And indeed, a short while after her death, he followed her. He was 75 when he died. Michael and Masia – beloved and pleasant, were not separated in their lives and in their deaths.

In honor of their memory.

[Page333]

Moishe Faerman (Winnipeg, Canada)

Moishe Faerman, z"l

by D. L. Granovsky

Translated by Sarah Faerman

Like thunder on a bright summer day, we received the devastating news that Moishe Faerman is no longer among the living. It is difficult to believe; the mind cannot accept it. Just the other day, August 5, 1964, I met with him and lively and happy, he shared his impressions of the World Zionist conference that was held in Bet Berl He spoke with great enthusiasm about the country which he hadn't seen for three years since his last visit to Israel when he was a delegate of the Winnipeg Labour Zionist movement to the twenty-fifth World Zionist Congress. The next day, on August 6th, we accompanied him to the airport in Lod and bid our farewells with the hope that soon he would come back and settle in Israel. On August 7th, a Friday, upon his arrival home, he managed to deliver a report on the conference that very evening to his comrades in the Labour Zionist movement. Two days later, on Sunday August 9th, he was no longer among the living.

Our sages, z"l say: "Whosoever sheds tears over an honest man, these tears are counted by the Almighty and saved." This saying was made to measure for Moishe Faerman. He was a man of great character, pure of spirit, a source of goodness, love and friendship and willing to help every person. He was a good and loyal friend and he served society with great dedication. During his whole life, he faithfully served the Labour Zionist movement in Israel and in the diaspora.

His father died when he was still a child and he came to Dubossar with his mother and a younger brother. From then on, for the following 55 years, we were bound together in a deep friendship that was not broken until the day he died. His death is a great loss for the Jewish community in Canada, for the Labour Zionist movement and for the Dubossar landsmen wherever they live. For me personally, however, Moishe's death is a double loss and a deeper pain. Since our "cheder" school days he was my best and most beloved friend and I am still shocked from this great blow.

From the early days of his youth, Moishe linked his fate with the Labour Zionist movement and at the age of twenty, in the years of 1918-1919, when the pogroms were raging in the Ukraine, he was one of the initiators and pioneers of the first Jewish kvutza (collective farm) in South Russia which would serve as a training ground for working the land in Eretz Yisrael. Later, when he emigrated to Canada, he worked once again on the land. He joined the Jewish Montefiore Colony in Saskatchewan, continuing the path he had taken in Russia, with the intention that it would lead to settling in Eretz Yisrael.

In Canada, Moishe was soon recognized as an honest and involved community activist. After a hard day of work, he would pick up his pen and write articles for the local newspapers relating to a variety of issues – working on the land, Zionism and the Poalei Zion (Jewish workers) movement. He was a devoted Zionist activist, a worker and propagandist for the Jewish National Fund, Keren Hayesod and the Histadrut Campaign (institutions and organizations in and for Israel) as well as being involved in cultural activities. He was also chairman of the Farband (Jewish National Workers' Federation) in his city. In his last years, he was executive secretary of the Talmud Torah School in Winnipeg.

After World War II, in spite of his heavy load of activities, he took on a new task. The great catastrophe had torn apart many families. Moishe searched out addresses and invested much of his efforts into uniting family members, often aiding them materially in their difficult situation.

During his last visit to Israel, thinking seriously of settling in Israel, he said to me while we were parting at the airport at Lod: "Who knows when and if we will see each other again?" He had an intuition that his time was near. We both shed a tear and quietly took our leave of one another.

Moishe died on foreign soil. He did not realize the dream of his youth. At the age of sixty-five, Moishe was torn away from us.

May his name be honored.

[Page335]

Moishe Faerman z"l

by Noah Wittman

Translated by Sarah Faerman

Moishe Faerman arrived in Winnipeg in 1921 at the age of 22 years, with considerable experience in Zionist activities in both his home town of Dubossar and in Odessa. He had been a member of the Central Committee of the Odessa Poalei Zion (Zionist Workers). He came to Winnipeg with an intense Chalutzic (pioneering) fervor and in the first few months that he was here, before he had even settled on the land, he already founded a Polaei Zion organization and soon after that, a Jewish Culture Society. Within one year he became one of the most active members of the aforementioned Poalei Zion. Deep in his heart however, this was not the most important thing in his life. He was a Chalutz through and through and his goal was to start the pioneering life even while in Canada. In Western Canada, he farmed in two of the Jewish farming colonies – the Hirsch Colony in Southern Saskatchewan and in the Montefiore Colony in Alberta – as well as farming on his own. In 1935, he and his family left for Eretz Yisrael where they remained for two years.

On his return to Canada he worked for several years as a storekeeper in the country and later in Winnipeg where he was offered the important position of Executive Director of the Labour Zionist Organization in Winnipeg. From then on he devoted all his efforts into activities on behalf of Israel and cultural programming in the city. He spent 8 years at this position and for the last ten years he held the position of Executive Secretary of Winnipeg's well known Hebrew school, the Talmud Torah with a student body of 700 children. The work provided him with a steady income but his thoughts and soul were bound up with Eretz Yisrael. He remained active in the Labour Zionist movement to the last minute. He had the honour of being chosen as one of the Canadian delegates to the World Zionist Congress that took place in Israel, July 1964. His daughter, Batya, has lived in Israel for 12 years and is well settled on the land with her fine family. It was Moishe's plan to move in the near future to Israel. Suddenly, two days after his return from the Conference, on Sunday, August 9, 1964, he was unexpectedly torn away from us.

May his name be honored.

[Page337]

Baruch Spivak (Kfar Vitkin, 1921-1945)

Baruch Spivak, z"l

Translated by Eti Horovitz

Baruch was born in Dubossar to his parents, Abraham and Dobsha Spivak, on the first day of Hanukah 1921. At the age of three, he came to Eretz Yisrael with his parents. He spent the first years of his childhood in Nahalal and when his parents were among the first to settle in the Hefer Valley, he was one of the first children of Kfar Vitkin. Baruch was the oldest child in the village, and mostly was lonely due to the lack of suitable company of his age. This fact and the difficulties the people of the village experienced as the first pioneers and occupiers of Wadi Howarat, made a mark on Baruch's tender and delicate soul, causing his face to express a seriousness incompatible with his young age.

Because he was the oldest child of Kfar Vitkin, he had the privilege of being the one to draw the raffle tickets in the main event in the village. This raffle was for the assignment of fields for the village members. The committee in charge of the raffle worked hard all day and finished when it was almost midnight. Then, someone suggested that the oldest child in the village should draw the notes from the ballot box. Baruch's father, Abraham, went to wake him up and before wiping the sleep from his eyes, he carried him to the ballot box. With his hands shaking and a smile on his face, he stood on the bench and announced each number drawn out of the ballot box. Thus, the members of Kfar Vitkin received their fields from his hands.

After graduating from elementary school in the village, he continued his studies at the agricultural high school Kaduri, majoring in Agriculture. He thought it was the logical way for a village boy in preparation for his future life.

Baruch was modest and withdrawn. When the Second World War started and the young settlers were called to go to battle against the enemy of the Jewish people, Baruch was among the first who complied with this obligation and tug at the Jewish conscience. He served in the British army for four years in the Hebrew Brigade, and endeared himself to his companions because of his kindness, his generosity, and his willingness to always lend a hand to a pal. Even in the army, he did not forget his origins and was active among the organizers of soldiers for settlement.

During his army service he got married and looked forward to the end of the war, so he could go back to his village as an independent settler. In the last year of his army service, he was infected with a disease that the doctors could not diagnose. He carried his pain silently and heroically with the belief that he would overcome the disease. When he finally went back to the village, he had many plans for his future. He went to the hospital for examinations intending to return to his village within a few days to start building his farm. However, destiny was cruel with him. He went into the hospital but did not get well. The malignant disease, which had struck him during his army service, ended his life when he was only twenty-three years old.

Baruch passed away on sixteenth of Elul, 1945, and was laid to rest in his village – Kfar Vitkin.

[Page338]

Miriam Ben Ami (Israel)

Miriam Ben Ami, z"1

(Daughter of Beryl Dudnik – The Melamed)

by Y. Kan-Tor

Translated by Eti Horovitz

Miriam was one of the first people of the Third Immigration and came to Eretz Yisrael in 1921. She was beautiful and pleasant and had a heart of gold. She lived in Israel almost forty years (passed away on 1960) and none of these years were easy. Unfortunately, her only son, who was so gifted and talented that people predicted greatness, fell ill during childhood and became disabled. Miriam worked hard all of her life, beyond her abilities, in order to be able to handle the therapy for her son. Despite her difficulties, Miriam knew how to hide her sorrow from strangers. She had a heart-warming smile and was very kind. She had a reputation among the people of our town and others as one who was willing to assist friends as well as strangers. Her door was open for anyone in need and her heart to anyone in pain.

Her home was modest, but no one ever felt unwanted or a burden in it. Whoever came to her home, could not leave without having a meal and if anyone ever needed a place to sleep – her home was never too small.

Her face never showed that she had suffered from continuous poverty. She always relied on herself and never asked for help, even in her most difficult times.

Miriam was a woman of valor, a pioneer and a devoted friend. She has been and now she is gone.

[Page340]

Dr. Krasnovitz, z"l

Translated by Sarah Faerman

Dr. Krasnovitz was a physician with a vast medical knowledge and experience. He was friendly with all and was much loved by the people. He was also the crown-appointed "Rabbiner" (non-orthodox rabbi) and many official community documents passed through his hands. In spite of the fact that he was a "Rabbiner", he was far from devout. He was also not nationalistic (Jewish nationalism) but he did many favors for Jews using his influence with the ruling circles. He was one of their crowd, eating and socializing with them. His unique position as friend of those with power was utilized to benefit not only individuals but the community as a whole.

Dr. Altman, z"l

by Y. Dunayevsky, z"l

Translated by Sarah Faerman

Dr. Altman was not born in our town. He came from Kishinev, from a poor family. His father was a tailor - one who mended patches. Thanks to the fact that his father had been a "soldier of Nikolai", he was able to get into university in spite of the quota system. While still a student in the Gymnasia (high school) and later in university, he would find time for Jewish studies, including the holy books.

Dr. Altman was an exceptionally solitary individual. He had no friends, belonged to no organizations and did not involve himself in community affairs. Aside from visiting his patients to check on their progress, he was not seen in the streets. Also, his outlook on life was singular. He was fanatically nationalistic (Jewish nationalism) and religious. He expressed his fanaticism in his own unique way: Mankind was compared to a huge army, organized into regiments, brigades and platoons. In the same way that each division is recognized by its distinctive uniform, so also is Mankind divided into different ethnic groups. And, in the same way that a soldier in the military cannot move to a different division and change his uniform – because it is tight or confining – as this would undermine the whole, thus also, a folk cannot take off its uniform, i.e. his uniqueness. The Jewish religion is the uniform of our folk and as long as we do not have a national-religious Jewish judicial body with the proper authority to carry out the changes that the times demand, every Jew is obligated, as a soldier in the Jewish corps to protect his uniform. It is our national duty to guard our Jewish religion; otherwise we will not survive among the nations.

Dr. Altman was somewhat of an "oddball" but he was a loyal soldier in his division and to his folk. he was, alas, not long with us for he died during his prime years.

May his memory be honored.

[Page342]

Hershl Zionist

by Yosef Visoky (Ram)

Translated by Sarah Faerman

All of his friends and acquaintances knew him by the name "Hershl Zionist". A quiet man was Hershl and modest, but with a warm Jewish heart. He made his living as a porter. During the cold, winter days when there was little work to be had because of the rain and snow, Hershl, unlike the other porters who frequented the taverns to get drunk and play cards, would make his way to the Tzeirei Tzion (Young Zion) organization. There, amongst the Zionist youth he would quench his thirsty soul and find rest for his weary body.

Hershl came from the lowest economic strata of society and from early childhood was no stranger to heavy physical labour. It is no wonder that he had almost no schooling at all. He was, however, blessed with a warm and sensitive heart and the spirit that reigned at the Tzeirei Tzion lectures that he listened to so attentively, planted in him a strong love of Eretz Yisrael and a deep belief in the fulfillment of Zionist goals.

With wholehearted zeal, he would apply himself to any and every Zionist task that was requested of him and he would carry this out faithfully and with diligence. If a speaker arrived in town and needed help with his arrangements, Hershl would undertake this assignment; if the Zionist youth planned an event, Hershl would do all of the heavy work even when it entailed missing a day's work and the income thereof; if there ever was a good deed to be done on behalf of the Zionists, he never avoided it. Knowing of his tight financial situation, we often wanted to pay him for a day's work but he positively refused saying: "This is holy work and that is my pay."

During his whole life, his heart yearned to fulfill his dream and settle in Eretz Yisrael. With the strength of this belief and hope, he overcame much suffering in the oppressive exile. Unfortunately luck did not light his way and he was murdered by the Nazi beasts that shattered his life and his dreams.

May these words serve as monument and memory of the good hearted, innocent devotee of Zion – Hershl – who did not live to tread on its soil.

[Page344]

Zelig The Dyer

by Y. Dunayevsky, z"1
Translated by Sarah Faerman

It was during the dawn of Zionist activity in Russia, which was in part legal and mostly illegal. The Zionist activities were carried out from five different locations. One of these was Kishinev (40 kilometers away) under the leadership of Dr. Bernstein-Cohen. Dubossar, with a very active Zionist organization was under the jurisdiction of Kishinev. Among those who frequented the Zionist events in Dubossar, was a simple Jew – Zelig the Dyer. Why he was called "the Dyer" I do not know for as far as I remember, he was a small wheat merchant. This Zelig was well known in Dubossar. He was a dear man and in his heart there was a great love for Eretz Yisrael.

One day, Zelig came to me and said: "I would like to request something from you. I want to be active in our organization but I am a simple person and can't see myself contributing in any way to the Zionist effort except, perhaps, like a beadle, be available to perform any task that needs to be done. I am prepared to do any work or carry out any assignment you would like me to do. With my whole heart, I would like to contribute my share, no matter what, for our Zionist goals." I was happy to fulfill his request and since that day Zelig would faithfully apply himself to any task that was assigned to him.

Years flew by. I went to live in Odessa and for years I neither saw Zelig nor heard from him. One morning, when I was sitting in my office, the door opened and in walked Zelig. This time he was all spiffed up, his hair was combed neatly and his face was beaming.

– "What good news do you have?" I asked him.

– "I came to bid you farewell and also to receive your blessing."

– "Where are you going, Zelig?"

– "What do you mean, where am I going!" answered Zelig, Where does a Jew go? To Eretz Yisrael!"

– "Are you going alone?"

– "No. We are all going – the old and young – Me, my wife and my five sons."

I was surprised. Zelig understood my bewilderment and added: "Why are you surprised? I didn't sit down to make any great calculations. One fine morning, I just got up, sold my meager belongings, bid farewell to my town and that's that... I'm leaving for Eretz Yisrael... and if you will ask me:"What about travel expenses?

Bah!! That doesn't worry me. What, will you and the other Zionists allow the ship to sail away and allow Zelig and his family to be left behind in Odessa?"

Zalman did not err in his reasoning. He was not left behind in Odessa. Sometime later, I received regards informing me that Zelig and his family had arrived safely in Eretz Yisrael. They were now more or less settled in and he was happy to have actualized his love of Zion.

[Page345]

David Puchis (Ein Ganim)

David Pochis, z"l

by Yeshayahu Kan-Tor

Translated by Eti Horovitz

One Shabbat, upon my arrival to Eretz Yisrael in the early twenties, I visited an immigrant from Yagorlik, David Pochis, who had come with the Second Immigration and who was a member of Ein Ganim. I came to his home for two reasons. One was to visit someone who came from the same area as I, and the second was to have an agriculture lesson from him, since he was a guide of agriculture and practical labor.

He lived by the principles of the "Cooperative Settlement" even before these were accepted as a way of life.

He had an orchard of 10 square kilometers and there he did everything that was necessary by himself: the hoeing at the end of the fruit picking, pruning, digging holes, watering, etc. When the time for fruit picking came he did all the labour himself – he picked the fruits and brought them to his packinghouse; He sorted the fruits, wrapped them, prepared the boxes, and after packing, brought them to the packing house. In addition to the orchard, he had a cow, a goat and a henhouse with eight hens that laid eggs.

He took care of all of them himself, including the selling of the produce. That way he complied with the principle of "Self-Labor" – the first element of the "Cooperative Settlement".

He used to help to whoever asked him – sometimes with loans, and some by collaterals. All pioneers needed help. More than once he paid from his own money, loans that vouched for and protected those that could not honor their commitment. "If they are not paying", he would say, " they probably cannot pay "Yet, he never received the same assistance even in his most difficult times. Then everybody he had helped forgot him. He was a giver and not a receiver.

By that, he followed the principle of mutual assistance – the second element of the "Cooperative Settlement".

David Pochis was not a man of ideology. He did not write principles. He carved them from his heart and engraved them with a shovel and a hoe upon his land. Because of that, the principles by which he lived his life were part of his being. In his work and in his way of life he molded his character – a character of a Hebrew farmer who works his land, a man of truth and integrity.

He was an innocent and honest man, humble and moderate, and after he passed away, no one bothered to commemorate him. May these few paragraphs remain as a modest memorial candle for the life and deeds of a person who shaped a generation of builders and self-actualizers who worked for his country and the idea of renewal with all his heart and not in order to be rewarded. May his memory be blessed.

[Page347]

Yitzchak Puchis. (Killed near Kfar Etzion, 1947)

Yitzchak Pochis, z"l

Translated by Eti Horovitz

Yitzchak Pochis was born in 1925 to his parents, David and Chaya, who were among the founders of Ein Ganim. He studied in the Ein Ganim Elementary School and continued his studies in Ehad-Ha'am High School in Petach Tikva. He served two years as a guard and in 1943 went to study Education in the Levinsky Teachers College. In 1944 he graduated from College and was hired as a teacher in a Night School for Working Youth in Petach Tikva, and as an instructor in the local playgrounds. He moved to Jerusalem, completed his studies in The Hebrew University and continued working in the Jerusalem Schools for Working Youth.

He was active in the "Haganah" from the age of 14 and achieved the rank of Commander. He was one of the founders of the magazine "Hashalom" issued in memory of Shalom Shtreit z"l, for poetry of youth.

He was a poet himself and wrote many songs with great talent. On 28th of Kislev (11.12.1947) he led a convoy that went to bring supplies to the warriors in Kefar Etzion on Mount Hebron. On their way, Arab rioters attacked them. Yitzhak fought heroically and lost his life in this battle.

An Individual from the Ranks

by Yitzchak Puchis, z"l

For the memory of a friend who died in battle

Young trees of the homeland,
lower your heads to the ground.
Dear trees of the homeland
your height has been cut off.

Be silence, do not move. The green
avenues -
the vile cutter is in your borders!
A shameful hand conspired against purity
Waved an ax at a martyr. -

It will dry-off, this soiled hand
the deep pain will not be healed

Be silence, friends! He is gone
He will never return here;
Look, in the rising darkness
the spark of his great legacy is still
burning.

[Page348]

Tzvi Hirsh (Hershl) Tulchinsky. (Winnipeg, Canada)

Tzvi Hirsch Tulchinsky, z"l

by D. L. Granovsky

Translated by Sarah Faerman

On the fourteenth of December, 1964, while driving in his car, Hershl Tulchinsky (Harry Toole) died suddenly at the age of 65 years. His sudden death was a painful blow in Winnipeg especially in his large circle of family and friends where Harry was much loved.

He was Moishe Faerman's step-brother, both of the same age and from the age of 5 years, they were raised in Dubossar. Both absorbed in cheder the love of yiddishkeit, the Jewish folk and Eretz Yisrael.

In 1922 he emigrated to Canada with his parents and together with his brother Moishe, settled on the land in Saskatchewan and Alberta. Later, upon moving to Winnipeg, Harry threw himself into commercial enterprises where he was very successful and became a respected business man.

All the years of his life, Harry remained a loyal Zionist, active in the national Farband (Workers' Federation in Israel) and donated to all Jewish causes with an open hand. In his last years, he was planning to move to Israel. Unfortunately his death cut down his productive life leaving his many friends and family wrapped in grief.

A dear, warm hearted, quiet man was Tzvi Tulchinsky and everyone who came in contact with him, loved him.

May his memory be honored.

[Page350]

Mendl Zeltzer

Mendl Zeltzer, z"l

by Y. Kantor

Translated by Sarah Faerman

Although Mendl Zeltzer was a big tobacco merchant, he was not wealthy. In his day to day routine, he presented himself as an affluent person, giving to charity with a generous hand. If any needy person approached him, he would never leave empty handed.

Mendl had a sweet, pleasant voice and it was a pleasure to hear him sing. He was therefore a guest at every poor wedding and with his singing would liven up the festivities and make the bride and groom, with their families, very happy. He was admired as a Baal Tefila (leader of prayers in shul) and synagogues would vie to have him daven (pray) at their shuls. Mendl, however, would never accept a fee for singing in a shul. On the contrary, he would turn down offers from the large, popular shuls and would pray during the high holidays at a shul that was experiencing financial hardships in order to help them out with his participation in the communal prayers.

His daughters, God forbid, did not marry without a very substantial dowry. Nevertheless – before going to the chupa (wedding canopy), the groom knew that the next day he would have to return this dowry to his father-in-law who had borrowed this sum from a friend. As far as the world knew, Mendl Zeltzer had provided generous dowries for his daughters.

In his old age, he became partially paralyzed and it was difficult for him to speak without a stammer. With great effort, he would go out in the street and with his last strength; he endeavored to present himself with a positive spirit. Every person he met, he would ask: "Have you by any chance seen Mendl Zeltzer?" He laughed at his own fate.

That was Mendl Zeltzer. Even in his worst days, his spirit was not broken.

May his memory be honored.

[Page351]

Kalman Levinshtein (Winnipeg, Canada)

Kalman Levenstein, z"l

Translated by Sarah Faerman

Kalman Levenstein emigrated to Canada from Russia in 1920. His first years were in Montreal and later he settled in Winnipeg where he remained for the rest of his life. All his years, he was active in the Poalei Zion (Zionist Workers' Party), an executive member of the Peretz-Folk School, affiliated with the National Workers' Farband, the Canadian Jewish Congress and other institutions as well. Wherever he invested his time and efforts, he worked thoroughly and with devotion. Modest and unassuming, he was loved by everyone. On the 9th day of September, 1963, he was torn away from his family and friends.

We mourn his loss.

[Page353]

Dubossary, Moldova

Photos and Lists of Deceased and Murdered
In Eternal Memory of those who died in Argentina
Translated by Sarah Faerman

[Page354]

In memory of those who died in Argentina

שרה בענדערסקי   זאב בענדערסקי

(פארצייבנט דער) (פארצייבנט דורך דער

נאנטער בומע און מאן שאבטער בומע און מאן

לעאן רוברן)   לעאן רוברן)

Sarah Bendersky   **Zev Bendersky**

רחל איצקאוויטש

(פארצייבנט דורך איר

זין משה און פרוי ראסא

איצקאוויטש)

Rachel Itzkovitch

פערל בערמאן דע
בענדערסקי
(פארצייבנט דורך דעם
שוואגער און שוועגערין
ליאן און מינע רובין)

מארקאס בענדערסקי
(פארצייבנט דורך זיין
שוועסטער מינע און
שוואגער ליאן רובין)

צבי בערסודסקי
(פארצייבנט דורך זיין
שוועסטער שיינדע
וועלדער)

Pearl Berman   **Marcus Bendersky**   **Tzvi Bersudsky**
Bendersky

יוסף מאנעם האלפערן
(פארצייבנט דורך זיין
ברודער אלכסנדר
האלפערן)

דוד און חנה ווינאקור
(פארצייבנט דורך זייער טאכטער רבקה וו. דין
טאמילאף)

דינה גענשענגארן
(פארצייבנט דורך אירע
קינדער: שמחת, פעסי,
צבי און אברהם)

Yosef Manes Halpern   **David and Chana Winoker**   **Dena Genshengaren**

Name(s)	Submitter(s)
Rachel Itzkavitch	son Moshe and wife Rosa
Zev Bendersky Sarah Bendersky	daughter Chume and husband Leon Rubin
Tzvi Bersidsky	sister Genia Zeltzer
Marcus Bendersky	sister Chume and husband Leon Rubin
Pearl Berman, nee Bendersky	in-laws Chume and husband Leon Rubin
Dena Genshengarin	children Simcha, Pessy, Tzvi and Avraham
David and Chana Vinakur	daughter Rivka Samilof
Yosef Manes Halpern	brother Alexander Halpern

[Page355]

Died in Argentina

צבי יערזאלימסקי
נרינדער פון
דובאסאריער פאראיין
אין ארגענטינע
(פארצייבנט דורך זיין
ברוי שרה)

קלמן זעלצער
(פארצייבנט דורך זיין
שאסטער חנה ז. דזן
מעלבאן אין פאמיליע)

צבי זעלצער
(פארצייבנט דורך זיין
ברוי זשעני און
פאמיליע)

Tzvi Yeruzalimsky   **Kalman Zeltzer**   **Tzvi Zeltzer**

שלמה סאמאילאף
(פארצייכנט דורך זיין
פרוי ריווע און קינדער)

Shloime Samailof

יוסף סאמאילאף
(פארצייכנט דורך זיין
זון חיים און פאמיליע)

Yosef Samailof

עזריאל כהן (כאגאן)
(פארצייכנט דורך זיין
פרוי חענע לאה און זון
ליזאן)

Ezriel Cohen (Kagan)

וועלוול פאלינסקי
(פארצייכנט דורך די
מאכמער גיטל און
פאמיליע)

Velvl Polinsky

לייקע פאלינסקי
(פארצייכנט דורך איר
מאכמער גיטל און
פאמיליע)

Layke Polinsky

טייבל ווינאקר
דע סאמאילאף
(פארצייכנט דורך איר
מאכמער עליסא)

Taibl Vinoker Samailof

Name(s)	Submitter(s)
Tzvi Zeltzer	wife Jenny and family
Kalman Zeltzer	daughter Chana Melman and family
Tzvi Yeruzalimsky (founder of Dubassar Assoc. in Argentina)	wife Sarah.
Ezriel Cohen (Kagan)	wife Hene Leah and son
Yosef Samailof	son Chaim
Shloime Samailof	wife Reva and children
Taibl Vinoker,nee Samailof	daughter Elisa
Laike Polinsky Velvl Polinsky	daughter Gitl and family

[Page356]

רבקה קיפניס־זעלצער און אירע טעכטער
אסתר, מלכה און עטי
פֿאַרצייכנט דורך חנה און וועלוויל זעלצער און
פֿאַמיליעס)

**Rivka Kipnis Zeltzer
and daughters - Esther,
Malka and Etti**

הירש און ציפע שטיינבערג
פֿאַרצייכנט דורך זייער זון לעאן און פֿאַמיליע)

Hirsh and Tzipa Steinberg

מרדכי ראשקעוואן
(מוסלעוו)
פֿאַרצייכנט דורך זיין
פֿריי גאלדע) (דובאסאר)

**Mordecai
Rashkevan**

Name(s)	Submitter(s)
Mordecai Rashkavan (Suslov)	wife Golda (Dubossar)
Hirsch and Tzipa Shteinberg	son Leon and family
Rivka Kipnis-Zeltzer and daughters Esther, Malka and Etty	Chana and Velvl Zeltzer

In memory of those who died in America

יוסף קיסנים
פילאדעלפיע (אמעריקע)

אברהם (אייבי) סאבאל
(ניו־יארק)

די מוטער פון לייביש
לואי לעווין (אמעריקע)

Yosef Kipnis (Philadelphia)

**Abraham Sobol
(New York)**

**Mother of Laybish Louis Levine
(U.S.A.)**

פנחם ספיטניק
(וויניפעג — קאנאדע)
(פארצייכנם דורך זיין
שוועסטער
רייזל לעווינשטיין)

**Yehuda Spitnik and wife
(Canada)**

**Pinchas Spitnik
(Winnipeg)**

**David and Serl Tulchinsky
(Winnipeg, Canada)**

Name(s)	Submitter(s)
Mrs. Levine	son Laybish, Louis Levine
Avraham (Abie) Sobol, New York	
Yosef Kipnis, Philadelphia	

In memory of those who died in Canada

Name(s)	Submitter(s)
David and Serl Tulchinsky, Winnipeg, Canada	
Pinchas Spitnik	sister Raizel Levenstein
Yehuda and Chava Spitnik	daughter

[Page357]

In memory of those who died in Argentina
No photos

Name(s)	Submitter(s)
Chaim Shmuel and Dobrish Nisenzon	by sons Shimon, Moshe ,Efraim and families
Mendl and Esther Koshnitsky	grandson Berl Finkle
Israel Koshnitsky	son Berl Finkle
Israel Yakov and Chava Rempel	daughter Sima Soibelman
Menachem Mendl Zev and Fayga Ranya Zeltzer	daughter Zena Zeltzer
Avraham and Judith Katzefman	son Shmerl Katzefman
Aaron (Orke) and Shaindl Kiner	son Moishe Kiner

[Page358]

In memory of those who died in Israel

ישעיהו און פערל דונאיעווסקי

Yishayahu and Pearl Donayevsky

בת שבע חכמאוויטש

Bat Sheva Chochomovitch

יונה-טאניא קנ־תיר

Yona Tanya Kantor

דוד חכמאוויטש

David Chochomovitch

שרה ספיטניק

Sarah Spitnik

דוד ספיטניק

David Spitnik

חיים ראקאוו

Chaim Rakov

ציפורה פרייבערג־דודניק

Tzipora Freeberg-Dudnik

מענדל מלמד

Mendl Melamed

העניע גאלדינער

יוחנן גאלדינער

בנימין איצקאוויטש
(פארצייכנט דורך זיין
זין משה און פרוי ראזא
פון ארגענטינע)

Henya Goldiner

Yochanan Goldiner

**Benjamin Itzkovitch
(submitted by his son
Moshe and wife Rosa in
Argentina)**

שמעון זשענין

רפאל זעלצער

אפרים איש הורוויין הלוי
(פארצייכנט דורך זיין
פרוי שיינדל און קינדער)

Shimon Zhenin

Raphael Zeltzer

**Efraim Ish Horvitz Halevi
(submitted by wife Shayndl
and children)**

חיים לעווין

Chaim Levine

מאסיא ליטמאנאוויטש

Masya Litmonovitch

לייב ליטמאנאוויטש

Layb Litmonovitch

Name(s)

Yeshayahu and Perl Dunayevsky

David Chachamovitch

Yona Mania Kantor

Bat Sheva Chachamovitch

David Spitnik

Sarah Spitnik

Mendl Melamed

Tzipora Freiberg-Dudnik

Chaim Rakov

[Page359]

In memory of those who died in Israel
No photos

Name(s)

Bracha Shochat

Rivka Shochat Sverdlov (wife of teacher Rafael Sverdlov)

Liba Filler

Rachel Feinbron

Aaron Feinbron

Mrs. Kris – mother of Tzvi Kris and Esther Brodsky

Laib Shteinberg

Orlinsky (Butcher in Atlit) and his wife

Yosef Visoky Ram

Gad Layb Rachav

Yechiel Zelnik and wife

Yosef Ben Ami

Michael Shteinberg and wife

Miriam Ben Ami

Yeshay Dunivsky and wife

David Chochomovitch and wife

Yona Kantor

Baruch Spivak

Chaim Rachav

Israel Zeltzer

Zika Yankelevitch

Harav R'Chaim David Dayan and wife

parents of Pinchas Spector

daughter of Yechiel Zelnick

Michael Tamashin and wife

Pinchas and Leah Bassin

In memory of those who died in Dubossar
No photos

Name(s)

Chaim Mordecai Kris (dedicated teacher)

Shloime Shochat

Hirsh Leyb Berman

Shmuel David Valovsky (father of Fruma Granovsky)

Avraham Yakov Filchikov and wife (A learned Talmud Chochem)

Chaim Dorfman

Aaron Maier Suslensky and wife – (murdered in Mashkutzy and buried in Dubossar)

Isaac Ben Moshe David Melamed (murdered)

Yakov Wargon (murdered)

Peretz Lambritzky (murdered)

Yitzhak Boider (murdered)

Shmuel Chirkis and wife.

{no page number after 359]

In memory of those who died in Israel
No photos

[Page361]

שאול און ציפורה ספיוואק   ר' דוד ליפשין און פרייי

Shaul and Tzipora Spivak   **Reb David Lifshin and wife**

רחל פיינשיל   דינה פילער   יצחק ספיוואק

Rachel Fainshi   **Dena Filler**   **Yitzchak Spivak**

ברוך קיפניס   סאסי קיפניס   רחמיאל פאסטאלאוו

Baruch Kipnis   **Sossy Kipnis**   **Yerachmiel Fastalov**

Name(s)

Reb David Lifshin and wife

Shaul and Tzipora Spivak

Yitzchak Spivak

Dena Filler

Rachel Feinshil

Yerachmil Fastalov

Sossi Kipnis

Baruch Kipnis

[Page 362]

סערל צעלניק

Perl Tzelnik

שאטל צעלניק

Tatl Tzelnik

ישראל צעלניק

Israel Tzelnik

הערש לייב קוטשוק

**Hersh Layb
Kotchok**

איסר צעלניק

Isser Tzelnik

יוסף קוטשוק
(יאסל מאשקאוויצער)
סבא של גב' גרנובסקי

**Yosef Kotchok
(Yosl Moshkovitzer,
grandfather of
Mrs. Granovsky)**

צישרה ספיוואק

עקיבא און גאלדע צעלניק

שרה סוחרמן-חכמוביץ
(נפטרה באַרץ)

Tzipora Spivak   **Akiva and Golda Tzelnik**   **Sarah Soicherman
-Chochomovitch
(died in Israel)**

Name(s)

Israel Tzelnik

Matl Tzelnik

Pearl Tzelnik

Yosef Kotchok (Yosl Moshkovitzer – grandfather of Fruma Granovsky)

Isser Tzelnik

Hersh Layb Katchok

Sarah Sukerman – Chachamovitch (died in Israel)

Akiva and Golda Tzelnik

Tzipora Spivak

[Page363]

הרב ר' שמואל פנחם ראבינאוויטש און פרוי
(פארצייכנט דורך זייער זון לעאן און פרוי קומע
רובין פון ארגענטינע)

Rabbi Shmuel Pinchas Rabinovitch and wife

העריטל און עטל שאפער

Hershl and Ettl Shafer

נח שטיינבערג און זיין פרוי פייגע

Noah and Batya Steinberg

Name(s)

Harav R'Shmuel Pinchas
  Raboniovitch and wife

Hershl and Etl Shafer

Noah Steinberg and wife Fayga
  (3 children in photo)

Submitter(s)

son Leon and wife Chuma Rubin, Argentina

[Page364]

Murdered by the Nazis

עזריאל גראנאווסקי

שלמה און צילא גראנאווסקי

מלכה גראנאווסקי
די מוטער פון דער
משפחה גראנאווסקי

Azriel Granovsky   **Shlomo and Tzila Granovsky**   **Malka Granovsky**

מיכאל מאלאמוד

ישראל און שרה וואלאווסקי פון יאגארילק

Sarah Spitnik   **Israel and Sarah Volovsky from Yagorlik**

הערשל לעווין   נח ליפשין און אירע קינדער חנה און עמנואל   נחמן לייזער ליפשין

Hershl Levin   **Chana Lifshin and children**   **Nachman Laizer**
                         Chava and Emanuel   **Lifshin**

Name(s)

Malka Granovsky (David Granovsky's mother)

Shloime and Tzila Granovsky

Azriel Granovsky

Israel and Sarah Volovsky (of Yagarilk)

Michael Melamud

Nachman Laizer Lifshin

Chana Lifshin and children Anna and Emanuel

Hershl Levine

[Page365]

רבקה טייטעלבוים־כ״ץ
(נחום טייטעלבוים׳ס טאכטער)

שרה דייזער מאכטער

פיניע כ״ץ

Rivka Teitelboim Katz	**Sarah Katz**	**Pinyeh Katz**
(Nahum Teitelboim's	**(their daughter)**	
daughter)		

אהרן טייטלבוים

ענע ביק
(ממשפחת טייטלבוים)

נחום טייטלבוים
(נחום דער בעקער)

Aharon Teitelboim

Anna Beck
(neé Teitelboim)

Nachum Teitelboim
(the baker)

חיה שרה פאליאק,
נחום טייטלבוים'ס
אן אייניקל

Chaya Sarah Polyak
(Nachum Teitelboim's
granddaughter)

Name(s)	Submitter(s)
Cohen Family – Pinye Katz, his wife – Rivka Taitelbaum Katz (Nachum Taitelbaum's daughter) and their daughter Sarah	
Nachum Taitelbaum (the baker)	
Anna Bick (Taitelbaum family)	
Aaron Taitelbaum	
Chaya Sarah Poliak (Nachum Taitelbaum's grandaughter)	Nachum Taitelbaum's daughter in America and Moshe Bick in Israel

[Page366]

לוי פיינשיל   הערשל פאסטאלאוום דריי קינדער   הערשל פאסטאלאוו

Levi Feinshil   **Hershl Postalov's three children**   **Hershl Postalov**

אידא קצבמאַן

Ida Katzavman

אסתּר הינדע קצבמאַן און זשעני בערלין

**Esther Hinda Katzavman
and Jenny Berlin**

ברוך קצבמאַן

Baruch Katzavman

אברהם דונאַיעווסקי
דערשאָסן געוואָרן דורך
די סאָוויעטן פאַר

**Avraham
Dunayevsky
(shot by the Soviets
for Zionist activity).**

רבקה קאַנטאָר־סרולעװיטש
און איר מאַן בצלאל
און זייערע קינדער

**Rivka Kantor-Srulevitch,
husband Betzalel and children**

פסח קיפּניס

Pesach Kipnis

Name(s)

Hershl Fastalov

Hershl Fastalov's three children

Levi Feinshil

Baruch Katzavman

Esther Hinda Katzavman and Jenny Berlin

Ida Katzavman

Pesach Kipnis

Rivka Kantor Srulevitch, husband Bezalele and their two children

Avraham Dunayevsky – (shot by the Soviets for Zionis activity)

[Page367]

מרדכי שאַרגאַראַדסקי און זײן פֿרױ בעלאַ

Mordecai and Bella Shargaradsky

עטל קיפּניס און איטע יאַנאָװער
איטע יאַנאָװער אומגעקומען

Etl Kipnis and Ita Yanover (killed)

אבא שאפער און פרוי

Abba Shafer and wife

פסח און פענע לעווין וויער און חיים
און זייערע אייניקלאך

רייזל פילשטיקאוו, דינה גורעוויטש, ברכה
פילשטיקאוו, חנה אימאם (אומגעקומען) אסתר
קיסניס — צדדיקעט שטייט — איז געבליבן לעבן

Pesach and Fenna Levine (Levy),
son Chaim and grandchildren.

Raizel Pilchikov, Dena Gurevitch,
Bracha Pilchikov, Chana Imam (killed),
Esther Kipnis (standing) survived

Name(s)

Ethel Kipnis and Ita Yanover (Ita murdered)

Mordecai and Bella Shargarodsky

Abba Shafer and wife

Pesach and Fenah Levin, son Chaim and grandchildren

Rayzl Pilchikov, Dena Gurevitch, Bracha Pilchikov, Chana Imas (murdered), Esther Kipnis (alive)

[Page377]

I Shall Cry Out No Longer

by D. L. Granovsky

Translated by Batya Fromm

No! I shall cry out no longer

and my bitter roar will terrify no longer

I shall become one with human suffering in hidden places

and mingle with my fallen, and wander among the graves.

My burning tear has also dried

among mounds of ashes, fires of life and labor

Day and night my heart will quiver

until my time will come –

I shall not be forever silent.

[Page 368]

Dubossary – Moldova
Murdered by the Nazis
Translated by Sarah Faerman

Aleph

Averbach, Elke and children: Sender, Ettl, Betty, Moshe, Chaikeh, Shmuel, Laykeh, Kalman, and Lyuba

Averbach, Abraham

Anitzkaner, Abraham and Kresl and child

Averbach, Noah (Noykeh)

Averbach, Isaac

Apt, Pesach and wife

Apter, Yehuda

Apter, Chaya

Apter, Lenya

Apter, Paulia

Apter, Reva

Apter, Clara

Aidelman, Matil, his wife and child

Aidelman, Buria and son

Itzkovitz, Ida and Zelig and children

Imas, Baruch

Imas, Dvorah

Imas, Ita

Imas, Zusi

Oksenhorn, Chana – Motl the shoichet's daughter

Oksenhorn, Lena – one year old

Oksenhorn, Zev Volodya

Orman, Yosef

Orman, Leah

Orman, Naomi

Orman, Chana

Orman, Isya

Orman, Shmuel

Orman, Moshe

Orman, Betzalel

Orman, Gitl

Aidelman, Motl and wife

Bet

Two sons of Burya

Borochovitch, Mariasy

Borochovitch, Sima

Borochovitch, Kayla

Borochovitch, Liza

Borochovitch, Mayer

Borlak, Chaikeh

Borlak, Sima

Berkovitch, Bluma and Zalman and children

Benderesky, Baruch

Benderesky, Nisl

Benderesky, Laya

Benderesky, Falya

Benderesky, Sarah

Brilyan, Moshe, Tobeh and children

Berelechis, Shmuel

Berelechis, Liba

Berelechis, Berl

Berelechis, David

Bragar, Hertz

Buzher, Yosef (kabab)

Buzher, Freda

Buzher, Nina

Buzher, Grisha

Bezfrizvani, Moshe, Elka and children

Barbarovitch, Chaim

Barbaraovitch, Hinda

Barbarovitch, Sarah

Barbarovitch, Fanny

Bartnik, Layb, wife and daughter

Berezovsky, Boris

Berezovsky, Leah

Berezovsky, Nachum

Berezovsky, Isaac

Berezovsky, Chaya

Bard, Isaac

Bard, Pessy

Bard, Shloimeh

Butashansky, Etka

Butashansky, Pinye

Butashansky, Nachum

Barnboim, Nisl, Reva and children

Batalsky, Yankl, wife and daughter

Benderman, Solomon

Benderman, Sarah

Benderman, Moshe

Benderman, Naphtali

Banderevsky, Arkey, Elya and son Hersh

Breitman, Zalman

Breitman, Leah

Breitman, Baruch from Yagarlik

Breitman, Gisia

Gimmel

Guravitch, Moshe

Guravitch, Gedalia

Guravitch, Zalman

Guravitch, Berl, Chaikeh and children

Goldenberg, Abraham

Goldenberg, Chaim David

Goldenberg, Ettya

Greenberg, Isaac – 100 years old

Greenberg, Simcha

Greenberg, Chaya

Giterman, Rayzl

Giterman, Noah

Giterman, Shmerl

Giterman, Chana

Giterman, Sosya

Glinberg, Naftali

Glinberg, Bluma

Glinberg, Faygeh

Glinberg, Mordecai

Glinberg, Isaac

Gostik, Rosa

Gostik, Layka

Greenberg, Shmuel

Greenberg, Toya

Greenberg, Zena

Greenberg, Shimon

Greenberg, Manya

Greenberg, Ida

Greenberg, Reva

Gantmacher, Sender

Gantmacher, Masya

Gantmacher, Velvl Chana and children

Goldenberg, Abraham

Goldenberg, Chana

Goldenberg, Baruch

Goldenberg, Reuven

Goldmacher, Sender

Goldmacher, Pesach

Guzinyatsky, Jacob

Guzinyatsky, Chana

Guzinyatsky, Chaim

Guzinyatsky, Fanny

Granovsky, Malka wife of Baruch and son Granovsky,Simcha, wife Malya, and children: Betty, Ita, Gavriel, and Chaya

Granovsky, wife of Yudl and children

Granovsky,Shloimeh,Tzila and children

Granovsky,Ezriel,wife and child

Granovsky,Israel ben Moshe

Guravitch, Jacob

Guravitch, Chana

Granovsky,Malka ,Noah and children

Greenblatt,Alter and wife

Gurayevsky,Nachum

Gurayevsky, wife of Moshe

Girayevsky, child Isaac

Gurayevsky , child Raya

Gurayevsky, Joseph

Goldstein, Abraham,wife and children

Goldenberg, Hersh

Goldenberg, Sarah

Goldenberg, Chaya

Gershkovitch, Manya

Gershkovitch, Yechiel

Gershkovitch, Liany

Dalet

Dayan, Moshe

Dayan, Toba

Dobchis, Aaron, Golda and children

Dayan, Baruch

Dayan, Izya

Dayan, Leah

Dayan, Shifra

Dishka, David, wife and daughter

Dunayevsky, Baruch

Dunayevsky, Chava

Dorfman, Godl

Dorfman, Rafael, mother and father

Dubitzky, Zelig

Dubitzky, Shmuel

Dubitzky, Zev (Velvl)

Dashevsky, Yudl

Dashevsky, Tzila

Dashevsky, Rosa

Hay

Hoichman, Shmuel

Hoichman, Shulia

Hoichman, Shalom

Hoichman, Sender, wife and son Shmuel

Horowitz, Abraham, wife and son from Yagarlik

Vov

Varshavsky, Eliezer

Varshavsky, Mordecai

Varshavsky, Faygeh

Vaysman, Shloymeh

Vaysman, Shifra

Vaysman, Esther

Vaysman, Bayla

Vayserman, Abraham

Vayserman, Shloimeh

Vayserman, Sonya

Vayserman, Liba

Vayserman, Monya

Vayserman, Tzvi (Hershl)

Vayserman, Arkeh

Vayserman, Shloimeh

Vayserman, David

Vayserman, Chaykeh

Vayserman, Maleh

Vayserman, Moishe

Vayserman, Efraim, Rivka and children

Volershtein, Abraham, wife and son

Vaysbein, Yasha

Vaysbein, Ida

Vaysbein, Vera

Vaysman, Shmuel

Vaysman, Faygeh

Vaysman, Rachel

Vaysman, Grisha

Volershteyn, Mica

Volershteyn, Riva

Volershteyn, Shimon

Vaysman, Shabtai, wife and son

Vinogradsky, Chaim, wife and son

Volovsky, Israel, Sarah and daughter Rosa with Rosa's husband and children

Volovsky, Shmuel, wife and children

Vaynshaynker, Chaim from Grigoriopol

Vitkovsky, Isaac, wife and children

Vitkovsky, Geta, wife and children

Weinstein, Abraham Layb

Weinstein, Tzirl

Weinstein, Chava

Weinstein, Bayla

Weinstein, Jacob

Weinstein, Laytzeh

Weilman, Ita Rayzel

Weilman, Yechezkel

Weilman, Jacob

Zion

Zeltzer, Jacob

Zeltzer, Pereh

Zeltzer, Bentzion

Zaytchik, Ita

Zaytchik, Chaikeh

Zaytchik, Tzvi Hershl

Zaytchik, Dobrish

Zaytchik, Etl

Zaytchik, Tzina

Zaytchik, Perl

Zaytchik, Shmaya

Zaytchik, Moshe – 102 years old

Zaytchik, Shloimeh

Zelyokovitch, Sholem

Zelyokovitch, Betty

Zelyokovitch, Fima

Zelikovitz, Sender

Zilberberg, Gutl

Zilberberg, Chaim

Zilberberg, Efraim

Zilberberg, Bentzi

Zelberberg, Sarah

Zhulkover, Chaya,

Zhulkover, Bella and children

Zhulkover, Abraham

Zhulkover, Chana

Chet

Chayat, Shaul

Chayat, Zev

Chayat, Jacob

Chayat, Sarah

Chayat, Betty

Chayat, Fanya

Chaytzin, Rafael

Chaytzin, Abraham

Chaytin, Shmerl

Chaytzin, Manya

Chaytzin, Klara

Chaytzin, Yossi

Chaikin, Abraham, wife and children

Chavarastian, Moishe

Chavarastian, Freda

Chavarastian, Sarah

Chavarastian, Isachar, wife and daughter

Chalemsky, Benny

Chalemsky, Manya

Chalemsky, Tanya

Chalemsky, Luba

Chalemsky, Arik

Chalemsky, Reva

Tet

Teitelboim, Aharon

Teitelboim, Moishe

Teitelboim, Toba

Teitelboim, Leah

Teitelboim, Joseph

Tamashin, Fayvl

Tamashin, Sarah

Tamashin, Abraham

Tamashin, Lyenya

Tamashin, Lyosya

Trachtenberg, Baruch

Trachtenberg, Ita

Trachtenberg, Pinya

Trachtenberg, Isya

Trachtenberg, Misha

Tchulsky, Moishe

Tchulsky, Rayzl

Tchulsky, Rachel

Tchulsky, Shimon and wife

Tchernyovsky, Tzvi (Hershl), Tova and children

Tchebatar, Sima

Tchebatar, Fanya

Tchebatar, Mila

Tchebatar, Yossi

Yud

Yatom, Eliezer

Yatom, Kresl

Yotam, Esther

Yatom, Rachel

Yatom, Shlomo

Yocht, Mordecai Shuv

Yocht, Chana Rivka

Yocht, Tzvi (Hershl)

Yerosalimsky, Shmerl

Yerosalimsky, Chana

Yerosalimsky, Shayndl

Yerosalimsky, Layb

Caf

Cohen, Isaac

Cohen, Mendl

Cohen, Layb

Cohen, Nechama

Cohen, Adel

Cohen, Layb

Cohen, Mendl

Cohen, Yossi

Cohen, Shloimeh and his mother

Cohen, Chaim

Cohen, Faygeh

Cohen, Shayndl

Cohen, Chava

Cohen, Chana

Cohen, Zev (Velvl)

Cohen, Baruch

Cohen, Jacob

Katz, Moish Layb

Katz, Chaya

Katz, Faygeh

Katz, Aba

Katz, Riva

Katz, Eliezer (Layzer)

Lamed

Liverant, Shabtai

Liverant, Ita

Liverant, Chantza

Livshin, Dvorah

Livshin, Shmuel

Livshin, Moishe

Laibovitch, Jacob

Laibovitch, Leah

Laibovitch, Burya

Laibovitch, Efraim (Froykeh)

Levit, Pinchas

Levit, David, his wife and son

Lerner, Eliezer, Chaya and children

Livshin, Chaim

Livshin, Bella

Livshin, Yossi

Livshin, Sarah

Lipman, Zev

Lipshin, Chanya, Shmuel and children

Lipshin, Chana

Lipshin, Emanuel

Levi, Pepa or Faneh

Levi , Chaim

Levi, David

Levi – 20 more Levi families – no first names

Ladizhensky, Pesach

Ladizhensky, Ida

Ladizhensky, Esther

Mem

Melamed, Tzirl

Melamed, Shifra

Melamed, Frima

Maidanek, Shaul, wife ,son, daughters

Musicman, Idl and wife

Musicman, Moishe

Musicman, Chaya

Musicman, Israel

Musicman, Abraham

Musicman, Mordecai (Motl) and children

Mimmer, Risl, wife, son and daughter

Melamed, Shmuel Natan, wife, children

Machnavsky, Frima

Machnavsky, Mordecai

Machnavsky, Chava

Machnavsky, Pinyeh

Machnavsky, Golda, father, mother, sister and brother

Milbert, Michl, brother and sister

Milbert, Nachum

Nun

Nestvayter, Zev (Velvl), Chantz, children

Nestvayter, Moshe

Nestvayter, Bronya

Nestvayrer, Yasha, Lyenya and children

Somach

Suslensky, Sarah,daughter, grandchild

Slavkis, Hinda

Slavkis, Moishe

Slavkis, Rayzl

Slavkis, Layb

Sirkis, Pinye

Sirkis, Shayndl

Sirkis, Rachel

Sirkis, Chaya

Sirkis, Burya

Sirkis, Misha

Sandler, Idl

Sandler, Mirl

Sandler, Abraham

Sandler, Moishe

Sandler, Tzvi (Hershl)

Sandler, Tema, husband and daughter

Sochav-Gurevitch and mother

Peh

Paskar, Shmerl (Bodner)

Paskar, Chana

Paskar, Tzvi (Hershl)

Polishtzuk, Lyuba

Polishtzuk, Tzvi (Hershl)

Polishtzuk, Noah

Polishtzuk, Layb son of Abraham Jacob

Pilchikov, Golda daughter of Tzalel Urman

Pilchikov, Faygeh

Piltchikov, Rosa

Pilchikov, Joseph

Pilchikov, Leah and her children

Pasis, Isaac (Itzik)

Pasis, Golda

Pasis, Israel

Pasis, Faygeh

Pecker, Shloimeh – teacher

Postolov, Tzvi, Sarah and children

Puchis, Shmuel

Putcher, Shmuel

Putcher, Shlima

Putcher, Jacob (Yankl)

Putcher, Rachel

Putcher, Zusi

Putcher, Freda

Puchis, Layb

Puchis, Mendl

Puchis, Jacob (Yankl)

Puchis, Chaikeh, David and children

Fidvil, Joseph

Fidvil, Chantza

Fidvil, Dvorah

Fidvil, Jacob (Yankl)

Fifelshteyn, Misha

Fifelshteyn, Golda

Filler, David Jacob

Filler, Chaykeh

Filler, Tzvi (Hershl)

Filler, Riva

Finkelshteyn, Isaac

Finkelshteyn, Blyuma

Finkelshteyn, Chana

Finkelshteyn, Baruch

Flekl, Shamai

Flekl, Chana

Flekl, Sima

Flam, Chaikeh, daughter and son

Fishl – Baker from Yagorlik, wife Maykeh

Fraydis, Chaikeh daugher of Dov Puchis

Tzadik

Tzveighoft, Moshe

Tzveighoft, Chana

Tzveighoft, Shifreh

Tzveighoft, Michael

Tzveighoft, Ida

Tzelnik, Zalman

Tzelnik, Mayer

Tzelnik, Sarah

Tzelnik, Ita and children

Tzelni, Shimon – Vaks

Tzveighoft, Israel

Tzveighoft, Joseph

Tzveighoft, Jacob

Tzveighoft, Layb, Faygeh and children

Tzelnik, Lipa, wife and daughter

Kof

Kotzovay, Naftali

    Kushnitzky, Chaya

    Kushnitzky, Golda

    Kushnitzky, David

    Kiner, Shmerl

    Kiner, Sarah

    Kiner, Tzaytel

    Kiner, Moishe

    Kiner, Dalya

    Kiner, Leah

    Kiner, Orka

    Kiner, Rachel

    Kiner, Mirl

    Kiner, Mordecai

    Kiner, Mirl

    Kiner, Golda

    Koifman, Israel

    Koifman, Esther

    Koifman, Joseph

    Koifman, Israel

    Koifman, Tzila

    Kalishevsky, Moishe

    Kalishevsky, Talya

    Kalishevsky, Eli

    Koblik, Frima

    Koblik, Riva

    Koblik, Sarah

    Koblik, Baruch

Koblik, Benjamin

Kutchyersky, Shprintzeh, Layb and children

Komisher, Chaim (Tzigayner)

Komisher, Bayleh

Komisher, Pesya and child

Kalinovsky, Abraham and wife

Kalinovsky, Rachel

Kalinovsky, Faygeh

Kazatzker, Michael

Kazatzker, Dvorah

Kudner, Zalman, wife and children

Kushnitsky, Chaya Riva and children

Kublik, Benjamin

Kublik, Sarah

Kublik, Rosa

Kublik, Tzvi (Hersh)

Kleiberg, Frima

Kleiberg, Isaac

Kleiberg, Nina

Kleiberg, Yurik

Kushnitsky, David

Kushnitsky, Leah

Kushnitsky, Yeshayahu

Kuperman, Moishe and wife

Kuperman, Peretz

Koshinsky, Benjamin, Chaya Sarah and children

Katzevman, Boris, 42 years, son of Abraham

Katzevman, Esther Hinda, 39 years, daughter of Pinchas

Katzevman, Polina, 17 years, daughter of Boris

Katzevman, Layb, 14 years, son of Boris

Katzevman, Ida, 2 years, daughter of Boris

Katzevman, Mordecai

Katzevman, Faygeh

Katzevman, Isaac

Krimershmois, Shayndl

Krimershmis, Yechiel

Kotzovay, Sarah

Kotzovay, Adl

Kipnis, Laybish, Chana and children

Krimershmoyneh, Eliyahu

Krimershmoyneh, Jenny

Krimershmoyneh, Izya

Raish

Rashkavan, Abraham-Moishe

Rashkavan, Shlima

Rashkavan, Sarah

Rashkavan, Toba

Rashkavan, Chaim

Rashkavan, Leah

Rashkavan, Bayla

Rashkavan, Adela

Rashakavan, Mila

Rashkavan, Layb

Rashkavan, Reuven

Rashkavan, Laytzeh

Rabinovitch, Chava

Radinsky, Rayzl and children

Roitenberg, Eli

Roitenberg, Zev (Velvl)

Rivilis, Isaac, Rachel and children

Rivilis, Daniel

Rivilis, Chana (Visoky)

Rivilis, Nachum and son Israel

Razmarin, Shaul, wife and children

Rashkavan, Mordecai, wife and children

Rashkavan, David

Rashkavan, Soibl

Rosenfeld, Mordecai

Rosenfeld, Leah

Rosenfeld, Sonya

Rosenfeld, Yasha

Rempel, Layb, wife and son

Rempel, Jacob

Rempel, Sarah

Rempel, Chaya

Shin

Shkolnik, Tzlalel

Shkolnik, Frima

Shkolnik, Chana

Shkolnik, Tabel

Shkolnik, Leah

Shinder, Chaikeh

Shinder, Faygeh

Shinder, Isaac

Shinder, Leah

Shinder, Berl

Shinder, Nechama

Shinder, Sarah

Shkolnik, Rachel

Shkolnik, Liba

Shkolnik, Shalom

Shuster, Ida, Moishe and children

Sholklaper, Leah

Sholklaper, Sarah

Shtilvasser, Buzya

Shtilvasser, Yuzek

Shtilvasser, Chana

Shoichet, Chananya

Shoichet, Esther-Chaya

Shoichet, David

Shoichet, Pesach

Shoichet, Zev-Velvl

Shoichet, Tibl

Shoichet, Freda

Shoichet, Shayndl

Shamis, Zev Velvl

Shamis, Shaindl

Shamis, Reuven

Shamis, Lyuba

Shamis, Mirl

Shoichet, Mendl

Shoicher, Leah

Shoichet, Frima

Shoichet, David

Shapliansky, David

Shapliansky, Rachel

Shapliansky, Jenny

Shapliansky, Yossi

Shreier, Isaac

Shreier, Masya

Shreier, Faygeh

Shreier, Tzipa

Shlita, Ben Tzion

Shlita, Dorah

Shainberg, Odl

Shreier, Misha

Shreier, Zusy

Shvartz, Israel, wife and children

Shneiderman, Reuven

Shneiderman, Miriam

Shneiderman, Israel

Shneiderman, Israel

Shneiderman, Isaac

Shoichet, David (Dovka)

Shoichet, Sarah Hindeh

Shneidmesser, Shmuel

Shneidmesser, Rivka

Shneidmesser, Burya

Shargaradsky, Mordecai (Motl)

Shargaradsky, Faygeh

Shargaradsky, Shloimeh

Shargaradsky, Ettya

Shitzer, Mordecai ben Avraham

Shitzer, Freda – Chaikeh

Shitzer, Leah

Shitzer, Rosa

Shitzer, Chana

We Will Always Remember
Dubossary memorial book – Picture Index
All these images are inserted in the book, however note that the page numbers give below are those of the original Yizkor Book, not the page numbers of this translation.

Caption	Page	Picture
Map of the Moldavian region. At the bottom is Odessa and the Black Sea. In the bottom quarter of the land mass by the big black dot in the center is Dubossar.	14	
Moshe and Golda Granovsky and children. Vanished without a trace.	50	
Yosef and Chaya Filler, grandparents of Baruch Bassin	59	
This picture which was taken from the Keren Kayemet (Jewish National Fund) golden book is of Aaron Horvitz z"l.	64	
Reb Naftali Ish Horvitz (father of Bernardo Gurevitch, Argentina)	97	

Members of the Zionist Organization ' Tzeirei Tzion', 1918 Alter Greenblatt, Ben Zion Shlita, Chaim Dorfman, Moshe Gorayvsky, Moshe Faerman, D. L. Granovsky, Tzvi Hirsh Tulchinsky, Tzvi Shpigel	137	
Chaim Finkelshtein. Murdered by the Nazis.	160	
Dubossar Landsleit in the United States To Plant Forest of 10,000 Trees	174	
Dubossar Landsleit Organization in Philadelphia	176	
Dubossar Relief Committee in America (New York) Harry and Henya Scheer, Bentchik Benjamin Shuster, Benjamin Finkelshtein (Philadelphia), Fayge Teitelboim, Yose Kipnis, Mendl Lerner, Nelly Teitelboim, Anshel Nirenberg, Moshe Bendersky, Moshe Feldman.	178	
Israel and Fayge Jenin and grandchildren in Philadelphia	180	
Dubossar Landsleit in Argentina	184	

Gluzman, Rabbi Puchis and wife Yenta, grandaughter of Miriam Bat Yakov, Gedalia and Rachel Rechev, David and Chaya Puchis with son Isaac.		
Sorting Tobacco in Rishon L'Tzion, 1925 Avraham Fier, Michael Tomshin, Mordecai Tomshin, Maier Rash, Yishayahu Kan-Tor, Avraham Moshkovitz	200	
A Big Reunion In Rishon L'Tzion, 1924, upon the Aliya to Israel of Michael and Masya Shteinberg	200	
Dubossarers In Israel Israel and Chana Tabachnik, their son Yehoshua (Aliya to Israel 1905), his wife Chaya Sarah, daughter Malka and her husband Yehoshua Levin with sons Moshe, Benjamin and Aryeh.	201	
Moshe Bick of Dubossar conducting a choir in Haifa	201	
Mordecai Volman, Lieutenant-Colonel in the Red Army. Died after the war.	259	
A Group of Dubossar Jews Days Before the Outbreak of War. **Murdered:** Yidl Zweighoft, Faygeh Vasserman, Esther Brilian, Shimon Kinor, Toba Rashkevan, Sarah Shkolnik, Shenkar, Rachel Poskar, Yitzchak Barenboim, Boris Katzavman, Menia Zemtzer, Chaike Tefler, Chaim Rashkevan, Layb Barenboim, Yakov Chayat, Isaac Shreier, Israel Koifman, Yakov Schinder, Layb Mordkovitch, Yakov Laybovitch, Sherl Kiner, Bentchik Shlit, Idl Sandler, David Shneiderman, Shifra Maydanik, Reva Barenboim, Menya Soibelman **Suvivors:** Riva Urman, Motl Urman,	273	

Zweighoft, Lena Berelechis, Velvl Festuyicher, Sarah Bashkansky, Avraham Livocht, Shmuel Tshoylsky, Hershl, Yosef Finkelstein, Yosef Volovick, Hershl Bander, Berl Bakman, Pessy Glimberg		
Pilot, Lieutenant-Colonel Litmonovitch	277	
Rabbi Gaon Reb Yerucham, son of Reb Shabtai Hacohen, z'l, z'tzl	298	
Rabbi Yehoshua Yissachar Abel z'l	302	

Caption	Page	Picture
Moshe Feldman in the Jewish Legion 1920	312	
Yosef Ram (Visoky), z'l	316	

Our Great Teacher Gad Layb Rechev	319	
Nachum Matenko	321	
Yechiel and Gittl Tzelnik (centre) and family	325	
Yosef Ben Ami (Nahalal)	329	
Michael and Masia Steinberg	330	
Moishe Faerman (Winnipeg, Canada)	333	
Baruch Spivak (Kfar Vitkin, 1921-1945)	337	
Miriam Ben Ami (Israel)	338	

David Puchis (Ein Ganim)	345	
Yitzchak Puchis. (Killed near Kfar Etzion, 1947)	347	
Tzvi Hirsh (Hershl) Tulchinsky. (Winnipeg, Canada)	348	
Mendl Zeltzer	349	
Kalman Levinshtein (Winnipeg, Canada)	351	

Died in Argentina

Caption	Page	Picture
Sarah Bendersky	354	

Zev Bendersky	354	
Rachel Itzkovitch	354	
Pearl Berman Bendersky	354	
Marcus Bendersky	354	
Tzvi Bersudsky	354	
Yosef Manes Halpern	354	
David and Chana Winoker	354	
Dena Genshengaren	354	

Tzvi Yeruzalimsky	355	
Kalman Zeltzer	355	
Shloime Samailof	355	
Tzvi Zeltzer	355	
Yosef Samailof	355	
Ezriel Cohen (Kagan)	355	
Velvl Polinsky	355	

Layke Polinsky	355	
Taibl Vinoker Samailof	355	
Rivka Kipnis Zeltzer and daughters – Esther, Malka and Etti	356	
Hirsh and Tzipa Steinberg	356	
Mordecai Rashkevan	356	

Died in U.S.A. and Canada

Caption	Page	Picture
Yosef Kipnis (Philadelphia)	356	
Abraham Sobol (New York)	356	

Mother of Laybish Louis Levine (U.S.A.)	356	
Yehuda Spitnik and wife (Canada)	356	
Pinchas Spitnik (Winnipeg)	356	
David and Serl Tulchinsky (Winnipeg, Canada)	356	

Died in Israel

Caption	Page	Picture
Yishayahu and Pearl Donayevsky	358	
Bat Sheva Chochomovitch	358	
Yona Tanya Kantor	358	
David Chochomovitch	358	

Sarah Spitnik	358	
David Spitnik	358	
Chaim Rakov	358	
Tzipora Freeberg-Dudnik	358	
Mendl Melamed	358	

Died in Dubossar

Caption	Page	Picture
Henya Goldiner	360	
Yochanan Goldiner	360	
Benjamin Itzkovitch (submitted by his son Moshe and wife Rosa in Argentina)	360	
Shimon Zhenin	360	
Raphael Zeltzer	360	
Efraim Ish Horvitz Halevi (submitted by wife Shayndl and children)	360	
Chaim Levine	360	

Masya Litmonovitch	360	
Layb Litmonovitch	360	
Shaul and Tzipora Spivak	361	
Reb David Lifshin and wife	361	
Rachel Fainshil	361	
Dena Filler	361	
Yitzchak Spivak	361	
Baruch Kipnis	361	

Sossy Kipnis	361	
Yerachmiel Fastalov	361	
Perl Tzelnik	362	
Tatl Tzelnik	362	
Israel Tzelnik	362	
Hersh Layb Kotchok	362	
Isser Tzelnik	362	

Yosef Kotchok (Yosl Moshkovitzer, grandfather of Mrs. Granovsky)	362	
Tzipora Spivak	362	
Akiva and Golda Tzelnik	362	
Sarah Soicherman-Chochomovitch (died in Israel)	362	
Rabbi Shmuel Pinchas Rabinovitch and wife	363	
Hershl and Ettl Shafer	363	
Noah and Batya Steinberg	363	

Murdered by the Nazis

Caption	Page	Picture
Azriel Granovsky	364	
Shlomo and Tzila Granovsky	364	
Malka Granovsky	364	
Sarah Spitnik	364	
Israel and Sarah Volovsky from Yagorlik	364	
Hershl Levin	364	
Chana Lifshin and children Chava and Emanuel	364	

Nachman Laizer Lifshin	364	
Rivka Teitelboim Katz (Nahum Teitelboim's daughter)	365	
Sarah Katz (Pinyeh and Rivka Teitelboim's daughter)	365	
Pinyeh Katz	365	
Aharon Teitelboim	365	
Anna Beck (neé Teitelboim)	365	
Nachum Teitelboim (the baker)	365	

Chaya Sarah Polyak (Nachum Teitelboim's granddaughter)	365	
Levi Feinshil	366	
Hershl Postalov's three children	366	
Hershl Postalov	366	
Ida Katzavman	366	
Esther Hinda Katzavman and Jenny Berlin	366	
Baruch Katzavman	366	
Avraham Dunayevsky (shot by the Soviets for Zionist activity).	366	

Rivka Kantor-Srulevitch, husband Betzalel and children	366	
Pesach Kipnis	366	
Mordecai and Bella Shargaradsky	367	
Etl Kipnis and Ita Yanover (killed)	367	
Abba Shafer and wife	367	
Pesach and Fenna Levine (Levy), son Chaim and grandchildren.	367	
Raizel Pilchikov, Dena Gurevitch, Bracha Pilchikov, Chana Imam (killed), Esther Kipnis (standing) survived	367	

An electronic version of this translation can be found at:
http://www.jewishgen.org/Yizkor/Dubossary/dub901.html

Notes

INDEX